INDIAN PHILOSOPHY, INDIAN REVOLUTION

INDIAN PHILOSOPHY, INDIAN REVOLUTION

ON CASTE AND POLITICS

DIVYA DWIVEDI
SHAJ MOHAN

EDITED AND INTRODUCED BY
MAËL MONTÉVIL

First published by in the United Kingdom by C. Hurst & Co. (Publishers) Ltd in 2024

Published in India by Westland Non-Fiction, an imprint of Westland Books, a division of Nasadiya Technologies Private Limited, in 2024

No. 269/2B, First Floor, 'Irai Arul', Vimalraj Street, Nethaji Nagar, Alapakkam Main Road, Maduravoyal, Chennai 600095

Westland, the Westland logo, Westland Non-Fiction and the Westland Non-Fiction logo are the trademarks of Nasadiya Technologies Private Limited, or its affiliates.

ISBN: 9789360450625

10 9 8 7 6 5 4 3 2 1

Typeset by Jojy Philip, New Delhi
Printed at Parksons Graphics Pvt. Ltd

CONTENTS

INTERVIEWS

FRIENDSHIPS AND SOLIDARITIES

ACKNOWLEDGEMENTS

In politics, no one takes a stand alone—quietly removed from the field of freedom, which is always of everyone; where the arteries tangle and part; where freedom explodes in those moments in arterial sprays to outline a new bastard horizon, revealing a new order of *imminence*. Such a thought of *standing alone against all* would be either the dream of a transcendent imperialism which aerially reigns over a terrain with its eyes in the skies and bombs on the grains of people below; or, it will be the fashionable evening tinkles of the *secret societies of silent resistance* found in the urban spaces of India and elsewhere. Therefore, if we spoke, we spoke from within the friendships and with 'the force', as Jean-Luc Nancy used to say privately, of the others. With—

Subhashini Ali, for agreeing (on politics as the fight for freedom) and disagreeing (on the specificity and disciplinarity of the creation of freedom) most fondly.

Hartosh Bal, the most excellent friend one can have, who introduced the political facts and the implications of philosophical arguments, and brought courage to every conversation.

Robert Bernasconi, who is caring and worrying to the point of occasional anger at the risks of a politics for egalitarianism, for which his mastery over the determination of *inherited communities* of all kinds—racisms, ethnocentrisms, philosophical racialisations—is essential.

Barbara Cassin conveyed the lessons of a world which does not take kindly to kindness and showed the astronomical map of the political ideas at work, recalled histories and stories of courage, and provided a fortress to work in rue Mouffetard where a number of these texts were written.

Rachel Dwyer, who discussed Indology—her early specialisation, shared references, memories of the great scholars, and hints of the tendencies of the politics of the discipline in discussions punctuated by the tales of elephants.

Meena Dhanda, demanded variations of the lines of arguments unfolding in these texts and she introduced the anti-caste currents developing in every corner of the world in conferences, the atlas she is who carries the responsibility of each word that leads to the annihilation of caste and comes bearing the brightest of smiles at all times.

Yashpal Jogdand, whose wisdom in ethics, politics, and research is never unaccompanied by cheerful laughter, calm courage, and literary idiom.

Patrice Maniglier, for a friendship that is possible only among philosophers, and for being the one who lives in the knowledge of what Stiegler said: '*there are only a few of us*'.

Maël Montévil, the bastard 'big' (*he really is big*) brother of this bastard family, who knows everything that is the matter for this book and nearly every occasion of their composition, dropped all of his cards of destiny whenever he heard of trouble, let himself be in the seizure of *indestinacy* the way Nietzsche thought it, and walked for hours with ice creams and gelato towards grace.

Hélène Nancy, who showed us the distinct calm belonging to turbulence as we struggled, discussed the politics with a view to resolution against the horizon of world politics, and gathered the crumbs that we come to be in certain moments into a corpus again.

Jean-Luc Nancy, *Jean-Luc*, the absolute friend of infinite love, who was always worried when we published each one of these texts, for our health whenever our voices changed, drew out the general principles for a wider world in conversations, and never ceased imparting by participation in the training in deconstruction even during our picnics or from his long hospital stays, and encouraged the more than deconstruction while unveiling the bastard family of deconstruction.

Our Parents, who knowingly carried us into the world and the words of Marxist Leninist politics of emancipation and equality; without ever asking for agreement, surrounded us with those books and conversations which affirmed politics as the fight for freedom and commitment as a precondition for writing; and, who keep giving love without ground.

Alok Rai, for important lessons, over a long weekend in Allahabad, in writing for the public sphere without surrendering philosophy and the revolutionary directives, and often said '*it is nothing to worry about*'.

J. Reghu (Reghu Janardhanan), the *fearless revolutionary* who imparted the lessons of his political life, collaborated on the politics and historical research, created a new surprising political articulation from the philosophical texts (*deconstructive materialism*) through the torsions of Rousseau, Voltaire, Marx and Lenin, and defended us with grit when many withdrew in fear.

Arundhati Roy, friend, neighbour (as Nicolas said, 'a tunnel between the homes') who shared texts, worries and sorrows for those moments of the people broken by the callousness of those in power, and donated levity to the unbearable through the humour of a cartoonist.

Bernard Stiegler, who often said 'as the head of this family'; convinced of the necessity of the annihilation of caste he pointed to the dangers ('they must be met') along that path, demanded more aggression in language, read and commented on many of these texts with an emphasis placed on their internationalism, and over that one cigarette and one glass of wine in the evenings spoke of revolutions of the future, 'or else it is all finished!'.

Vijay Tankha, who often witnessed the 'not so easy' moments of anguish and the writing seized by the ruins of this anguish, lent outrage and solemnity to the coming to terms of the words to the events, and continued the ancient Greek education, or the lesson among the ruins.

Romila Thapar, who kept the virtue of difference, as that which produces future, in all conversations; and at the same time the theoretical field underlying her corpus itself generated the differ*a*nce of history; with the naughty twinkle in her eyes she brought the lesser known records and unwritten histories to us, and shared her own ideas of a socialist egalitarian future India.

Siddharth Varadarajan, who kept the place open to many of these texts, sent strong words of caution, and often caught the undercurrents of the mischievousness to which language inevitably draws most of us.

For the reasons they know well, not all names can be taken, and some can only be mentioned *Khalid Anis Ansari*, *Emily Apter, Anthony Ballas, Kamran Baradaran, Michel Bitbol, Anne Cheng, Katja Freistein, Bertrand de Harting, Nicolas Idier, Laurence Joseph, Danielle Cohen Levinas, Achille Mbembe, Anish Mohammed, Ivana Perica, Aarushi Punia, N. K. Raveendran, Philippe Rogers, Giuseppe Scuto, Rajesh Selvaraj, Robert J. C. Young.*

The places where many of these texts could appear are courageous, for the Indian public sphere does not take too well to the politics of the Dalit-Bahujan position and accept the call for the annihilation of caste (such an upper caste decision to suppress the discussion of caste oppression is reflected in international media)—*Asian Lite, Libération, Le Monde, Raiot, The Indian Express, Iranian Labour News Agency, Naked Punch, NDTV, News Click, Outlook India, The Wire.*

INTRODUCTION
PHILOSOPHICAL TESTIMONIES

Maël Montévil

In the sense of a philosophical response appropriate to the deteriorating political conditions of India which are alarming the world, this book of essays by Divya Dwivedi and Shaj Mohan is the best positioned for the term 'Indian philosophy'.

Mohan and Dwivedi are the most well-known philosophers of their generation and belong to the tradition or 'the bastard family' of deconstruction. They developed their philosophical contributions in the intimate friendships with Jean-Luc Nancy and Bernard Stiegler (it was Stiegler who, in fact, introduced me to them both many years ago), both of whom in turn were friends of the renowned inventor/discoverer of the project of deconstruction in the history of philosophy, Jacques Derrida, who used to refer to them as 'post-deconstructive' thinkers. That is how Dwivedi and Mohan have come to be known outside of India—as the philosophical heirs to a tradition which begins at least from Husserl. When philosophers write about anything whatsoever their reflections are grounded in their philosophical intuitions and projects such that everything is philosophical.

The essays gathered here have two kinds of unity. They are grounded in the egalitarian political desire of the lower caste majority of India on the one hand, and on the other hand they show a progressive expression of the revolutionary interpretations of Indian politics and society through the philosophical architectonic of their authors. In that sense, this book provides two kinds of introductions: first, it is the introduction from the point of view of the lower caste position in politics to the increasing authoritarianism and the destruction of democratic norms in India under the RSS and the BJP led today by Modi. Second, it is also an introduction to the complex philosophical corpus of Dwivedi and Mohan with its revolutionary implications not restricted to India alone. What philosophers write has a value beyond their time, as memorably shown by Derrida through his interpretation of the laundry notes of Nietzsche. In that Nietzschean sense, these texts bring the present moments into contact with eternity. I will highlight the ways in which the themes of this book connect with each other and constitute a deeper philosophical contribution.

This book presents the contemporary history of the rise of the Nazi style movement of *upper caste supremacism* in India, which today goes by the name of 'Hindu nationalism'. Most of the damage done to India by its international observers comes from the lazy acceptance of the simplified account of India's politics as the opposition between 'Hindu majoritarian nationalism' and 'religious minorities', or between 'Hindu fundamentalism' and 'religious pluralism'. This false opposition, Dwivedi and Mohan argue, has been fed to the 'west' by the upper caste elites (both 'left' and 'right') with whom alone the so called western media interacts. This kind of 'native informant' is also the problematic of colonialism where the colonising powers interpreted the societies of India through the discourses and the interests of the upper caste minority who had been leading the oppressive caste system for millennia. In other words, the colonial practice of keeping the upper castes as the rulers who would control and contain Indian society on behalf of the elites of the world continues even today. It is enabled by the innocent and not so innocent practices of 'western' journalists and academics.

The theoretical and political positions from which Dwivedi and Mohan's articles follow are revolutionary in their refusal to accept oppression and 'heritable forms of power' as the norm. In that way, this book breaks many more myths about India, of which the most prominent is that caste-based discrimination is a theologically sanctioned process internal to 'Hinduism', and to no other religion. The caste line dividing Indian society into minority upper castes and majority lower castes extends into all religions of India. There is untouchability and caste supremacy among the Christians, Muslims, and the Sikhs in India. It is in the interest of the upper caste elites of all religions to present the political problematic of India as 'Hindu majority' versus 'religious minorities', which allows the upper caste elites of all religions to hide the voices and even the bodies of the lower caste peoples and to present the upper castes as the representatives of each religious group. In order to achieve the suppression of the truth—namely, the political will of the majority lower castes to find democratic emancipation through the principle of egalitarianism—people from the religious minorities are butchered on a regular basis through orchestrated pogroms. As Dwivedi asks: 'Hinduism is the instrument through which lower caste aspirations can be slayed, for which religious minorities are a mere medium. We should wonder what is more sinister: That this is the reality of politics in India or that we accept this reality in our everyday life?' This moral rage and the ethical courage to express this rage without the fear of consequences to their own lives is the testimony presented through these essays of Dwivedi and Mohan.

Dwivedi and Mohan speak from the lower caste majority position, or as they themselves say, they speak as *the servants of the lower caste majority position*. This position grounds a true and transformative account of Indian politics, and exposes what has been taking place according to the minority upper caste position as something pernicious and macabre. The Indian subcontinent has been ruled by the upper caste minority—Brahmins, Kshatriyas, and Vaishyas (or Baniya)—for three thousand years. From among these oppressor minority castes, the Brahmins and the Kshatriyas were celebrated under their self-designation as 'Aryan' at the great price of the holocaust and the Second World War in Europe. The lower caste majority position is that the only worthy aim of politics in India is the annihilation of the oppressive caste order to create an egalitarian society. This was explicitly the ambition of the Dalit intellectual, constitutional scholar and political philosopher Dr B. R. Ambedkar who framed the constitution of India.

The *upper caste supremacist project* of 'Hindu nationalism' was an explicit response against the anti-caste mobilisations from the mid-nineteenth century on the Indian subcontinent. For this reason, many of these texts refer to and interpret the history of Nazi-style movements in the past in other parts of the world. This volume thus provides an analytic instrument to study and respond to the present rising threat from racialised, fascistic and neo-Nazi movements across the world, especially in the US and Europe, and to understand the crisis of democracy appearing everywhere in our world. The article 'Democracy and Revolution' shows the absolute commitment to democracy as a political necessity and revolution as a democratic necessity to protect democracies from being taken over by anti-democratic interests by using those very democratic institutions.

These essays also comprise the history of the decline of democratic politics and the suppression of the struggle for justice and rights by the lower caste majority people of India (more than 90% of the Indian population) by upper caste controlled media, academic spaces, judiciary, the police and the mafia. From the last two sentences it should be evident that what we read here is not the usual story of India that we read in the newspapers, which projects a 'Hindu majority' oppressing the 'religious minorities' and (only) occasionally mentions the people considered as lowest in the racialised caste order, the Dalits (formerly untouchable). Their new history shatters that familiar and much easier to digest tale of India. Instead, it is underpinned by a theorisation of history which is implicit and explicit across the works of Dwivedi and Mohan.

In this anthology, the essay 'Looming Objects and the Ancestral Model of Historiography' presents an important aspect of the new theory of history and historicity. This theory, deeply articulated in Mohan's works and demonstrated through the engagements with philosophical corpus in Dwivedi's works,[1] follows from deconstruction. The deconstruction of history rejects the Hegelian and Marxist models which rest upon the foundations of classical logic from out of which contradictions in theory and history are derived—such as the master versus slave dialectic in Hegel or class dialectic in Marx—and these histories are manipulated to show these contradictions resolving into a higher concept or a stage of history. In a yet to be published text on Louis Althusser, Mohan has shown that dialectical theories of history are unified or given an identity, and therefore a totality, by *teleology* which is a process that proceeds through the resolution of contradictions towards a goal or purpose. This concept has been discarded through three steps: through the deconstruction of certain features of classical logic itself by Derrida; the deconstruction, later on, of the meaning of a people—such as European or Hindu—by Nancy; and most recently, the deconstruction of the very category of *Telos* or goal of history by Mohan, who proposes in its stead the concept of *teleography*.[2]

To do so, Mohan has discarded classical logic as such through an examination of identity, showing that all the classical laws of thought—the law of excluded middle and the law of non-contradiction—are meant to conserve identity. If we discard identity, there is no classical logic. This is the basis for the new theory of history or *anastatic theory of history* of Dwivedi and Mohan. History, instead of spiritual or natural processes endowed with *telos*, is written and experienced through the adoption of political goals. Mohan calls this practical adoption of telos and the explicit development of specific schemas for historiography by the name teleography. There is such a teleography at work in this book for the sake of the emancipation of the lower caste majority in the creation of an egalitarian India.

The theme of 'revolution' runs through these texts. In some moments it is the 'French revolution' in particular, which is underscored by the very definition that Dwivedi and Mohan give of the writer as the revolutionary. In a text published in April 2016, they write, 'The writer is also a revolutionary in language. Revolution is the modern theatre of politics where a cut with the past is made in a single event.' In January 2020, they jointly published a text where they stepped over the class oriented revolutionary theory of the communist parties of India and asserted the new meaning of revolution in India: 'In the Indian context, revolution has only one sense, the end of the caste system, and "Citizen" has only one sense, the people of the state who have shed caste and racism.' In a publication from February 2020, Mohan[3] would argue that the political desire to create a world where nobody enjoys (the upper castes, the racists, 'inheritors of power') or suffers (the poor, the lower caste people, racially oppressed peoples) any form of exception is revolution: 'revolution implies this: We must go beyond "resistance" to struggle for people, without exception'. When Dwivedi said in October 2022, 'India will be unable to emerge from this stasis [of caste oppression] without the equivalent of a French-style Revolution that transforms the social order and can disrupt the heritable form of power and opportunity that is caste', she trended once again on social media and received abuses and threats. The interview 'became viral and controversial'[4] and the international community of philosophers became seriously concerned about the well-being and security of the two philosophers.

The question whether there is a theory of revolution in the philosophical works of Dwivedi and Mohan has been asked. For example, J. Reghu, an important interpreter of their works, says 'There is something which can be called a revolutionary theory, but not under that name. Dwivedi and Mohan call it *anastasis*, in the sense of that which displaces the stasis of a society (*Gandhi and Philosophy*, 2019). In India it is caste that is the stasis'.[5] Reghu shows that this theory of revolution also has a relation to deconstruction: 'There is revolutionary possibility in their works under a different name as "deconstructive materialism" by placing an emphasis on politics [...] deconstructive materialism is about the possibilities released through the analysis of an object or of a society [...] when you deconstruct gender, all kinds of materialist possibilities appear for people to live by. This is the making of freedom or politics.'[6]

I myself have discussed the possibility of a revolutionary seizure of the sciences through their thinking, where what I find to be central is the rejection in Mohan's works of the 'classical laws of thought'.[7] The concept of anastasis as a theory of revolution in philosophy is at the moment the subject of ongoing discussions in the journal *Philosophy World Democracy*, and in a series of seminars being held at the École normale supérieure (Paris) since 2021. These texts can serve as an introduction to those projects as well. In so far as this is an anthology of the texts and interviews about contemporary India by Mohan and Dwivedi as philosophers concerned with the grounds of justice, democracy, and equality in their country and in the whole world, this writing is courageously *Indian Philosophy*.

And yet, in India, the feelings evoked by their names are complicated. It is important to remark on the perilous and stressful situation from which these two philosophers engage with politics. Dwivedi and Mohan were introduced to me by Bernard Stiegler, and we worked together in a research group called 'Internation' which was tasked with producing a report on the various crises of the world and providing recommendations to the United Nations. Being a theoretical biologist and a philosopher of science I firmly believe that science and philosophy are committed to politics, and conversely that politics can be meaningful only through an active engagement with science and philosophy. For me, the encounter with Dwivedi and Mohan was from the very beginning a great friendship, as they are philosophers committed to science (especially in the works of Mohan) and to politics. Soon after we were introduced, Stiegler alerted me to the political situation of India and shared his worries for their safety.

It all began with the publication of an essay, 'Courage to Begin' on 2 October 2019 in one of India's most prestigious English dailies (included in this collection) where they remarked, and not for the first time, that Hindu religion was an upper caste invention of the twentieth century to represent the lower caste majority. Further they urged the Congress party to become the instrument for the political aspirations of the lower caste majority: 'The mega-organisational structure that belonged to the Congress can today serve a new end if it lets itself be seized by the oppressed majority of millennia'. Two days later, Divya Dwivedi spoke on the then liberal centrist television news network NDTV[8] in continuation of their article. There she said, 'Hindu Right is the corollary of the idea that India is a Hindu majority population and this is a false majority. The Hindu religion was invented in early twentieth century in order to hide the fact that the lower caste people are the real majority of India'.[9] According to a leading journalist this was 'unthinkable'[10] in India until that moment and the video became viral and controversial. Threats appeared on social media, including the threats to assassinate them.

In December 2020, Dwivedi and Mohan together with J. Reghu, published a long scholarly essay establishing the thesis of the creation of Hindu religion in the twentieth century, the political aims of its creation, and how this false religious identity had been the cause of evils in modern India. This time *Le Monde* reported that Dwivedi and Mohan faced threats including of decapitation. Jean-Luc Nancy wrote in the newspaper *Liberation* defending them. In October 2022, when Dwivedi spoke against the destruction of democratic institutions of India and the need for a social revolution to overcome the stasis that caste oppression is, threats mounted again. I initiated a petition with an international community of philosophers including many of our friends such as Etienne Balibar, Antonio Negri, Stuart Kauffman, Slavoj Žižek, Barbara Cassin, Patrice Maniglier, and Hélène Nancy. The words of the petition form an important background for the reception of these texts today, and for a sense of the dangerous conditions from which they appear before the reader:

> Mohan and Dwivedi are among the most important philosophers in the world alive today. They have developed their thought beyond the 'western' concept of philosophy within a community of friendship with Jean-Luc Nancy, Bernard Stiegler, Achille Mbembe, and Robert Bernasconi. Their extraordinary commitment to justice, equality, and the political freedoms of people everywhere in the world comes at a serious price. In India, where they reside, they face harassments and death threats on social media on a regular basis. These threats are significant. In recent years, while foreign intellectuals have been denied entry in India, Indian intellectuals have been jailed or assassinated.[11]

In October 2023, I had visited India with a view towards reading more about its bio diversity and to witness this diversity. India is beautiful, with stunning natural diversity in all directions, and its culturally diverse people are gentle, kind, and generous; and, evidently, the political class is the minority who seem to be an exception to the bustling streets, rumbling highways, and the mountains full of unheard of ancient gods. It was the week when India had hosted the G20 summit. The roads and buildings of Delhi were prepared for the summit with posters of Modi. Dwivedi was requested by the France 24 news network to participate in an interview on this occasion on the 8th of October in New Delhi. In it, she spoke of the economic and political inequalities among the G20 countries and within them. She said that the GDP is not the measure of political progress. Her expressed desire and confidence in the future of India without the caste order was necessary for the world to listen to and to think about—there is an apartheid of 3000 years. But as is almost always the case, the interview became viral, and has been viewed more than 2 million times. The next day I called Dwivedi from a South Indian city as I began to discover the despicable threats to her in social media. She told me, 'the sadness I feel is in seeing the attention being brought on me, but it should instead be upon what I said'. The threats and intimidations are continuing to rise as if they could persuade her to surrender.[12] In the words of Meena Dhanda in the days that followed: 'What is unique about Divya is that she had the gumption to express this critical thought in public.[...] She is threatening to her opponents within India because she is thinking against the grain, when others are falling in line.'[13]

As a criterion of selection and organisation of the texts in this book, I kept in mind ease of reading, thematic unity, and the progress towards the politico-theoretical goal of egalitarianism in their works. I have retained all the texts which are accessible to any reader, especially those readers without familiarity with the philosophical works of Dwivedi and Mohan, and the phenomenological and deconstructive tradition to which they belong. Many of the texts have been previously published, but several of them were censored during their publication, hence the original versions are presented here. Some of the publications have disappeared from the internet which is to be expected under the political conditions in which they were written. Some remain inaccessible due to paywalls. A few of the articles were published originally in French, and are included here in their English versions. There are several unpublished texts in this book—in most cases they were found unsafe in their context by the media.

The texts have not been ordered chronologically, but rather as genres: thematically grouped essays followed by interviews, and ending with *éloges* to friendship, solidarity and the courage of their contemporaries and predecessors. This division is guided by the criterion that the reader be introduced to the political milieu they address and to the conceptual and theoretical field through which this milieu is determined. Nevertheless, the reader can follow the chronology through my chapter introductions which also provide the contexts of all these texts and to enable those readers who are not too familiar with the political situation in India to immerse in them. The introductions, when necessary, contain some philosophical explanations.

While editing the collection, I have had to modify certain sentences which were bound to their immediate contexts in order to make them accessible. Dwivedi and Mohan always write with references and notes. Some of these are part of the original documents and were excised by the newspapers and other media to suit their formats. I have restored these annotations and have also added extensive notes of my own whenever a term, an event signified by a year, authors, organisations, concepts, and historical episodes are mentioned or alluded to. There is a continuity in the writing style of Dwivedi and Mohan across their philosophical and political works in that they are precise, rigorous, and proceed through distinctions. However, their philosophical works are often compressed in their execution while they make allusions to many domains including the sciences, myths, literature, music, and the philosophical tradition. In contrast, their political texts are much more direct, even as they also contain allusions and humour. In some cases, where it does not affect the style of the text, I have added notes to illuminate these moments. At the end of the book, the readers will find a short glossary of their concepts including terms such as anastasis, ceremonial society, functional isolation, homology, resistance, and stasis.

ESSAYS

1

THE PATHOLOGY OF A CEREMONIAL SOCIETY

In the summer of 2014, the Hindu nationalist party BJP led by Modi came to power in India. Soon, there were signs that India was not going to be the same again. Upper caste supremacist projects were announced. Up to April 2016, the public sphere in India had not yet fully surrendered itself to the terror of upper caste supremacism. Writers were returning state given awards as a form of protest and universities were still able to protest. The upper caste supremacist organisations led by the RSS and the BJP government officials mocked and opposed these acclaimed writers, violent attacks by cow vigilantes became a fact of everyday life, religious conversions were targeted, and academic institutions were assailed. In this atmosphere, Dwivedi and Mohan invoked revolution: 'The writer is also a revolutionary in language. Revolution is the modern theatre of politics where a cut with the past is made in a single event. Hence, modernity was also obsessed with scientific, literary and philosophical revolutions.' This text explains the kind of society India, or any country swept by fascism, could become, a 'ceremonial society'. This is a concept with Kantian, Marxist, and cybernetic elements to it, which is an important component of the philosophical system in *Gandhi and Philosophy*. According to this concept, any society which tries to conserve itself must

> conserve and reproduce the means through which it perpetuates itself in the most faithful manner. This evidently points to the caste system as such, the system which reproduces the rules of strict endogamy and occupational restrictions to ensure the perpetuation of the privileges of the upper caste minority. This form of self-perpetuation of upper cate supremacy is referred to as the 'Aryan doctrine' in their works, expanding the more limited sense which is usually and incorrectly restricted to Nazism in Germany.

Ceremonies have a certain morbidity—as events that are not open to debate. An annual ceremony this year repeats the ceremony of the previous year, which repeated that of the year before, and so on. Any deviation would be disrespectful to the original event which the ceremony commemorates. Likewise with magical utterances or *mantras*, deviation would draw supernatural punishments. A purely ceremonial society, where each day is a faithful repetition of the days gone by, is called primitive—a theoretical ideal for ethnology. A primitive society has no need for history books. Gandhi himself preferred a certain form of ceremonial society which he called 'village swaraj'. He contrasted the permanence of the villages of the subcontinent with the achievements of the ancient Greeks and the Romans—'Such ephemeral civilisations have often come and gone and will continue to do so'.[1]

In being a ceremony in itself, a primitive society does not need quotation marks. We use quotation marks to set off an older statement from a new one. We quote in order to distance ourselves from the statements and traditions of the past—these punctuation marks are an institution which sets off the past from the future.

Modernity conceived itself as a progressive distancing from primitive societies. It created institutions—copyright, the university, refereed journals—to safeguard the ideal of a surge towards the future. This vision is also reflected in the academic norm of limiting the amount of quoted material permitted in a book, and the vigilance against plagiarism. Without the use of quotes there is no recognition of the new statements. Without the new statements there can be no meaning for quotes. Modernity is the game of finding the ideal ratio between the past and the future separated by quotation marks.

We write, therefore we are

For this reason, the writer is the heroic figure of modernity. The act of writing involves a certain aggression that rushes towards the unknown and the unwritten, and creates new statements. The writer's new statements maintain the ratio between the past and the future such that we live with a sense of history. Without the writer, we will have slipped into a society in which there are only quotes, or a society that merely recalls and repeats. The writer is also a revolutionary in language. Revolution is the modern theatre of politics where a cut with the past is made in a single event. Hence, modernity was also obsessed with scientific, literary and philosophical revolutions.

Quotes are quite complex in their deployment. We quote in many ways, such as by prefacing what we speak with 'as said by', 'allegedly', 'in the interest of neutrality', 'it is believed by some that'. The academic uses quotes to mention that statement from which she secedes in the history of that discipline. She deploys quotes to gather thoughts, often separated by centuries, and the differences between these thoughts, into a corpus for the free thinking animal that we are.

No one in religious institutions would preface their ceremonial chants with 'allegedly' or 'it is debatable'. If, in the ceremonial colony of the Germany of 1939, a man were to say that *Czechoslovakia is not a part of Germany*[2] it would have been seditious. If he shouted 'Czechoslovakia is a part of Germany' while winking or drawing quotation marks in the air with his index fingers, he would have quoted academically and earned a ticket to a camp.[3] The quote marks would make the statement secede from its ceremoniality and ritual power. The pure recitation of the past is ceremonial. This is what is currently being demanded of the great international Sanskrit scholars Wendy Doniger, Michael Witzel, and Sheldon Pollock by the clergy of the subcontinent where the rationalists M. M. Kalburgi, Govind Pansare and Narendra Dabholkar have been killed for this.[4] Obedient recitation rather than academic citation.

Let us imagine a time without writers. All that we write and speak are quotes: restricted to the same set of permissible and unburned books, mandatory slogans, and the drill. Bereft of the aggressive use of language to lure in the future, quotation marks will become redundant. The same number of statements—whether they are in quotes or not will make no difference anymore—will repeat. There will be no new novels written, no breakthroughs in science. This will be the end of our politics, sciences, and the arts. We will no longer refer to a past and project a future. Guns, tanks, and khaki shorts are going to be the only difference we will then have with the primitive societies, from which this coming society will in all other respects be indiscernible.

The right to remain silent

When new statements are suppressed by being declared seditious, the potentiality of language secedes from us. In India, we are now beginning a fight for our right to *not speak* the words that are against our conscience, such as declaring our allegiance through slogans and songs for a fair skinned upper caste housewife swathed in silk and gold, who loves to straddle wildlife, and lusts for real estate all the way from Iran to the Philippines.

In 2008 'the assailants chanted [...]' before a nun was raped in Kandhamal.[5] When Kanhaiya Kumar[6] suffered custodial beating it was apparently to force him to speak the words that were not his own: 'We thrashed him for three hours and we also forced him to say [...]'. If the thugs who boasted about this incident spoke the truth, then, the machinery of the state will have been an accomplice to compelled speech. When it was said, 'an amendment should be made in the law so that everyone says it'[7] we wondered about the rituals to be followed. Are we to chant it before all meals? Are we to chant it when we are not speaking other matters? Are we to chant only it, and utter no other word? Now, they tell us that this slogan needs more *lebensraum*: 'We want the whole world to chant [...]'.[8] The unmistakable suggestion of the lust for the 'whole world' is alarming. The right to remain silent is necessarily implicit in the right to speak freely. *We will say what we want to. We will not say what you want us to.*

If we do not fight back and write back we will have achieved the subcontinental version of the ceremonial society of Nazi Germany. Leni Riefenstahl's propaganda film *Triumph of the Will* captured the primitive society that Germany became: all men and women content to repeat the words of the Führer, the drill, the uniforms, the marches—a people celebrating the sacrifice of all their faculties in order to take the modern form of the ceremonial society. The repugnant drill that is carried out in the playgrounds by the men in khaki shorts[9] could soon be all of us, our everyday.

Today, our statements towards the future are suspended—allegedly—by physical threats and penal intimidation. We are beaten—allegedly—for language still clings to us. We are shot in our homes—allegedly—for putting pathetic ceremonies in quotes. We are imprisoned—allegedly—for we are not blind to injustice. We are being amputated from each other, since we will soon have no words left to exchange—allegedly. We watch language seceding from us with the tranquillity of an animal that is being eaten alive.

Our regression into the ongoing discourse about *who chanted which profane slogans* and *which sacred slogans all must chant* is the desiccation of language and the withering of lives in the subcontinent.

It is not too late to enquire into the ways in which we are letting the whole of language slip into quotes and become ceremonialised. Centuries of ceremonial mnemonics practiced as knowledge in the subcontinent, and the ritualised social order, were repeated in the postcolonial decades too. It is not merely a discriminatory education system that sent the poor and the lower castes to entirely inadequate schools, colleges and universities; it is also the 'rote learning' system which enforces conformity upon all young minds: the outdated syllabi, the doctrinal history books, absence of philosophy in the schools, question papers that repeated for decades, the answer sheets in circulation since the first questions appeared, the class rooms that demanded obedience and ceremonial repetitions. That is, we systematically inhibited the possibility of free thinking people and aggressive writers.

The aggression of language

It is this pathology that makes us play our politics through quotes today when we demand our freedoms by invoking the long gone greats: we do not have to quote Tagore to say that any kind of nationalism is a mass movement for psychopaths; we do not need Gandhi to speak about the illegitimacy of having a sedition law; we won't be helped by quoting Bhagat Singh to demand the freedom to be irreligious. There are many things spoken by the great figures of the past that are entirely disagreeable to us. And, as we can see, these authoritative quotes are worth nothing today. We need to write our own revolutionary statements.

Without the aggression of language that breaks free of every holy land, we risk being embargoed into a ceremonial colony, even geographically, in the subcontinent. The writer is someone who breaks through the ceremonial idolatry and the desiccated surfaces of a tired language in order to bring new matter, be she the practitioner of fiction, history or philosophy. The writer, free of the quotation marks, gives something new to contest. She may inaugurate a new polemics as when Hannah Arendt reported on the trial of the Nazi, Adolf Eichmann. He may obtain for us a new region in language, as when Eduardo Galeano brought politics and the tragic into football writing. He may speak of the unspeakable, as when the French philosopher Sartre wrote about the French involvement in the Holocaust. She may draw new lines of demarcation, as when Ada Byron wrote the first computer program.

A writer represents the aggression of language, someone who gives new matter for the inverted commas to swaddle, as new points of departure for the others. The writer is the step leader for lightning to strike. Rohith Vemula's final message is our step leader, and it contains the following words: 'I always wanted to be a writer'. The measure of the writer is the terror she inspires in the ceremonial orders of power. Each writer brings into language a new style of aggression. When Perumal Murugan wrote, 'Writer Perumal Murugan is dead',[10] he practiced the style of proscription—declaring the secession of his language from fascism. He left his statement to us as an augury as dreadful as that of a land where nature withdraws into aridness. There is another style of the transmutation: when our writers condemned the state for its intolerance, the honours and awards bestowed by it became shingles, which they threw back.

Today, we are in need of all our writers, the writer in all of us. We are in need of lightning strikes. So that we can write, grinding our teeth: *Back off!*[11]

2

HIDDEN BY HINDU

In June 2020 Dwivedi and Mohan published 'Ce que l'hindouisme recouvre' in the French language revue *Esprit*, an old and prestigious philosophy journal. 'Hidden by Hindu' is the English version of that text. There is much here that is continuous with their controversial and now cult essay 'The Hindu Hoax' published in the *Caravan* magazine in 2021. This text explains the central thesis in the political stand point of Dwivedi and Mohan. It is a precondition to understand the particular meaning of their theory of 'anastasis' as revolutionary in the Indian context. Implicit in it is a theory of history. To address it directly the authors have composed a new text for this anthology, 'Looming Objects and the Ancestral Model of Historiography'.

The contemporary image of India is that it is the land of the people who gained independence from British colonial rule through a great freedom struggle under the leadership of the Congress party and the spiritual guidance of M. K. Gandhi. Today, India projects and propagates its culture as the sum of Hindu religion, yoga, peace, and Gandhi as their mascot. This image was produced through concerted efforts such as the Oscar winning propaganda film *Gandhi* made by Richard Attenborough and the National Film Development

Corporation of India in 1982. We know that everything gets complicated once we begin to wander the texts and the streets of each country. Behind this image is hidden away and continues, unopposed, the millennia old oppression of nearly 90 per cent of the population in India, the lower castes people by the nearly 10 per cent upper castes people.

Constitutionally, India is still a secular and socialist republic of a union of states. The government data shows that it is a country of a Hindu religious majority. Today, it is ruled by Hindu nationalists who want to change the secular constitution and declare it a Hindu nation. Many would think of this word 'Hindu' as the name of an ancient religion.[1] The fact, however, is that it is the most recent of religions, of the twentieth century to be exact. What is designated by this term 'Hindu'? Achamaenid Persians used the term 'Hindu' in the 6th century BCE to talk about the geographical region around the Indus river (also known as Sindhu) which is the north-western region of the Indian subcontinent.[2] Alexander's army would call this region Indus, from which the modern name of the subcontinent and the name of the country 'India' are derived. The Arabic variant 'Al Hind', too, referred to the geographical region, and it is from this term that 'Hindu', as the name for the non-Muslim and non-Christian populations of Al Hind and the regions beyond it, came into usage. In the nineteenth century, Indologists and British colonial administrators were the first to use 'Hindu' in a loose but consistent fashion to refer to the people of the whole of the Indian subcontinent; and, more rarely to speak about the customs of the upper castes, especially the Brahmins.

From being the name of a region where diverse groups of people had many customs and practices of their own, how and when did 'Hindu' become the name of one religion for a large population nominally combining all these diverse groups—this is the story of the recent invention of this religion for conserving ancient social hierarchies in a modern political milieu.

The ancient oppressive caste order

The birth of 'Hinduism' can be understood only if, when studying this recent period of history, we do not lose sight of the most glaring and obdurate fact: *the oppressive caste order has been the only invariant of the Indian subcontinent for millennia*. The caste order is maintained through strict ceremonial endogamy. The notion of 'purity' of touch and sight maintain the distance between castes and severe punishments were prescribed for their breaches. Any threat of miscegenation is punished with death even today.[3] The caste system observes caste-rules as *the means* in order to repeat the system as *the end* generation after generation. That is, the caste system does not permit the exchanges between means and ends. The means and ends given to an individual is to perform his caste duties, which is the message of the text *Bhagavad Gita*. We have called the general principle of such systems as calypsology elsewhere.[4]

The ground of the caste order was described as early as the *Puruśasukta* in the *Rgveda* (1000–800 BCE). Also called the *varnāśramadharma* (office assigned according to skin colour), it was presented as the essence of the socio-cosmic order in several Brahminical texts including the *Manu Smriti* (200–400 CE). It stratifies society into the hierarchy of 'Varnas' in which the upper castes are Brahmins (priestly class), Kshatriya (warrior), and Vaishya or Baniya (trader), and form less than ten per cent of the Indian population. Below these three are the Shudra (worker) and the untouchable castes (who in the twentieth century began to call themselves *Dalits*[5] or 'the oppressed'), and these lower castes together constitute the more than 90 per cent of India's population.

For millennia, a great wall has stood between the world of the upper caste minority and the lower caste majority. Through this wall, certain limited transactions advantageous to the upper castes are allowed, including the manual labour of the lower castes for the upper castes and the transfer of the excreta of the upper castes towards the lower castes.[6] The only relation the lower castes have had with this wall, and for most purposes still have, is that they are forced to look up to it and thereby remain beneath the upper castes in terms of wealth, power, knowledge, and above all to surrender their dignity to it. The lower castes were never allowed near the temples of the upper castes, which is not very different from today.[7] They are not allowed to eat in front of the upper castes, even today.[8] They were not allowed to even listen to the very Vedas that prescribed their inferior social position. The punishment prescribed for it in the *Manu Smriti* was to pour molten lead into the ears of the lower castes who listened to the recital of the Vedas. The heroes of the Sanskrit epics were exemplary in punishing with death the Shudras who tried to transgress this knowledge barrier. The Shudra and the untouchable castes were never allowed to have knowledge of the goings on in the world of the upper castes.

The revalation of the real majority

For millennia, the upper castes have been the minority that controlled the majority of the land, the labour of the lower castes, and all cultural, bureaucratic institutions. The caste based oppressive social order and the population differential between the upper caste minority and lower caste majority became apparent only during the British colonial rule. When the census operations began in 1872, the officers found that there were too many religions and too many castes in India. There was certainly clarity regarding the religious denominations of Christians, Muslims, Sikhs, Buddhists, and Parsis. But the population that was none of the above was not classifiable without complications.[9] This population was made up of groups adhering to several localised religions, or sects and cults as they were called, including Shakta, Shaivism, Vaishnavism, Lingayat, Aalvaar, Nayanar and so on. Further, people often recorded the name of their religion and of their own caste as the same term—*religion? Brahmin, caste? Brahmin*. This is not surprising since a caste is a group that is socially and ritualistically endogamous. Caste observances determine most domains of life, worship, kinship, land-ownership, judicial functions, labour, and relations to other castes in the hierarchy.

The 1921 Census of India Report noted that 'No Indian is familiar with the term "Hindu" as applied to his religion'. In 1911, the census commissioner E. A. Gaits issued a circular with certain questions to help the census officers to determine the viability of 'Hindu' as the religion common to all those disparate groups. Most of these questions pertained to the wall of separation between the castes. For example, the circular asked all castes to answer if they had access to the upper caste temples; whether they had access to a Brahmin priest for the ceremonies in life such as weddings; whether they were familiar with the gods of the upper castes.[10] If it could be demonstrated that the disparate caste groups shared, at least occasionally, the same cultural spheres and activities, then there could be a case for a single religious category encompassing them all. The answers recorded for these questions made it obvious that this was not the case, and that the upper castes were then a small minority in the subcontinent. The upper castes soon saw the danger, protested against the circular, and forced it to be withdrawn. Their leaders expected that similar circulars would be used again. They therefore proceeded to invent the very customs and enforce the very practices which would be able to meet the Gaits criteria in the future, including temple entry programs for the lower castes, which are euphemistically called 'social reforms'. These cosmetic changes left the material conditions such as land ownership and political power of the lower castes unchanged, which was of course their goal. Hence, the very criteria that had failed in the 'Gaits' circular' would form the basis for the new 'Hindu' religion.

The subsequent census operations of the Raj, especially the 1921 and 1931 census, made the demographic difference between the upper and lower castes even more apparent. Even the Muslim religious minority were found to have outnumbered the upper castes. This fact would not have had any special sense if not for the modern legal and electoral procedures that were being introduced by the Raj, such as the 'Caste Disabilities Removal Act' in the mid nineteenth century, the increasing devolution of government to elected Indians in 1919 and 1935, and separate electorates for lower castes. Thus, under the colonial introduction of reforms, religious conversions, modern democratic electoral processes, and laws criminalising caste-based discriminatory practices in the early twentieth century, the lower castes had an opportunity for the first time in millennia to become visible as the claimants of public good, and to seek freedom and equal rights. These freedoms were not spectacular but as quotidian as the right to walk the same streets as everyone else, the right to drinking water of a village, the right to education, and the right to ask for a wage for the labour performed.

However, these freedoms are still not available to the majority of the people.

The reform measures of the colonial administration were met with extreme reproach by the upper castes who were fighting for 'transfer of power' under the leadership of the coalition of interests that was the Congress party. They anticipated that the social hierarchy of the caste order would not survive in a constitutional democracy based on principles of political, material and social equality. Under the Congress coalition, upper caste leaders including Gandhi launched agitations against these very reforms. But they were also confronted with the growing agitations from the lower caste people; in 1924 in Kerala, the lower caste people began their agitation for their right to walk on all streets including those in front of the temples which considered them as 'polluting'. In 1927 B. R. Ambedkar led the agitation of thousands of Dalits in Mahad (a place in Maharashtra) to drink water from the public tank. When the upper castes opposed it with the use of force, the Bombay High Court had to intervene and rule in favour of the lower castes.

The fabrication of the false majority

The pinnacle of the confrontation between the upper and lower castes was between 1930 and 1932 when three roundtable conferences for constitutional reforms in India were held by the British government. B. R. Ambedkar demanded in the first conference that separate electorates should be provided for the lower castes peoples and the Congress party predictably walked out of the conference in protest. Separate electorates for the lower castes would have changed the destiny of the subcontinent. It would have given the lower castes political power through representational democracy for the first time; it would have revealed and established the fact that the upper castes are a minority, smaller than the Muslim population.

The Congress party and Gandhi stubbornly opposed the demand of the lower castes. In a letter to the British prime minister Macdonald in 1932, opposing the introduction of separate electorates for the lower castes, Gandhi wrote, 'I sense the injection of a poison that is calculated to destroy Hinduism'. By 'Hinduism' Gandhi certainly meant the reign of the upper castes over the lower castes. In a statement to the press in the same year Gandhi admitted that he did not know the religious criteria by which the untouchables were to remain in 'Hinduism'; he wrote, 'There is a subtle something—quite indefinable—in Hinduism which keeps them [the lower caste people] in it even in spite of themselves'. The horror of this 'subtle something' which folds the lower castes into the 'Hindu' 'in spite of themselves' is quite evident. It is the very same 'subtle something' which folded the African slaves of America into slavery and the Jews of Nazi Germany into the Nuremberg laws 'in spite of themselves'. Seeing the insistent demands of the lower castes, Gandhi threatened to kill himself, or as the euphemism goes, commit 'satyagraha' unto death. Fearing the backlash from such an event, Ambedkar and lower caste peoples were forced to relent. Their surrender to Gandhi and the upper castes closed off the possibility of freedom for the majority of the subcontinent.

From the early twentieth century the upper caste leaders had invested in the process of creating a majority under the category of religion which they could then represent on the basis of scriptural and traditional authority. The term 'Hindu' served their need. Gandhi and other upper caste leaders like Lala Lajpat Rai had to convince the Brahmins to accept the term 'Hindu' which they found repugnant as it was of Arabic origin, or a 'mlechcha'[11] (foreign or impure) sound. Further, they had to direct the lower castes—who were agitating for their right to use the streets in front of the temples, but not quite interested in these temples themselves—to enter them and be part of this new religion. In the state of Kerala, the temple entry movement would eventually be presented as the generous and condescending reform offer of the upper caste people.

Hindu religion, which was gestating in the minds of the British and the upper castes since the late nineteenth century, began its birthing process in the twentieth century to avert 'the danger' that the lower caste majority posed for the upper caste Reich of two thousand years. The majority of the 'Hindus' would come to know about their own membership in this new religion and what they lost through this membership only years after the declaration of independence.

The false problem in politics: Hindu Right vs Hindu Lite

The construction of *the false religious majority* instituted *a false problem* in Indian politics. The primary enabling condition for the deflection, as we found earlier, was the setting up of a demographic opposition between the new 'Hindu' identity and Islam resulting in the partition of India. India's political discourse in the mainstream had been suffused with Pakistan as the external enemy and the Muslims of India as internal enemies. Since 1947, the politics, cultural developments, and intellectual and academic praxis participated in this nationalised deflection. The majority of academics, and what passes for 'the left' in India, discuss Hindu-Muslim religious harmony alone as an 'Indic' definition of secularism. They plead with this false 'Hindu majority' to not be majoritarian, and remind this fictitious entity of its fictitious better self in the past where 'Hindus' were a non-violent people. We can call it the opposition between *Hindu Right* and *Hindu Lite*.

The dominant Indian paradigms of academic research are continuous with the politics of Hinduness. Postcolonial theory is a revisionist project that seeks to criticise the colonial element in contemporary India and at the same time recover the lost 'native' elements of the past of the upper castes. Subaltern theory studies the 'failure' of the modern legal system to accommodate the caste obligations of the *Savarnas* (upper castes). In her classic example of the subaltern who cannot speak, Spivak discussed a Brahmin woman's obligation to wait till her menstruation to commit suicide such that her family would not face the dishonour of gossip about extramarital pregnancy. But since the mid-nineteenth century, the majority of India, the Dalits and lower castes had rejected and opposed these 'native' Vedic, Brahmanical traditions for the sake of emancipation, egalitarianism, constitutional values, human rights, the sciences, English and modern education. In what are called 'Eurocentric' values—sciences and reason—the lower castes find the replacements for the values of their oppressor. They do not, nor should they, fit the figure of the subaltern constructed by the Subaltern school, which did not address caste oppression in most of their writings. Despite suppressing the real problems of the real majority, both postcolonial and Subaltern theory have been the reigning paradigms for 'South Asia' in both USA-UK-Australia and in India for the past three decades. In this sense, the international academic community has been unwittingly participating in the oppression of the majority of India. The upper castes have manipulated both the *Darstellung* (representation as speaking about and classifying other people) and the *Vertretung* (representation as speaking for and in the place of other people).

After 1931, the Indian state has refused to make public the caste composition of the population due to the fear that the numbers of the upper caste will be exposed as dangerously low. Since then, there have been ongoing struggles and agitations to make these numbers available to the public. Based on the available government data, 'If the OBC numbers are about 60 per cent of the total population and the SC/ST, the only known figures, are 30 per cent, *the upper castes can only be 10 per cent of the population*'.[12] In 2011, due to pressure from the lower caste political parties, a caste census was conducted, but the present government refuses to publish its report. Meanwhile, untouchability persists across India; 71% of Dalit farmers are landless; 65% of all crimes are committed against Dalits; less than 9% of jobs in the national media are held by lower castes; Dalits and the tribal people account for less than 9% of the faculty in the branches of India's prestigious Indian Institute of Technology (IIT) and Indian Institute of Management (IIM). There are hardly any lower caste members in the present central government, and hardly any Dalits in provincial governments. The upper caste minority is still ruling over the lower caste majority using the state machinery, the judiciary, and the police as instruments. All this ensures that the voices, the cries for help, the political aspirations, and the theoretical inventions of the lower castes are never heard in the national media, with notable exceptions such as *The Caravan Magazine*.

The upper castes and the lower castes have opposite attitudes towards the colonial era, English language, 'Eurocentrism', the sciences, and modernity. The lower castes consider these very terms, which the upper castes reject through postcolonial theory, to offer a new set of values that can displace the old oppressive values of 'dharma' and 'karma'. The aggressive 'Hinduisation' (also called 'Saffronisation') taking place today in Indian academic institutions and their counter-parts in the west is working to avert the low caste majority from the 'other' future which they have been accessing through 'Eurocentric' categories. The 'left' academics are promoting education in 'Hindi' and 'vernacular' languages in order to keep 'English' and what is called 'western education' away from the low caste people. The hypocrisy of this postcolonialist gesture is that most of these academics and politicians place their children in private schools and western universities where they get 'western education'. But the majority have been alert to the false problem and the deceptions. Their protests have not ceased since the mid-nineteenth century, since the efforts of Phule, Periyar and Ambedkar; they are intensifying. The Hindu Right-Hindu Lite model is nearing its end today.

3

THE 'ARYAN DOCTRINE' AND THE *DE-POST-COLONIAL*

'Aryan doctrine' is the concept through which Dwivedi and Mohan analyse the political field of India in relation to 'the west'. Dwivedi has investigated the effects of the 'Aryan doctrine', the development of racism in Europe and its still persisting effects in philosophy. Mohan has often recalled the concept to show that the construction of the 'history of metaphysics' is tied to the 'Aryan doctrine', which in effect has created a canon of philosophy shorn of its formative diversity.

This is an introductory essay on the 'Aryan doctrine', its relation to the postcolonial academic practices of India, and the decolonial academic and political projects underway in India. It argues that these seemingly disparate processes are unified through the 'Aryan doctrine'. The concept points to the logic of the racialised apartheid of the caste system that denigrates the lower caste people to exclude them from all social transactions, and at the same time they are dominated in economic activities through their inclusion as the lesser men or less than men. Dwivedi, in her philosophical works has shown the way in which it inspired the race theorists of slavery in America. The most famous of these decolonial activities are the rapid name changes of places including the hints of a change in name of the country itself. The proposed name 'Bharata' for India (which subsists in the constitution of India) is after an 'Aryan' tribal chief in the stories and myths of the ancient north western Indian subcontinent.

An edited version of the first two sections of this text was published in *Revue Des Deux Mondes* (a magazine founded in 1829 in Paris) in October 2023 under the title 'La "doctrine aryenne"'. I decided to include the full version since it contains an extended and previously unpublished critique of postcolonial and decolonial discourse.

Remember the phrase of Joseph Conrad, *under western eyes*.

The world sees India, experiences it, dreams of it and even criticises it *under upper caste eyes.* The *post-de-colonial* common sense insists that India, like all other ex-colonies of the west, has been grasped through the méconnaisance of western epistemology. It prefers to not see the 'debt' (debt as such having been immortalised by Marcel Mauss and Durkheim as a famed mark of 'Indo-European' *being* in whose hyphen the 'Aryan' still *looms*) which the European 'Aryan' race theory owes to the Brahmanical institution of castes, the original 'Aryan doctrine'. It prefers that the world not see the effects that this doctrine—the oldest racism in the world—continues to precipitate in India and now in the Indian diaspora.

The 'Aryan doctrine'

Caste is the determinant of nearly every aspect of life in India. Castes are endogamous groups classified in a scale of superiority and inferiority where the 'essence' and life-course of each person is determined by birth and descent. Castes are ranked according to degrees of purity, degrees of freedom, and thus, degrees of the power to determine the occupations, property, wages, and the very value of their lives and deaths. For three millennia, this pyramidal social institution has remained in place with regional variations and minor mutations, beginning with the arrival on the subcontinent of the people who called themselves 'Aryan' (noble, superior) and denigrated the indigenous inhabitants as *dasa* (slave), *a-nasa* (barbaric, ugly), and *mlechha* (impure, untouchable). Across three millennia, including the interlude of colonial rule, the subcontinent witnessed the consolidation of the apartheid named *varna-ashrama-dharma*, that is, the divinely ordained law and duty of segregation in accordance with divinely created and biologically heritable colour-coded character traits. Up until today, the caste order continues to secure upper caste supremacy by organizing *inherited inequality*: the social and economic capital of the upper castes is drawn from the exploitation of the lower caste peoples—assured through physical and psychic oppression rather than consent (which Louis Dumont's *Homo hierarchicus* had wrongly canonized). The upper castes comprise no more than 10 per cent of the population of India. Yet, they occupy 90 per cent of all positions of power, influence, and profit in all the spheres of life which continue to be reserved for them century after century, and from which the rest, the majority lower caste peoples are excluded so that for them may be reserved the toil, the deprivation, the precarity—most stable!—and the humiliation.

Under upper caste eyes, the world, including most international scholars, sees the lower caste majority as a hapless senseless mass, or else it remains invisible. Its *longue misère* does not perturb the promissory *moksha* of 'Hindu' spirituality devoid of ethics. This image of 'India' was lodged in the retina of the world when the philosophers and scholars of what came to be 'the occident' identified with the 'Aryan doctrine' of the Brahmins. It still remains an implicit component in the self-construction of 'the occident' which has once again surged in the European and American far right.

What is the 'Aryan doctrine' which the world has identified solely with the Nazis at great peril? It has two mutually dependent components.

The first is the Idea of a special group of people who created a complex linguistic culture of poetry and religion, and at the same time excelled in the brutality which created the foundations for social organisations, for a large region of the world.

The second is the *denigrate-dominate function* which allowed upper caste supremacists to denigrate and dominate a population in the subcontinent for nearly three millennia through the caste order.

The caste order is the oldest and longest lasting system of social enslavement and apartheid in human history, the oldest racism. Caste was at the origin of European racism. It was the driving force of the *Indomania* (as Léon Poliakov called it) which gripped European scholars and thinkers from Voltaire, Herder and Friedrich Schlegel to Humboldt, Max Müller, and Gobineau.

The analogy between the functions of castes and 'races' which Dalit scholars and activists would rightly emphasise in the UN World Conference Against Racism in 2001 in Durban to denounce caste as a descent-based oppression, was first observed by European race theorists themselves from the eighteenth century onwards to justify oppression. For eighteenth-century European race theorists, the 'Aryan' had already perfected the strategy of *self-designated supremacy* for heritable domination long before their own civilization. The logic of birth-based descent sustained the *hypophysics* which the orders of both caste and race are, since every hypophysics consecrates value (for instance, inferior/superior) inside or within or under[1] each thing rather than as separately attributable to it. This consecration is the more un-dis-lodgable since birth can posit transmission at the level of nature (existing organically by itself rather than through artifice)—the value of a person cannot change or be acquired because it came with birth and was thus established under (*hypo-*) the natural-born existence (*physis*). It makes the value appear as intrinsic and inalienable from the thing. Hypophysics robs the thus-defined thing of its freedom to be other than what hypophysics deems it. Let it not be forgotten that no theory or perspective can imprison a thing without the application of force to prevent other theories and perspectives from emerging.

The hypophysics of caste-based descent assures that the power to oppress and exploit can be inherited. Intrinsic value, once forcefully imposed on things including humans, can be classified on a scale or a measure of degrees—better/worse, inferior/superior, touchable/untouchable—from the point of view of the profitable ends that the gradation can serve the ones who had the force of imposition at their disposal. The upper castes demonstrated their mastery of this social technology not only in their ancient scriptures—the *Manusmriti* contains, in fact, a racist's code of crime and punishment—but also in their testimonies to colonials and missionaries who subsequently came to the subcontinent. Upper caste ideology had already perfected the totalizing link between birth, culture, and power.

Starting with comparisons between the white Europeans and the 'fair' northern Indians—and never with all 'Indians'—the Europeans came to see themselves at first *as similar to* and soon enough as *originated from* the 'Aryan' masters. They saw themselves under 'Aryan' eyes. Philological race-making and racial anthropology competed as the most valid race science but also augmented each other in aggregating a 'white', 'occidental' identity. While the precise definitions and borders of these group- and civilizational identities varied across Europe and Britain, the analogy to the 'Aryan' masters of caste had been transformed into a homology or logic of common origins.

Arthur de Gobineau, the enormously influential race-theorist to have shaped the nineteenth and twentieth century racism in both Germany and the USA, found in the Brahmin nearly the sole bulwark against race-mixing and the decline of the 'Aryans'. He was impressed by the Brahmins' efficiency as custodians of caste, dharma and its scriptural archives, which made them the caste which described the 'degeneracy' of caste-mixing (whether in marriage or in change of occupation) and arrested it using the very weapon of caste (ability to prescribe punishments and deter transgressions, revolts and revolutions). The pursuit of technology and philosophy teach us that any end can be achieved by different means, and any means can serve more than one end. However, caste is an order in which the ends and the means are one and the same: enforcing caste-obedient conduct as the means towards the end of reproducing and perpetuating castes.

The identification of means with the ends prevents that wandering and inventiveness of human actions which the 'Ode to Man' in Sophocles' *Antigone* sings of and which is none other than the very vocation of art, technology, politics, and philosophy. Like the adventurer Odysseus trapped into an island, forgetting his wanderlust and inventiveness, under the spell of Calypso, the caste order too is a *calypsology* which traps human beings into forgetting the very possibility that they could be other than what they were born as. The observance of caste is the means towards the end of the *eternal* (Sanatana) reproduction of caste: the upper caste supremacists have never wavered from this imperative of the eternal, and so in the nineteenth century they tried to give it a religious (and hence fortified) status by adopting *Sanatana Dharma* as the new name for the denigrate-dominate programme.

The subjugating outsider or the upper castes across religions

The Aryan doctrine is the doctrine of the power to conquer and establish the *denigrate-dominate function*. The homology of caste and race established the synonymy between 'Aryan', 'Indo-European,' 'white', and 'occidental', just as the subcontinent began to witness a twin process which established the synonymy between 'Aryan', 'Sanatana', 'Hindu' and 'Hindutva' by the beginning of the twentieth century. The far right in India which calls itself 'Hindutva' (the Hinduness programme) is continuous with the mainstream upper caste dominance and its modern mask of 'Hinduism.' This far right does not itself make any distinction between Hindu and Hindutva, which the liberal left is anxious to make on behalf of the deeper caste structure.

'Hindu majority' is a hoax through which the 'leaders' of modern India asserted a religious category which would include the lower castes at the level of law and exclude them at the level of life. The hoax religion created a hoax majority which resulted in the partition of British India into a Muslim majority nation and a Hindu majority nation.[2] The latter must be made to appear organic—hence ancient—and this can only be done according to the hypophysics of descent and of superiority by birth, which is racist. Muslims and Christians are projected as foreigners, outsiders, and interlopers, or else as traitors who have betrayed their 'Indic' religion of birth by converting into faiths that are 'Abrahamic'—an appellation which, through its opposition to the 'Indic', purveys the older opposition between the 'Semitic' and the 'Aryan'.

In order to keep the 'Aryan' apart from the conquered denigrated peoples the doctrine employs a calypsology which ensures that there is no miscegenation. However, in the politics of modern nation states, the Aryan doctrine has run into a peculiar contradiction which it deftly manages while slandering those who expose it. Modern nation states are founded, at least implicitly, on the ground that the people of a particular geographical boundary are *one* 'people' of *one* 'common' origin. This '*oneness*' is asserted either as eternal (Sanatana) as in India, or else through the determination of a past sufficiently in the distance as in other countries where 'Aryan-ness' is invoked. The 'oneness' of and with the people who were already present in a land is the very argument that is used in contemporary politics against migration, even though human kind is essentially a migrating animal.

The upper castes, or those who claim the 'Aryan' position in the social hierarchy in India, isolate themselves also by asserting their superior origin from outside of the subcontinent. The religious texts of the Brahmins, such as the Vedas, recorded the origin of the population which identified themselves as 'Arya' from outside the subcontinent (which has been confirmed by archaeological and population studies; the 'Aryan' population either invaded or migrated suddenly into the Indian subcontinent from Asian steppe regions). These very ancient texts of the upper castes record the local population of the subcontinent encountered by the 'Arya' as slaves, demons, and non-human. In the Brahminical rituals, such as 'Agnichayana', a ceremonial map is used to assert the north-western geographical origin—far removed from the subcontinent—of the 'Arya' ancestral population and their movement towards the south-east.

While for the upper caste Indians, being unconnected to the older inhabitants of the subcontinent (whom they called 'dasyu') is essential for the maintenance of the denigrate-dominate function, they also find it simultaneously necessary to lay claim as the original inhabitants of the subcontinent to assert their dominance in the politics of the modern nation state. For this reason, certain upper caste politicians of the nineteenth and twentieth centuries took the position that the North Pole (the 'arctic home' of the Vedas and the 'Aryans') had itself been in India a long time ago, and that the 'Aryans' migrated from out of India into Europe to spread their language and culture.[3] For this very reason, the upper caste supremacist organisations posit Muslims and Christians as 'outsiders' and 'invaders'. Thus, other religious groups are oppressed as 'foreign' in order to direct attention away from the much quieter self-assertion of the upper caste supremacists as 'Aryans' who came to the subcontinent from elsewhere.

The separation between the high and the low is determined through the outsider and the insider, and is unfortunately at work today in most religious groups in the subcontinent. For instance, among Muslims too,

> The sociological descriptions usually indicate three kinds of Muslim status groups (in decreasing order of prestige): (1) the Ashraf, or the high-caste sections combining Muslims of foreign descent with native converts from high-caste Hindu origins; (2) the Ajlaf, converts from Shudra (Backward) occupational origins; and (3) the Arzal, converts from the formerly untouchable (or Dalit) origins.[4]

In these ways, we have the meaning of being lower caste in the eyes of the upper castes of all religions: *the lower caste people are those who were already there in the subcontinent at the time when the people who identified themselves as 'Aryan' arrived, encountered them, and subjugated them. The upper castes, in their own eyes, are from a superior elsewhere, both biologically and geographically.* This sense of caste is carried over into other religions of the subcontinent including Islam, Christianity and Sikhism.

The false 'Hindu majority' enforces the upper caste norms—their gods, their dietary regimes, their cultural symbols—on the real lower caste majority, as well as on indigenous tribal groups, and other religious minorities. Caste apartheid survives in all the religions of India and Dalit Muslims (*Pasmanda*) and Dalit Christians are the main victims of a fake majoritarianism. Dalits of all religions are the victims of vigilante violence against inter-religious and inter-caste marriages (honour killings), religious conversion and eating beef. Endogamy always entails violent control of women's labour and sexuality. Old patterns of exploited labour continue, having partially transformed into new forms of precarious work including child labour and sexual labour. The state itself has coerced the Dalits into a false Hindu identity by restricting the reservations in public institutions to those Dalits who are classified as 'Hindu'. The post-decolonial project provides the theoretical justification for a nativism falsely constructed on the components of the 'Aryan doctrine' and the insider-outsider logic.

De-post-colonial: the latest purity-programme

The *de-post-colonial* academic project and upper caste supremacism in India are both determined by the same category—the Brahminical notion of *purity*, the hypophysical core of the Brahmanical 'Aryan doctrine' which has animated the caste order across three millennia. Both these projects are, therefore, opposed to impurity, to contamination, to the bastard offspring that all culture and all history is. We should regard the academic arm of the purity programme not through the quibbles between 'postcolonialism' and 'decoloniality' but through the portmanteau word *de-post-colonial*, the bag of tricks with the past.

The relation between the de-post-colonial project and the upper caste supremacist project to dominate India through the category 'Hindu' can be understood through a familiar, though reticent, analogy. Postcolonial theory approaches the nominal, legal, moral, textual, conceptual and historical sites by defining them as sites of the colonial entombment of the originary past of the upper caste people. From there on, postcolonial theory commences a *speculative archaeology* of these sites, that is, an uncovering of the past which, unlike actual archeology of material sites, is necessarily speculative. It necessitates and upholds speculation about the past since it proceeds from the axiom that colonial epistemological acts restructured the knowledge of and the ability to know India so thoroughly that the purity of the past has been lost forever. It thereby designates the actual sites of history and knowledge as impure, obstructive of the speculated pure past, and thus worthy of demolition. It should be remembered that the past about which postcolonial theory advances its axiom and its speculative archaeology is only the upper caste past—the scriptures, the rituals, the epistemology belonging to the upper castes who held monopoly over the means of preserving their own knowledge and culture while they erased those of the subjugated populations. Thus, postcolonialist archaeology 'discovers' those traces of the upper caste past which it has, in fact, merely speculated. The theoretically condemned sites are now ready for the decolonial project to take over: demolition of places and monuments, dismantling of institutions, disappearance of archives, and the construction of new monuments on the basis of the speculative models of what *might have been buried* beneath the colonial monument.

In sum, *postcolonial* is the project which accepts the double bind of a colonised present from which the pure past is lost behind colonial sites and can only be speculated, and thus asserts a right to assign legitimacy to speculatively identified traces of an upper caste past. And *decolonial* is the project which asserts the right to demolish the ethico-juridical and archeological sites of colonisation and to erect new North Indian upper caste monuments which are modelled on the strategies of denigration-domination over the lower caste majority under contemporary political conditions. The analogy of the RSS and the upper caste de-post-colonial academia betrays the homology between the two: de-post-colonial projects of India assert, along with the RSS, a 'return' to the recently invented Sanskritised language which has usurped the name 'Hindi'; an 'indigenisation' of education founded on a speculated indigeneity which confines the lower caste people to their caste occupations; and a renaming of many cities to re-vitalise and legitimise the 'Aryan doctrine' which is oppressive to the psyche of the lower caste majority and other religious groups. The only difference between upper caste supremacist organisations and de-post-colonial project is the occasional 'nuance' which distinguishes the arrivals of different colonial and foreign contaminations. The former identifies the arrival of impurity with the Mughal rule and the latter with the arrival of East India companies.

In India, postcolonial discourse has a clearly identifiable context in the 1980s in which it arose alongside the BJP, both of them obscuring the developing currents of anti-caste politics, and their alignment in that decade can be seen as a response to the real possibility of a lower caste majority revolution that was presenting itself. A few places and dates will indicate this context: Bihar had witnessed the near decimation of the political leadership of the upper castes (especially the culture of Brahmin chief ministers in the Northern states) by the 1970s. In Gujarat, the 'caste wars' over reservations made the political participation of the lower caste majority a necessary condition for any party to come to power. Tamil Nadu, too, was developing a new current of anti-caste discourse and politics. The Mandal commission report was tabled at this juncture and was itself not without precedent: the Kalekar commission report[5] on caste based inequalities had been tabled already in the 1950s revealing that anti-caste politics could never be suppressed in India but only that it could always be written off or silenced in historiography. The tabling of the Mandal commission report initiated a wave of upper caste protests throughout the country. The media, which was then as today owned and controlled by the upper castes, took a stand against the minimal reservation in limited zones of life offered for the lower caste majority (given that the policy affected the public sector which makes for not much more than 4 per cent of employment). The Congress proving to have become weak and ineffective in inhibiting the new wave of empowerment of the lower castes, the BJP was ushered in by the upper caste public sphere along with its voluble 'Hindu' political project of the Rama temple. This phase of the anti-lower caste project was achieved through the demolition of the Babri mosque, and the conversion of all political struggles into murderous religious conflicts: the killing of both the lower caste people and lower caste Muslims became the norm and the normal from then on, having served as an effective and repeatable strategy to silence anti-caste politics.

Postcolonial discourse and the subaltern school historiography adopted as their lineage the anti-colonial and the anti-Eurocentric discourses arising in European languages, especially the works of Fanon, Sartre, Gramsci, Derrida, and Foucault, which were taken as the orienting and legitimising canon for postcolonial theory. However, there were two fundamental discrepancies between the self-diagnosed 'Eurocentrism' of philosophers such as Derrida and the absence of any such self-critique in the postcolonialist discourse. First, the anti-colonial discourse of Fanon and Sartre is still relevant to the regions addressed by them where the exploitative influence of former colonialists persist, while this is not the case in India. Second, the anti-colonial politics of India was never uniform since, on the one hand the lower castes experienced colonial rule through the self-serving mediation and collaboration of the upper castes, and on the other hand they experienced the colonial 'epistemic violence'—the loss of upper caste cultural and social pride—as the first ever disruption of the upper caste epistemology which had conducted the denigrate-dominate function for millennia. The lower caste intellectuals and leaders astutely analysed this non-uniformity and non-monolithic character of the 'Indian' colonial experience, and they welcomed the modern and rational aspects of colonial law and the new rights and possibilities for political participation.

There should be a reckoning of the difference in the response to colonial rule by the upper caste minority and lower caste majority, and of their reciprocal dynamic. There should be a reckoning of the ways in which the anti-colonial movements of pre-1947 India were concerned with suppressing the voice of the lower caste majority, often criminalising them (for instance, the chastisement of the Tamil representative in the Constituent Assembly by Vallabhbhai Patel), the entrapping of the lower caste majority within the newly invented Hindu religion, the baptism of upper castes as the representatives of false 'Hindu majority' and the silencing of the lower caste majority, the transfer of power from Britain to the upper castes and the extension of their 3000 years of rule using the modern constitutional system.

The officiated historical memory of India is that of the upper caste minority and corresponding to it is the fable of an ancient theocratic empire extending over most of south Asia with different 'Aryan' names: *arya-varta*, *bharata-varsha*,[6] *Jambu dweepa*. It is this same 'Aryan' memory that was and is being celebrated by the world. The self-description of India in the school and university curricula post-1947 suppressed the facts and memories of the political struggles of the lower caste majority. Postcolonial theory (and the consequent decolonial project) is continuous with this suppresion.

Postcolonial theory posits an *idyllic a priori*[7] in which the lower caste majority figures as an amorphous mass of labour required for the conveniences and luxuries of the pre-colonial world of the upper castes. In this world, colonial rule emerged as a disturbance of the millennia-old upper caste privileges, pride, and easy supremacy, whose celebration became difficult, at least without some embarrassment, after the appearance of modern jurisprudence and other international conventions. The upper castes felt humiliated, and their epistemology violated, by the uncovering of the humiliation long suffered by the lower caste majority and the dawn of its reddressals during colonial rule. As though the sorrow of a slave master after the emancipation of his slaves has a higher cultural value than the sorrows and sufferings of those who were once enslaved. This height (nobility, 'Arya') of upper caste feelings (pride, sorrow) guides postcolonial theory, and unfortunately its international reception.

The upper caste idyllic a priori

The theoretical grounds of postcolonial discourses are the self-critiques of 'Europe' by philosophers including Marx, Lenin, Heidegger, Derrida, and Foucault, who wrote in European languages. These critiques have had a double effect. On the one hand, they addressed the metaphysical and philosophical conditions under which 'Europe' was to be understood, and on the other hand they became the matter from out of which the de-post-colonial project of the upper caste supremacists could criticse Europe while itself averting self-scrutiny.

For Marx, Europe was the creation of the two stages of exploitation of its people, feudal and industrial. Europe's industrial phase of exploitation and self-creation also exploited other countries as resources. At the same time, Marx insisted, and not always incorrectly, on the positive social effects of colonialism in India. For Martin Heidegger, it was the suppression of the question of the meaning of Being which produced Europe as a techno-centric self-automating power. He saw Europe's as a story of decline from the Greeks to the engineering theory of cybernetics. At the same time, he asserted that Europe alone (in fact, Germany) held the power to re-open the question of the meaning of Being. This remains the case for the other philosophers of this tradition too.

Thus, it was through the very critique of 'Europe' that these philosophers produced the most metaphysical of all identities for Europe. And, through their critique of 'Eurocentrism' they succeeded in Europeanising 'philosophy' itself while excluding from the map of philosophy all those historical tributaries and distributaries in other regions and languages that were labelled as 'non-European'.

When, however, the Indian postcolonial theorists appropriated this self-critique as an instrument against the coloniser 'Europe', they had neither the reference of something like a 'Europe' nor a 'German nation' to correspond to, to produce their own regional self-constituting self-critique. They could not posit a territorial map nor a linguistic or an ethnic identity on whose basis such a critique were to be deployed. For, a positing of an identity is possible only through self-critique which shows the boundaries within which such a thing may be identified and the limits across which it would cease to be that particular thing. Instead, postcolonial theory deployed the language of 'loss of memory' asserting that the 'European' categories of history, modernity, reason, and critique had mediated what contemporary Indians thought, knew and remembered. All this while, postcolonial theory implicitly assumed the territorial state created by colonial rule, or the Raj, as 'undivided India', and it silently served the position of Europe in the self-constituting self-critiques of European philosophers. The Postcolonial claim was that since the 'Eurocentrism' of colonial rule had thus irreversibly transformed the memories of (upper caste) 'Indians' today, there was no access to a pure memory that could testify to the lost *idyllic a priori*. In fact, this memory remains available through Mughal court documents and even other upper caste texts, but it is the inconvenient memory of the privileges of the upper castes and the misery of the enslaved majority peoples. Moreover, the upper caste supremacists and the postcolonial discourse find this available memory to be less in 'height' and stature than the exorbitant *idyllic a priori* which they project in the hoary, even immemorable past: fantasies of being at the origin of atomic physics, relativity theory, plastic surgery, and aeronautics 3000 years or so ago.

In this way, a 'lost' memory, which is in fact that of an *idyllic a priori* rather than of anything that actually ever took place, is posited as that which must be founded again, and postcolonial discourse gives this manoeuvre the name of an aporia (non-passage, non-access): that which is defined as inaccessible must be created as though it were being 'recreated'. This postcolonialist aporia created an empty field for the past of India and the field laws could now be prescribed by the RSS and the BJP. The RSS asserts through its ministers that in the 'lost' past of the upper caste supremacists, the superior groups (mythic sages and heroes) had already anticipated all the developments and achievements of 'Eurocentric' discourses including the European sciences. The comedy of this strategy is that now every invention in the past of the upper castes can be posited only after this invention has been made in present times in Europe, USA, China etc. Only once they learn about it from today's newspapers can the de-post-colonial agents assert that it is but an ancient 'Indian' invention that was 're-appropriated' by the 'Eurocentric' sciences and philosophy. *The upper caste supremacists therefore await the findings of the James Webb telescope and the further development of stem cell research so that they may then step in and 'discover' more about their own ancient idyllic a priori.*

Whereas postcolonial theory was the accounting of the loss of upper caste pride according to the measure of their *idyllic a priori*, decolonial politics in India is about the aggressive restoration of that very *idyllic a priori*. The present constitution of India curtailed—to a minimal extent until the rise of RSS with the Modi government—the upper caste dominance in its extremes in urban centres of India. If postcolonial theory emerged with the appearance of the BJP in Indian politics, the decolonial project emerged with the rise of Modi led, openly fascistic, and brutally illiterate upper caste supremacism since 2014. The abandon with which decolonial strategies—including 'indigenous' education, 'vernacular' education, Sanskrit supremacism and Hindi imposition—were prepared in the so called 'leftist' campuses of JNU, Jadavpur, and Delhi University was matched by their carnivalesque adoption by the BJP governments. This resulted in the Sanskritization of Hindi and the loss of its 700-year-old existence starting from a contact language born in the marketplaces; the renaming of cities and institutions according to Brahmanical connotations; and finally the substitution of the name 'Bharat' for India by nearly all political parties.

To understand this situation and to reckon with its future effects—especially when conjoined with 'decolonial' as a slang, like

'Global South', for a Sino-Indo-centric global order—we should necessarily address the theoretical terrain. Against these dominant theories about India, the lower caste majority's perspective on the subcontinent has not yet come in full view because the discourses from the lower caste majority position have been disavowed in the media and academia; because those who speak from the lower caste position in the media and academia internationally are excluded and ostracised; and, due to the criminalisation of lower caste educational and political projects (including teachers and students) as Maoism and terrorism by the various governments of India.

Meanwhile, India remains a poor country today, and the poor are the majority lower caste population. The *World Inequality Report 2022* directed by Lucas Chancel, Thomas Piketty, Emmanuel Saez, and Gabriel Zucman reveals that only 13% of national income and only 5% of national wealth are possessed by the bottom 50% of the Indian population—which overlaps nearly entirely with the percentage of reservations for ex-untouchables, tribes, and lower castes under the official policy of positive discrimination. Which means that it overlaps with *at least* that population of lower castes and Dalits whose numbers the government itself acknowledges. The caste census finally conducted in Bihar in summer 2023 has now shown that this number is underestimated, that the upper castes are only 13% of the population. The top 10% population holds 57% of income and 65% of all wealth. The world is told that India has lifted many people above the poverty line in recent years, but its method is that simply by lowering the poverty line further down, many more people can be lifted above this line: the *line* today is set at an individual earning of a little less than half a Euro. The poor are cheated even about the fact of their poverty to the satisfaction or rather the wish-fulfilment of the upper castes which would today like to be 'proud' of India. This evil game with imaginary lines accompanies the de-post-colonial game with the *idyllic a priori* of the 'Aryan Doctrine'.

4

NEVER WAS A MAN TREATED AS A MIND[1]

A series of events in the university campuses began to challenge the Modi regime in its early years. There are two historiographies of these events: one, the upper caste story covering up the real history and the other the lower caste majority students and activists who were the ones to precipitate these events. The lower caste majority position is sharply asserted in a later chapter of this volume titled 'Sex and Post-colonial Family Values'. The very first act of defiance and analytical approach against the Modi government came from the lower caste students of the IIT Madras Ambedkar Periyar Study Circle. In Hyderabad Central University, the lower caste students organised in a similar manner, protested the death penalty to Yakub Memon and screened 'Muzaffar Nagar Baqi Hai'(a film about the pogroms in 2013 against Muslims in Uttar Pradesh), and they supported autonomy for Jammu and Kashmir. The lower caste students seized Pune Film Institute next. Then, Dalit students in JNU celebrated 'Mahishasura Martyrdom Day', which provoked the sharpest reaction from the then Education minister. But soon after, the upper caste student body, its leaders, and the upper caste faculty of JNU took over the protests with the help of mainstream 'liberal' media and suppressed the clamour of the lower caste majority by framing everything into 'good nationalism versus

> bad nationalism'. This framework of discussing India is a version of 'good Hindu versus bad Hindu' and 'Hindu majoritarianism versus religious minorities'. It is against this background that this article should be seen: as a text appearing in the middle of an upper caste management of political events by what is called the left and the right in India. It asserts that 'the Aryan doctrine' guides upper caste politics and that confronting it requires the assimilation of the knowledge of its effects in Nazism and other such moments in Europe as well.

The enduring figures—or the eternal forms—of humanity are made-up of free thought and free thinkers. The eternal forms are not things stolen from a divine world, the way the myth of Prometheus would tell us. Instead, even the idea of stealing from a divine world, of making a divine domain for ourselves through the fiction of a theft, is one that we have ourselves forged. Thought takes time as it makes new forms and gives them endurance; for example, Darwin's revolution has endured over a hundred years. Those who think freely and speak freely give history and form to this human world. The thinker relays what she made in the moment allotted to her to those who will come after her; this relaying of free thinking accumulates over time and adds up to a body of thought which encompasses our sciences, philosophies, arts. This relaying—that creates ideas and gives them endurance—is the very body of humanity.

The logic of thought

The figures might be the name of ideas—reason, geometry, constitutional democracy, computation, cubism—or the names of people—Aristotle, Einstein, Darwin, al-Khwarizmi, B. R. Ambedkar. What are we, the people of this ominous moment in the subcontinent today, going to relay to those who will come after us? Which are the names and figures that we will hand over to those unborn, whose gaze we can feel on the skin of our thought, full of dread, and whose footsteps we can hear on the tympanum of our ideas, retreating from us? The weight of this question, even as it crushes us, tells us that we have no greater responsibility than keeping freedom (*Azadi, Freiheit,*

Viduthalai,[2] *Liberté*) alight, a lighthouse, an orienting star[3] for those unborn who are coming towards us.

The lesson of the last century, a lesson obtained through the ashes of millions of lives lost in the wars and the holocaust, was to not let this light be snuffed out ever again in the name of anything, be it race, nation, territory, language, religion. The declaration of human rights asserts that the species we strive to be through our institutions is the animal that thinks freely, the animal that thinks freedom, the animal that needs freedom to think in order to be. When compared to the primate that walked out of Africa several millennia ago, our species, defined by this freedom, is rather fragile.

The institutions of humanity—the constitution, parliament, the courts, the university, the book shops—exist as shelter for this fragile animal, for thinking freedom. Other than that, there is no legitimacy for human institutions.

The lesson since 1945 has been that those who destroy this fragile animal will be punished. Their crimes are not protected by national boundaries, for those are crimes against humanity itself, against this fragile, free-thinking animal. The concentration camp guard who stands on trial today,[4] toothless in his 90s, unforgotten and unforgiven, is a reminder of this stern lesson.

Unquestioning obedience to superior orders—'*Befehl ist Befehl*'[5]—will not absolve anyone from the guilt of seeking the destruction of this fragile animal whose protection is the sole r*aison d'etre* of any institution.

The logic of action

In the early 1930s, Martin Heidegger, 'the last universally recognizable philosopher' according to Alain Badiou,[6] turned into a Nazi sympathiser and sought to spiritualise National Socialism. He tried to ground Nazism metaphysically on 'resolve and action' as against the paralysis of too much thinking. In his view, 'Europe lies in the pincers between the alarming non-spiritualism of the communist Russia and the equally non-spiritual capitalism of America.'[7] Germany was to take a 'great stand' in this 'darkening of the world' or 'the emasculation of the spirit', in such a way that it could create spiritual awakening through a resolute German people who would *act*. Action-without-thought was the proffered solution.

This 'solution' became the savagery and destruction of the Second World War; the concentration and extermination camps were the finality of this unfolding solution. In an interview to *Der Spiegel* in 1966, Heidegger put forward an evasive apologetics for his 'judgement: insofar as I could judge things', but this was no better than the sympathy for 'a puppy run over by a car'[8] and was in no way an apology. He suggested that the prevailing mood of pessimism called for total mobilisation, and the politicisation of the sciences called for casting out traditional academic freedom; only once in a private exchange is he said to have admitted this as 'the biggest stupidity of his life', which is as bad as 'the saddest day of my life'.[9] In a similar TV interview in 1969 he shifted the discussion very cunningly onto Marx's call to action in the 11th thesis on Feuerbach –philosophers have merely *interpreted* the world in different ways; now the task is to *change* it—from which he now distanced himself. He found that there was, and is, too little thinking in the world and that that is the root of the problem: an undertaking to change the world must be preceded by thinking; indeed, one must first understand this present world, and then also think and explain the meaning of the new world that one seeks to actualise.

Heidegger's crime was not that he was not thinking but that his actions contributed to the taking away of the right to think freely from millions of humans on the basis of their race and religion. These humans, reduced from the free thinking animal to labouring animals, were further reduced in the concentration camps into wood for the 'Aryan' fire. As we can see today, in the subcontinent too, our 'Aryans' are envious of the arrival of a gathering of thoughtful and free young people (or 'children'). Given their 'Aryan'[10] style of thinking, they can recognise these children only through their 'immediate identity'. It should trouble us a lot, since the distance from being reduced to 'immediate identity' to becoming ashes is not very much. That is the other lesson of the Holocaust.

The call to action that we hear around us is contrasted with democracy. That is, democracy is held to be too encumbered since it gives freedom equally to everyone to think; since it shares and relays thinking so that 'immediate identities' break down; since it thinks too much and thinking leads to paralysis. This style of action-against-thinking characterised the birth of fascism. There is a minority of power-hungry people around the world speaking in this form today—action-against-thinking—in Europe and the Americas, all the way from the stock markets to the war machinery. It is a good moment for the world to pause and think.

Further, the big lie is the mark of all totalitarian systems: to 'repeat long enough the lie' that we are in a state of danger and that thinking is a luxury that can be poisonous. The right to think freely alone can give us a conscience worthy of the free-thinking animal. In the subcontinent, we are familiar with the tale of a man who stopped to think in the battlefield when faced with the task of killing his kinsmen. He thought freely, beyond the bounds of his caste rules and capabilities, and the weight of conscience which increases with thought made him put his weapons down and step off his chariot. The rest of the tale is about the removal of thought-driven paralysis so that there can be caste-based action, bringing death and destruction. Gandhi was never happy with this reality of the tale of a man who silences his conscience and goes on to kill. So, Gandhi insisted that this 'action' did not take place, that the war was a fiction inside the tale.[11]

Action and reaction

The 'Aryan doctrine' of the subcontinent is a very clever business. Freedom is not a matter of this world, of these mortal moments. The notion of having and needing the freedom to think is an illusion, we are always told. Instead, we are to have faith in the freedom that awaits us after death—*mukti*, *moksha*, *nirvana*.[12] This postmortem freedom that cannot be experienced in these mortal moments is believed to accrue to us in proportion to our obedience to caste laws. So, the argument today appears to be the same as it ever was: Our 'notional body' is sick, its infection is nearly complete; it needs the critical care of the defence system and desperate remedies; do not go about feeding it whisky and beef. Or, when the only thing that matters is the physical existence of the national body, all of us should be nothing other than a hymn singing corps for military men. Language is only good for hymns and slogans now.

The word 'action' has a limited and idiotic meaning in these instances. It means that humanity is only worth the repetition of its meals and ablutions. We should also remember that those who ask us to stop thinking and only act, do not believe that all actions are equal. They will never concede the following to be worthy of being called action: the letters written by a Dalit scholar who killed himself; the struggles of the students of the subcontinent to think freely and act freely; the labour of the kindergarten worker; the labour of the woman who stitched clothes to send her son to the university; the toil of the peasant.

The would-be Aryans are ignorant about action too. Let us note that only the free thinking animal acts and the other animal only 'reacts' with hurt sentiments. They proudly admit to this fact that they cannot catch that interval of time between stimulus and response in which one thinks freely and generates action. Is it not a fact that only the free thinking animal who acts is getting enmeshed in the legal systems of the subcontinent today? Is that perhaps why the criminals who vandalised court premises and assaulted journalists have not been found fit for trial so far? What is being called the acting animal today is a species of the *reacting animal*, created by each wave of fascism, one that is predatory and feeds like a parasite on those who think freely.

Authors' Note: *We have borrowed the title of this article from Rohith Vemula's suicide note.*

5

THE MACABRE MEASURE OF DALIT-BAHUJAN MOBILIZATIONS

In September 2020, a Dalit girl was raped by upper caste men belonging to the Thakur (Kshatriya) community in the state of Uttar Pradesh. She died after struggling with severe injuries for days in the hospital. In Delhi in 2012, when an upper caste girl suffered the same fate the state and the country came to a standstill. The rapists received capital punishment. It became one of the factors which removed the Congress party from power in the Delhi state and Indian Union governments. However, in the case of the Dalit victim, the BJP rule continued unimpacted.

This is certainly the most visceral text of this anthology, written with a rage that seizes the reader from the very first words. It is also a strong anti-caste text which asserts through Ambedkarite literature and icons that there shall not be a retreat out of fear. Dwivedi demolishes the pretences of upper caste academia, including postcolonial theory, and of upper caste media, which makes it an essential reading for understanding the truth of the public sphere in India. The publication of this text was delayed by leading media houses holding on to it and in the end rejecting it. It may seem unusual that this happened to Divya Dwivedi, but is not uncommon in India. Eventually, the text was published in Newsclick on 23 October 2020, whose offices were raided on 3 October 2023.

Another Dalit girl is dead after being brutally raped, tortured and mutilated by upper caste men (Thakur caste belonging to the savarna Kshatriyas) on 14 September 2020 in Hathras village in the state of Uttar Pradesh, where 10 rapes are committed every day according to official statistics,[1] while many others go unreported.

Hereby another human identified as untouchable by the subcontinent's millennia-old racist, slave-driving, segregationist order of caste has been *reduced to her immediate identity and nearest possibility*—in the immortal words of Rohith Vemula, written just before his institutional murder, to describe the way his university reduced him, too, to his Dalit identity.[2]

The 19 year old girl died on 29 September under the following conditions: the severity of assault, the delay in receiving appropriate treatment for her torturous wounds at a leading public hospital in Delhi, and the neglect of the policemen to whom she had made a clear dying declaration of her sexual assault and the perpetrators' identities.

Her death too is an institutional murder. But the character of this institution which oppresses, enslaves, tortures, traffics, rapes, mutilates, and murders has to be examined closely to the point from which the condescending and duplicitous gestures of this institution should no longer be repeatable.

The unabashed and manifestly illegal effort of the upper caste police administration, obedient to an upper caste chief minister (himself a Kshatriya) of an upper caste party (directed by a Brahmin organisation, the RSS), was: to hurriedly declare an absence of sexual assault[3] even before trial had begun, and despite the final testimony of the victim and the medical report of the first hospital; and to destroy evidence by cremating the body at 3 am without the consent or presence of the girl's parents and siblings.[4]

'हमारी बहन को कचरे की तरह जलाया गया', *our sister has been burnt like waste*—saying this, Chandrashekhar Azad Ravan, chief of the Bhim Army, an organization of, by, and for Dalit-Bahujans, named the essence of this choreography of actions which would have been impossible if the victim were an upper caste girl. He did so on 2 October, the birth anniversary of M. K. Gandhi who was a defender of the caste order and who preferred that the people of the untouchable manual scavenging caste should voluntarily embrace the profession to which they were already condemned by birth, and should strive for excellence in cleaning shit.

It is impossible to overlook the political posturing and manoeuvrings that are still played out in Gandhi's name by what is liberally called the left and of late the Hindu right, who are both committed to the 'Hindu' upper caste dominance of Indian society.

That this pattern manifests itself most acutely in Uttar Pradesh (UP) has everything to do with this state being the core component of the 'Hindi-Hindu-Hindustan' belt, that is, the north-western region of India with the maximum expression of the drive for a nation whose language, religion and social structure strictly correspond to an 'Aryan' identity. India as a 'Hindu' nation that will revert to the glory of the 'Aryan' supremacy, which in reality is the supremacy of the upper castes of Brahmins, Kshatriyas, and Baniyas has been constructed predominantly from the north-west Indian perspective.[5]

UP has a large upper caste population which has held political, administrative and cultural power for the largest part of the period before and since the transfer of power in 1947. The largest number of members of parliament are returned from this state. The newspaper with the highest circulation—in Hindi language and promoting the upper caste project of a Hindu nation—is run from UP. Rajasthan and Madhya Pradesh, which are the other significant constituents of the Hindi belt, also record very high rates of crimes against Dalit-Bahujans and against women in general.[6]

The treatment of the victim, leading to, in, and after her death, has faithfully exhibited the millennia-old attitude of the upper castes towards those they enslaved and segregated. This phenomenon is ubiquitous and very well-known but deliberately un-acknowledged in the Indian Union for reasons that themselves pertain to the perpetuation of the caste order.

In the early 2000s, the pattern of crimes against Dalit women and their oppression through both quotidian and grievous acts, was meticulously researched and documented; these country-wide findings were published in 2011 in a book, accurately titled *Dalit Women Speak Out*, edited by Aloysius Irudayam S. J., Jayshree, P. Mangubhai, and Joel G. Lee. They analysed then what is still recurring with ceremonial regularity today, and most acutely so in Uttar Pradesh and Rajasthan:

> Dalit women are more likely to face collective and public threats or acts of social violence than dominant caste women, who tend to be subjected to violence more within the family due to strict controls over their sexuality and freedom of movement.[7]

Irudayam et al revealed the essential character of caste-based crimes—they are in fact *punishments* dispensed by the upper caste guardians of the caste order to Dalit women 'when they transgress caste norms, such as those relating to caste endogamy or untouchability, or assert their rights over resources: public or cultural spaces.'[8] It is not by negligence or corruption, but rather with great care that these acts of punishment follow a norm which is outside that of the constitution of India and the criminal code, from which these acts are shielded with great care. *Dalit Women Speak Out* had exposed this 'procedure' a decade ago:

> An unofficially established trend exists today of police collaborating with dominant caste perpetrators to file false cases against the Dalit women or their families in order to pressurize them to withdraw cases or make out-of-court settlements. In many instances Dalit women are threatened into compromises or forced to become hostile witnesses to ensure a case acquittal.[9]

These deadly crimes happen with a regularity that is indifferent to the laws and norms of the world. They annihilate a person's capacity for becoming anything different from what the caste order dictates for them. Its aim is to guard against the future liberation of the Dalit-Bahujan and a possible representation of this real majority community in politics. For this, the guardians of the caste order send out terminators of all kinds equipped with all the new technologies—the modern police system, the judiciary, the social media, the academia, latest social science disciplines and theories.

It is a well-known 'secret' that the upper castes are a severe minority population of the subcontinent which has been oppressing the majority population, the Bahujan. The falsity that there is one religion of the majority population of India—a falsity that would soon be baptised as 'Hindu' religion—was exposed as early as 1855 in an essay by Mukta Salve, a teenaged pupil of the Phules' school, which has been rightly hailed as perhaps the first feminist text of India. She wrote:

> If the Vedas belong only to the brahmans, then it is an open secret that we do not have the Book. [...] then we are not bound to act according to the Vedas. [...] Let that religion, where only one person is privileged, and the rest deprived, vanish from the earth and let it never enter our minds to boast of such a (discriminatory) religion.[10]

Since the mid-nineteenth century, Dalit-Bahujan had been mobilising to annihilate caste. Progressive views and reforms for women's equality were first envisaged and implemented in the form of girls' schools by Joti Rao Phule. Long before Gandhi was even born, Phule said:

> In their opinion, women should forever be kept in obedience, should not be given any knowledge, should not be well educated, should not know about religion, should not mix with men, and they bring out extracts from our Shastras in which women are so deprecated in support of these idiotic beliefs, and ask whether anything written by the great and learned sages be untrue.[11]

Neither these transformative achievements nor the strenuous counter-efforts of the upper-castes to obstruct them have been taught in our history textbooks.[12] Instead, we have all suffered an arrested political and intellectual development due to the brazenness of the upper caste fantasy that our current problems are the *remnants* of colonial rule.

This most malicious and elaborate fantasy also goes by the name of postcolonialist theory whose proponents are nearly all upper caste. It is the project to recover the lost pride of the upper castes who lost control of their traditional powers over the lower castes during British rule. It is the enemy of any attempt to emancipate the majority of the subcontinent from the oldest indignity, inequality and oppression of the caste order. Postcolonialist study of contemporary India is a witness to something that has no objective reality, a mock fight against a spectre that is no longer haunting anyone.

The upper castes have been interposing themselves in the place of Dalit-Bahujans to 'speak for them' and even for their alleged 'subaltern' inability to speak for themselves. It is not that the Dalit-Bahujan do not speak, but rather that their speech is made to disappear. Besides minimising the history of the lower castes—who were neither abject nor subaltern but were rather the pioneers and participants in an enlightenment that is still dawning on the subcontinent—the upper castes have cunningly practiced several other strategies of erasure in politics and the public sphere:

An intellectual obligation has been imposed to treat the category of 'caste' as a colonial construct. All discussion of our social reality is forced to look for its adequate terminology and truth in the Brahmanical terms from various periods like 'shudra' or 'harijan' (children of Vishnu) rather than in the experience of reality that the lower castes have had or the political identities they forged for themselves, like 'Dalit'. The more recent Brahmanical imposition has come in the form of the term 'subaltern'; the use of 'internal colonialism', a convoluted analogy of foreign rule, to describe caste; the term 'vertical diversity' as another perverted euphemism for caste to give it a positive spin; and the demand that Indian feminists should prefer Draupadi, the Kshatriya heroine of a Sanskrit epic, as an icon for their plight. Similarly, caste atrocities are evaluated from an upper caste perspective, such as *could Bhanwari Devi have been raped by upper caste men since she was untouchable?* The government of the upper castes has recently prohibited the media from using the word 'Dalit'.

Most important in the present context is the cunning of Indian feminists who rejected European feminism by saying it was only concerned with white women and that it colluded in the colonialist oppression of brown men and women. Thus, the upper caste women became the self-appointed representatives of all women, but they in fact addressed only their own concerns and hid the problems of caste and of Dalit-Bahujan women and men.

Anu Ramdas occasioned a necessary reflection and debate on whether 'feminism is Brahmanism' when we observe that the canon of feminism did not represent any Dalit-Bahujan voice or material concerns.[13] The upper caste discourse erased the fact that Phule was making feminist demands *avant la lettre* and decades before upper caste feminists, and he had not tried to advocate the equality of lower caste women alone but for all women. For him gender came before community, as Tejas Harad pointed out. But not for Indian feminists: when they were reminded of their prejudice, most recently in the moment of Raya Sarkar's list, their response was through anger and self-praise.[14] But feminism has already been criticalised by Dalits who exposed the fact that on the subcontinent gender comes after community and that postcolonial feminists are upper caste first and women later.

When Dalit scholars and activists spoke about the intersecting and compounding relations between caste and gender, the upper caste feminists sought to discredit 'intersectionality' as an imported term—perhaps they expected everyone to accept their postcolonialist common sense that 'foreign' knowledge, especially of Black feminists, is bad and upper caste feminists' thoughts are more acceptable because they are indigenous and 'pure'. Priyanka Samy has once again patiently outlined 'the interesting factors behind structural violence against Dalit women' in the Hathras case.[15] For such reasons, the new discipline of 'women's studies' practiced by upper caste feminists has alienated Dalit students. Rupali Bansode articulated their scepticism, writing that 'Dalit girls feel there is nothing called "Sisterhood", nothing called "Oneness", rather they feel excluded always'.[16]

Moreover, upper caste scholars and commentators in the public sphere regularly appropriate the very emancipatory discourse of the lower castes to talk about them. Many of the theoretical breakthroughs of the Dalits have been appropriated and folded into a discourse which the upper caste scholars can wield and direct, even as others have been discredited. The foremost instance of this was the effort to prevent Dalit activists from raising the issue of caste-discrimination at the United Nations World Conference Against Racism and related discriminations at Durban in 2001. Theirs and every later attempt to discuss caste and racism in the same breath was dealt with savarna-splaining and condescension by many leading sociologists and political scientists.[17]

Another recent example, in the media, is the Hathras case in which the Bhim Army, the very organisation of Dalits themselves which had first started massive protests in Delhi, was given last priority in reportage as well as in access to the family of victim. Its leader, Chandrashekhar Azad Ravan was the first to raise the matter to the necessary point where it could not be ignored or buried. Yet, he was the last to be permitted to meet the victim's family, after the leaders of the Congress (although it was commendable that they and other opposition parties took up this issue).

Caste is the only political problem of the sub-continent. All spheres of activity—business, judiciary, army, politics, media, academics, art, literature—are controlled and dominated by the upper castes, keeping the Dalit-Bahujan in an 'underworld' where they have no representation and participation even though they are the real majority. Using this control and for the sake of maintaining it, the upper castes have created an alternative reality in which caste is seen as a thing of the past. For many decades, they even succeeded in wasting much breath on discussing *is caste a reality in twentieth century India?* or *has caste withered in the 21st century?* or *why bring caste into an incident which is simply violence of a Hindu against another Hindu*? More recently, instead of fighting the well-known reality they have taken to broadcasting their own uncertain awakening. Uncertain, since it is still snuggled in devious apologetics and diffractions of casteist reality.

For instance, many people have been outraged by the Hathras incident in a specific way suggesting that the main problem was whether opposition or media can access the family or not—whereas the problem is recurring because it is systemic. Many upper caste commentators in various domains have analysed the incident predominantly in terms of patriarchy, police irregularity, goonda raj[18] lawlessness in UP, Hindu nationalism, colonial remnants—this last will need special attention—and with as little reference to caste as can be gotten away with. This is also consistent with those looking for solutions in the judicial system, demanding—

from whom?—a 100 per cent percent conviction rate. They know that the outgoing chief justice of India was accused of sexually exploiting a Dalit employee of the Supreme Court, and he was able to himself preside over her compliant and judge it to be false. He was thereafter made a nominated member of the parliament. Some even asked for presidential rule which would be more of the same 'Aryan' supremacist rule as currently in UP, both being controlled by the BJP-RSS.

All these institutions have been serving upper caste interests—as also revealed in the way that the few progressive anti-caste laws are being diluted. These include provisions related to the very SC/ST Prevention of Atrocities Act under which the perpetrators of Hathras were finally arrested. Also being diluted are the provisions of reservations, which were restricted to 'Hindus' so as to prevent them from converting to other religions, and also to prevent the Dalits-Bahujans of the other religious communities from receiving the constitutional guarantee of reservation. The ideals of just institutions are unachievable until the majority finds representation in them through membership rather than trusteeship or proxy.

The caste order works to convert all men and all means into one sole end—the perpetuation of the caste order. Like Calypso in the Greek legend it seeks to hide or avert everyone who is on and from the subcontinent from actualising the fundamental homological powers of humans to become something different from what they are or what they are born as. It is stasis—a conversion to end all conversions—it *interns* and *inters*. It is the most perfected calypsology known in history, the longest lasting form of racism. It is the death mask. This can be quickly observed through a contrast.

Michel Foucault, in his project *Lives of Infamous Men*, had attempted to demonstrate the birth of a modern form of power in the eighteenth-century internment records of ordinary, poor and marginal individuals.[19] In these records, their direct voice is absent, their lives are vanishing lives, their names are not recognised or remembered, but nevertheless the very institutional documents of their internment carried the trace of their 'clash with a power that seeks to annihilate them or to obliterate their lives … they had met with power and provoked its forces'. This nascent form of power would expand and consolidate into the twentieth century's forms of totalitarianism and contemporary surveillance state according to him.

The Dalit-Bahujans, too, impart the trace of their clash with a power that seeks to annihilate them, the power which they provoke. But in a way very different from Foucault's 'infamous men'. The actions and articulations of the lower caste and outcaste peoples are not mute traces of 'low-life' nobodies shining through the verbose and formulaic eloquence of the official internment records. Rather, they are cogent, creative, and resounding mobilizations—both intellectual and organizational, individual and collective—for nearly two centuries starting at least with Joti Rao Phule and Savitri Phule's work from the 1840s. Far from being ignored by the upper castes, they have been and are still being actively suppressed, forgotten, turned to ash like the Dalit girl from Hathras. Because their defiance of caste rules is intolerable to the upper castes.

Hence, the prose of power of internment held up by Foucault stands in sharp contrast to the great internment of caste. Up to and in 2020, the calypsological caste order functions through the avoidance, distortion, defacement and erasure of records—of first information reports, postmortem reports, census reports, documents of the archives, history textbooks, historical monuments, archaeological sites and reports, repositories of ancient manuscripts, worship practices of non-upper caste people, commemorative statues of B. R. Ambedkar the great intellectual, constitutionalist and leader of Dalits, memories and commemorations of the military defeat of Brahmins by Dalits in the 1818 battle of Bhima Koregoan, incarceration of Dalit-Bahujan scholars, journalists, activists and those who support their cause in any way, prolonged incarceration of under-trials, destruction of bodies living and dead.

If the discussion on caste is now growing, this is solely because of the insistence of the Dalit-Bahujan activists, poets, scholars and politicians. Extreme efforts are being made to silence them. Anyone raising themselves from grinding poverty or caste-occupation is assaulted, lynched, shot, humiliated, jailed, forced to exit institutions, forced to commit suicide. Humiliating physical abuse is routinely inflicted on Dalit men as well.

The most extreme upper caste strategy today is to frame Dalit leaders and comrades under serious charges and incarcerate them indefinitely. Azad and his party members have now been charged under several laws and might be arrested soon.[20] In relation to the protests started by him, another case has been filed claiming that there is an international plot and Islamist funding behind the protests.[21] Meanwhile, caste meetings of the Thakurs took place unhindered in Hathras to explicitly support the accused men.[22]

This step by the government of upper castes in UP is extremely significant. It follows the upper caste scheme in the protests in 2018 to commemorate the Battle of Bhima Koregaon, which too was called an anti-national Islamist conspiracy and several Dalits and others are now jailed under-trials.[23] It is being done again against the protestors of the anti-CAA protests.[24] It also follows an even older pattern of deflecting caste conflict and presenting it as Hindu-Muslim conflict initiated by Muslims.

Owing to their brilliance in theoretical inventions and fortitude in organisation, Dalit-Bahujans have begun to successfully mobilize despite setbacks, and they should not rest until the social transformation of India is achieved—the majority must attain adequate representation in power in all spheres and assert themselves to attain equality. Seventy years since the transfer of power, this alone will be true independence which India has not experienced. This unprecedented moment has introduced an intense fear in the upper castes that they will lose their vice grip on power, and their response is to inflict terror on the majority. The ferocity of this drive is only increasing, which is the macabre measure of the emancipatory agency of the Dalit-Bahujan and of the resistance of the upper castes to a new anti-caste social order.

6

THE MEANING OF CRIMES AGAINST MUSLIMS IN INDIA

This is a previously unpublished text which is essential to understand the reason why Muslims are endangered in present-day India, and it should be heeded if the Muslims are to be saved from a worse fate in India. From the outset, it proceeds to develop its title. The fact of non-publication of this text itself is important, as it happens often with several other texts of Dwivedi and Mohan, which is also a comment on the media in India.

India is at the receiving end of international condemnation for the Islamophobic remarks made by the high office holders of the ruling Bharatiya Janata Party (BJP). The BJP, as usual, has distanced itself now from these 'outspoken' members by calling them 'fringe elements'.[1] A spokesperson of the BJP who made statements insulting the prophet has also claimed that 'the entire "senior leadership", starting with the Prime Minister's Office, had reassured her saying "we are with you".'[2] The term 'fringe element' has been used tactfully by the Indian media and the BJP for many years now. Those actions which are unacceptable in the present, but at the same time the central goals of the parent organisation of the BJP, the paramilitary organisation National Self-server's Corp (RSS), are initiated through 'fringe elements' who would soon come to be the mainstream. It is important to note that the present prime minister and the present chief minister of the state of Uttar Pradesh were once upon a time called 'fringe elements'. That is, what is taking place today will come to be the norm which will be accepted by the world soon.

But what should concern us equally are two other aspects to the present situation of Islamophobia and widespread crimes against Muslims committed by both the state and the Hindu organisations in the recent months. First, this is not the first time that the members of RSS and BJP have made hate speeches against Muslims. Last month, a BJP leader who is a member of the legislative assembly from the state of Bihar asked for Muslims to be set ablaze.[3] In recent months, several Indian states have been using bulldozers to demolish the businesses and homes of poor Muslims and the term 'bulldozer' has come to be a euphemism for crushing the aspiration of Muslims.[4] The bulldozer may come to be the national symbol internationally.[5]

We can go on, sadly. However, all these incidents did not receive international condemnation, particularly from the 'Islamic nations' which have responded furiously to the recent remarks on the prophet. Does it mean that there is a difference between the killing and the dehumanisation of Muslims, and 'hurting of the religious sentiments' of Muslims. Or, what is the difference between 'Islam' and 'Muslims'? If we do not have the courage to address this question the fate of all religious groups and the non-dominant (but majority) lower caste groups will be in peril.

The second aspect of the problem is that we rarely ask the question why Muslims and Christians are at the receiving end of the pogroms and humiliating actions by the Indian state. Rather, the answers usually given and received are outrightly wrong and deliberately misleading. The blindfolding answers include the superstition that religious and ethnic groups 'naturally' hate each other, and that India is a 'Hindu majority' state where Muslims are perceived as a 'mysteriously' threatening foreign population. Dispelling these superstitions of the public sphere are essential to ensure that another genocide in India is not months away.

As we have written, following the works of many important historians, 'Hindu religion' is a recent invention of the twentieth century. It was invented to cover over the fact the 'upper caste' people, who have ruled over India for millennia, are a minority of 10 per cent of the population. The real majority are the lower caste people who form 90 per cent of the population.[6] In fact, this ratio between the majority lower caste people and upper caste people remains the same for other religions too in India, including Islam. That is, Islam and Christianity in India practice caste. Two related consequences follow from these facts.

What are called 'Hindu organisations' are headed by the upper castes. The RSS leaders have always been Brahmin, with a Kshatriya[7] leader as an exception. Whenever the lower caste groups demand rights or create organised struggles asking for rights the 'Hindu organisations' create pogroms against Muslims as a distraction, which has been well recorded. The present situation is not an exception. Since 2018, lower caste organisations have been increasing their organised agitations and most of the leaders of these movements are languishing in prisons without trial.[8] The fact is, in recent months the killings of both the lower caste people and Muslims have increased in India, although crimes against the lower caste people receive less attention.[9]

The second consequence, which is equally important, is that for centuries since the arrival of Islam, Christianity, and colonial rule the lower caste people saw religious conversion as a way to escape caste oppression and humiliation. Today religious conversion—the most important act of religious freedom—is illegal in most states in India. It is not that religious conversion provides total equality in India, as Islam, Christianity, and Sikhism practice caste discrimination; but moving out of the recently invented 'Hindu religion' provides a measure of relief. Religious conversion is feared by the upper castes because it has the potential to expose them as the exploitative minority they are.

By not addressing the most enduring form of racial oppression in human history—caste discrimination—the upper caste controlled Indian media and the economically blinded world (which is always looking for a better trade deal) are allowing Muslims, but not Islam, to be the sacrificial lamb on a theatre of orchestrated confusions.

7

WHO GETS TO KILL WHOM IN THE UNION OF INDIA?

By 2017, it was clear that India as it used to appear to the world, as a relatively peaceful democratic country on the path to progress towards economic prosperity and cultural importance on the world stage, was finished. The cow vigilantes were killing Muslims and Dalits in front of camera crews, the police were filing cases against the killed, Dalits were getting beaten and killed regularly, and Modi himself was no longer speaking about the rights of the living but of the dead. That is, he demanded more cremation grounds for 'Hindus' and opposed burial grounds for Muslims as a central problem in Indian politics. As the title declares, this is a chilling article which shows the truth of Indian society, that there are those who have the right to kill, and there are those whose only option is to be killed. This article shatters the myth that India was something like a flawed but progressive democracy and in this it is more a critical account of even the previous governments led by the Congress party which held power in India for the longest time. It gives a quick account of the pogroms against Muslims and the crimes against the lower caste people in the previous decades, and shows how they were clearly paving the way for the present outrightly upper caste

> supremacist regime. A deep and subtle philosophical question moves through this text, or it can equally be said that it is this question which moves this text: what is politics for? What kind of life is worth living? These questions, and the text itself, continue the revolutionary spirit which animates the political writings of Dwivedi and Mohan.

The country is witnessing the law of the living manifesting in the space of death.

The holy mobs in the Union of India kill men without any conflict with the law, as though the killing took place in an abattoir. The belief that beef is more sacred than human flesh has come to be a religion of the abattoir. What does it mean to kill in the Union of India?

This question is important especially now that the government of India has objected to the province of Ontario in Canada legally recognising the 1984 anti-Sikh pogrom as genocide.[1] The Bharatiya Janata Party (BJP), which leads the government, has kept talk of the 1984 pogrom alive only so that its loudness covers over the anti-Muslim pogroms of 1989,[2] 1992,[3] 2002,[4] and the anti-Christian pogrom in Odisha of 2007–8.[5] Assuredly, recognising 1984 as genocide would also draw attention to the role of Hindu nationalist organisations and other dignitaries of today[6] in that event. It would also set the precedent for terming as genocide the events we are now only able to whisper of as '2002'.[7] But it might be that much more is expected in the near future of the same hue.

From Lebensraum to Todesraum

Who gets to kill whom in the Union of India? We need to survey the conditions under which we are to ask this question. There is the indecent innocence with which the apologists of 'Hinduism' and 'Hinduness' rue that 'development' is being eclipsed by the killings. They would like some balance between broken eggs (the killings) and the omelettes (mining contracts and bullet trains) on the table.

There is no alarm on television about the tales of holy-mobs expressing with murder and loot their devotion for whatever is holy for the day—the flags, the national house-wife,[8] beef,[9] cremation, anti-love, the heroes of old television serials.[10] We have become adroit at not hearing the essential electoral question today: '*Shamshan* (cremation grounds) or *Kabristan* (burial grounds)?'[11] Although we do know that the former is to be built upon the latter, and that it is the ideal image of the 'Hindu' Rashtra (Hindu nation state, the establishment of which is the goal of the RSS). We stand in awe before this invention by the 'Hindu' nationalists, of a difference with their spiritual fathers: the Nazis asked for *Lebensraum* while the advocates of a Hindu Rashtra are asking for *Todesraum*, space for death.

On television, the hate speeches were kneaded with 'it is just election speech, don't take it seriously'.[12] Then people began to die and the dead meat in the refrigerator was interrogated.[13] The slain are investigated and their birth—Muslim, Dalit, South Indian, North-East Indian—is on trial.[14] There are television news anchors who are better spokespeople of the 'Hindu Rashtra' than its politicians.[15] That the holy-mobs kill Muslims, Dalits and Christians in order to prepare death-room for the Hindus is a fact that has eased itself into the living room of the Union of India.

Life and living: genocide and ethnocide

The question 'who gets to kill whom?' leads us to the meaning of the state in the Union of India. There are several ways to enter the problematic of the state. In its modern form the state is the first order condition for there being many *ways of living* and an openness to the inventions of ways of living. In the classical sense, the state is that institution which received the right to use force from everyone by an accord to which it refers for the legitimacy of its exercise of force at each instant. It ensures that there is *life* so that there can be ways of *living*; the securitisation of the state refers to this concept.

The precise way to think of the state in the subcontinent or anywhere else would be as that institution which has appropriated to itself the right to kill. That is, individuals do not have the right to kill, the state reserves this right for itself, as in the provision of capital punishment, in its immunity from prosecution in the territories it 'disturbs' under the Armed Forces Special Powers Act, and in its obligation to protect the weak in the case of pogroms, where it in fact does not exercise this right.

Corresponding to *life* and *living* there are, following the anthropologist Pierre Clastres, two distinct crimes—*genocide* and *ethnocide*.[16] The former is the killing of a people and the latter is the destruction of the ways of living—such as the freedom to love, the many expressions of love, food, clothing—of a people. The 'Hindu' mobs have been working towards both goals, as is evident from the destruction of the ways of living of the Dalits and the Muslims through legislation, displacement, killings, and intimidation.

The progressive delegation by the state of the right to kill to 'Hindu' mobs reveals the meaning of this institution. The killings may appear sporadic, such as the recent beef killings and floggings in Dadri (of a Muslim), Alwar (of a Muslim), Una (of Dalits). In fact, every decade since the 1960s has seen incidents which should be termed pogroms.

The Marichapi pogrom against Dalits in the state of West Bengal in 1979, which killed more than 2,000 Dalits, is hardly ever discussed by us. The pogrom in Marichapi was presided over by a left front government led by the Communist Party of India. It could be the worst pogrom in India since 1947 considering the number of dead and the displaced.[17] In 1984 the anti-Sikh pogrom took the lives of more than 3,000 people. Then there was the pogrom of Malliana and Hashimpura in 1987. As pogroms under the Congress party's rule and with its leaders implicated in it, these events—and especially 1984—are used to justify all the other pogroms led by the Hindu mobs ever since. Perhaps it should have been the sole responsibility of the Congress-led UPA government to see to the completion of the legal proceedings against its own members and former members who took part in 1984. Certainly, other parties have shown no particular interest.

Somewhere along the way, we have all forgotten the pogrom in Bhagalpur, Bihar in 1989. It was initiated through the movement organised by the BJP and the Vishwa Hindu Parishad to build a Ram temple in place of the sixteenth-century Babri mosque in Ayodhya. On December 6, 1992, the mosque was demolished by the holy-mob led by the BJP and the VHP. In what was then Bombay alone, the subsequent pogroms would kill over a thousand.

The most notorious pogroms took place in 2002 in Gujarat, which in the narrative of the 'Hindu' organisations is linked to the Ram temple movement. The most recent one in Muzaffarnagar (western Uttar Pradesh) killed dozens of Muslims, displaced thousands of them from their homes and destroyed their livelihoods in 2013, which prepared the ground for Modi's ascent to power. The central government (then led by the Congress) and the state government (then led by the Samajwadi Party) did little to prevent this pogrom which is seen as a precursor to the BJP's electoral victory at the centre in 2014 and now in Uttar Pradesh in 2017.

The state and the grounding law of the living

By naming pogroms 'riots', the Union of India has been suggesting something—that it is *a failed state*. If a state cannot exercise force, which it has appropriated from individuals, to protect the weak, the poor, the minorities—religious or otherwise—it has no legitimacy. This failure is not innocent, in the way an unarmed man is as he stands helplessly before the holy mobs there to kill his family. Rather, the mighty Indian state—as we are reminded everyday on television—has allowed itself to be instrumentalised by the 'Hindu' upper caste organisations and, in the event of 1984, by the Congress. Today, when the 'Hindu nation' is being ushered in, *the state is becoming the holy-mob*. We are told that this is a strong state led by strong men. But political theory tells us that the stronger a state becomes the more forsaken it is of any legitimacy.

The legal discourse and the institutions of law are complicit in this failure of the state to protect individuals. By acquitting the guilty despite the evidence and in delaying and denying verdicts, the legal institutions have removed their blinds. The Supreme Court recently expressed its wish that the Babri Mosque issue be settled outside the court rooms.[18] As in Kafka's parable 'Before the Law', *the house of law leaves its gates open at all times only to tell you that you cannot enter it and make your case*. In the Union of India, don't the minorities stand before the law anymore?

The holy-mobs can reach anyone as they are adept at finding a way. In the University of Hyderabad and JNU, it was nationalism and beef. In Kerala, it was public expressions of love which drew out the holy-mobs, which were then opposed by the inventive protest movement 'Kiss of Love'. In Muzaffarnagar, the holy-mobs militarised the love between Hindus and Muslims by calling it 'Love Jihad'.[19] They will find a way eventually into every home.

When the legal institutions fail, another law, *the grounding law of the living*—the law which legitimises the legal institutions—shows itself and reigns: *You shall protect your own life and that of your loved ones*. The accord which created the state was possible only because we entrusted to the state this grounding law—that *we must protect ourselves*—such that the state exercises this right on our behalf without failing in any instance. This fact is evident in the constitution—*the individual has a right to defend himself*—and is hence unchallengeable.

A failed state is an interesting place for political thinkers, since it is where the grounding law—*we must kill in order that we are ourselves not killed*—becomes visible. In states which more or less function, the appearance of the grounding law is an obscenity, like the entrails of the living laid outside an abattoir.

The command that 'you shall not take the law into your own hands' is as dreadful in these circumstances as Gandhi's advice to the Jewish people that they should let themselves be killed by the Nazis. The obedience to it is meaningful so long as the state functions. In a failed state this command should be translated as 'you shall let yourself be killed when our people come to take your life'. Instead, Muslims and Dalits must refuse to be killed.

The choices in Todesraum

With the exception of Kerala, the 'Hindu' mobs have been able, everywhere in India, to disrupt, assault and kill with impunity, without fear of state action or of retaliation. In Kerala, the RSS program began, as it did everywhere, through hate speeches and campaigns against the Muslims. It culminated in 1971 in events known as the 'Tellicheri riots'. According to the report of the Justice Joseph Vithyathil Commission which enquired into the riots, 'In

Tellicherry the Hindus and Muslims were living as brothers for centuries. The "Mopla riots" did not affect the cordial relationship that existed between the two communities in Tellicherry. It was only after the RSS and the Jana Sangh set up their units and began activities in Tellicherry that there came a change in the situation'. In Kerala, the Communist Party of India (Marxist) has retaliated in kind against the RSS since then.

The recent escalation of the killings of CPI-M workers and RSS members by each other is holding off religious bloodshed in Kerala. CPI-M workers in effect act out the grounding law of the living—*you shall kill the ones who seek to kill those you love.* The unison of the media in condemning the CPI-M indicates that the norm is being violated—that the 'Hindu' mobs shall run their human abattoirs without any distractions.

The scenario where two organised groups kill each other is termed civil war. When an organised group of people kills another group which it identifies under a religion, caste, or political position, it is termed genocide. The choice is now available in the Union of India—genocide or civil war. This choice would deny the meaning of *living* or of *the ways of living* for a whole generation. Instead, they will be forced to dwell on *to remain alive*; to find *ways of remaining alive* each day in order to defer death for another day—fleeing, arming, hiding, slaying, dying.[20]

Perhaps it is still not too late in the night for this choice to seize us. After all, the people of the Union of India are the bravest of all, who stormed the gates of the residence of the president and brought parliament to a halt several times in the recent past during the Congress rule. Such moments, named 'civil society movements' and 'the people', might be staged again by the same courageous actors. However, we must not wait idly for the mysterious 'people' to appear again.

8

COURAGE TO BEGIN

The article exhorts everyone to have the courage to confront the reality of India, namely, that this is a region with the longest lasting racialised oppression in human history. This 'everyone' includes India's Congress party, intellectuals, and also the international observers.

The text was published on the occasion of the 150th birth anniversary of M. K. Gandhi in 2019. This was also the year their book *Gandhi and Philosophy: On Theological Anti-Politics* was released and was receiving attention for its philosophical inventiveness in India, but not quite their politics. This could be the reason why this text could be published in one of the oldest newspapers in India, *The Indian Express*. This text is one of the early articulations in their writings of what Dwivedi and Mohan call the lower caste position in politics in India, although there were already French publications and interviews to legacy media such as *France Culture*[1] and *Mediapart*[2] in which they discussed their thesis at length. The article brings three components together in a strict relation. It discards the upper caste—both left and right—point of view that Indian politics is concerned with 'Hindu majority' and 'religious minorities'. Instead, it asserts that Hinduism was invented as recently as the twentieth century to suppress the fact that the lower caste people are the real majority of India.

> It assigns the responsibility for the creation of 'Hinduism' and its maintenance to the Congress party and also M. K. Gandhi. Further it shows the only remaining possibility for politics in the good sense in India, which is to assume the lower caste position and work towards the destruction of the caste system to create an egalitarian society.

When a newspaper in 1784 asked 'What is enlightenment?' the answer, by philosopher Immanuel Kant was: 'sapere aude'—to have the courage to reason.[3] This motto came to define modernity soon after. The modern temerity—the confidence before the openness of the future and the belief that the present can sufficiently be the origin of new worlds—is opposed to the inconfidence with which aging societies refer to their past for authority and security. But today, in India, we are reaching further into the past in panic. And when we speak of the past, especially on M. K. Gandhi's 150th birth anniversary, it is important to consider: can Gandhi be separated from the attempts to deploy him for the purposes of lending authority to the Hindu nationalist project?

This courageous question concerns much more besides the posthumous life of Gandhi. More explicitly, it asks: is it not time that we finally became modern? The answer is yes, but its implication is that it will no longer give us a Gandhi who would deliver any political objectives in the Indian union—he will lead a different posthumous life.

When two or more distinct laws entered into a conflict in a polis, it implied a 'stasis' or stagnation for the ancient Greeks. There has been a 'hidden' stasis in the subcontinent for millenia: the conflict between the reign of an 'upper' caste minority over a 'lower' caste majority through social norms and anti-miscegenation rules, and the freedom struggle of the oppressed lower caste majority. Releasing India's political constellations from the paternal gravity of Gandhi will also release into politics the crisis or stasis that can no longer be 'managed'.[4]

We cannot arrive at Gandhi's posthumous life without taking into account the implicit conditions under which this patronym is repeatedly invoked. The independence movement under the

Congress party was a chimera, made up of distinct parts of disparate creatures. Those parts of the Congress that could not endure together disintegrated, of necessity, into several oppositional parties—the communist parties, socialist parties, Muslim parties and the Hindu parties. Gandhi shared his legacy and responsibilities with this Congress chimera.[5]

Nevertheless, the Congress of the British colonial era is not a mere conglomerate of incompatible micro-interests. Under its organisational mega-structure, those conflicting interests—Hindu, Hindi, Dravidian, Southern, Northern, Bengali, Capitalist, Socialist—could convene as a sufficiently large force to negotiate the 'transfer of power'.[6] We are dreadfully aware of the 'shared interest' over which most members of the Congress-chimera found agreement: namely, that the social order, or the caste system, which reproduces itself faithfully as the only invariant of the subcontinent, must be conserved. That is, the strict observation of caste rules as a means reproduces the caste order as the end generation after generation. (Elsewhere we have called the general principle of this reproduction Calypsology).[7] Today we hide the realities of the social order under the neologism 'Hindu'.

'Hindu' is derived from the Arabic 'Al Hind' which began its life as the name of a religion in the colonial writings of the nineteenth century. The census officers of the 'Raj' found that people filled the columns for declaring their caste and religion with the same term—their caste. This implied that there were far too many religions but administrative convenience required much less. Further, the E. A. Gait census of 1911 also showed that the upper castes were a minority in the subcontinent.[8]

In that precarious moment in which all political destinies, including the 'annihilation of caste', were still open for the subcontinent, this revelation of the census could have had deleterious effects on the Congress project. In order to mask this fact, a new religion had to be created with the consent of the colonial administration. Its goal was to bring under its umbrella all the caste groups without disturbing their hierarchy, and then distinguish the new and demographically largest religion from the other religions of the subcontinent, including Islam and Christianity. The baptism of this religion was both in the statistical needs of the British colonial administration and in the upper-caste minority's need to pose as the spokesman of a seeming majority.

Gandhi had an important role in the invention of 'Hindu' religion. He understood that if the majority of the population, the lower castes, were not let into the upper-caste temples, a common religion called Hindu would not be legally recognised.

Although many upper caste leaders found the foreign term 'Hindu' objectionable. Gandhi also contributed to the later invention and promotion of Hindi with Madan Mohan Malaviya and others. Hindi was explicitly conceived as the language of the 'Hindus'. This is evident in the directive principles of the constitution which dictates that this new language shall draw its vocabulary primarily from Sanskrit.

The stasis has been accelerating since modern law arrived with colonial rule. The 1850s 'Caste Disabilities Removal Act' legally recognised caste discrimination for the first time. Since then, there have been, at a minimum, two laws contending over the political character of the Indian subcontinent: the law of equality on which the modern constitution is premised, and the law of social hierarchy which tenaciously mobilises even the modern state apparatus. These two laws are in outright conflict, which is the modern manifestation of the ancient stasis. It is accelerating today as the oppressed majority is organising with relative indifference to electoral politics. As Suraj Yengde said, 'the musical whispers of those people who are warned not to cross the lines and remain in one's place like a permanently fixed graveyard' are in motion. The mega-organisational structure that belonged to the Congress can today serve a new end if it lets itself be seized by the oppressed majority of millennia.

It would amuse another generation that the prominent academic schools to emerge from India—post-colonialism and subaltern theory—are continuous with the Hindu-Hindi politics and that they refer to Gandhi for paternal authority.

Postcolonial theory is a revisionist project that seeks to criticise the colonial element in contemporary India and at the same time recover the lost 'native' elements of the past of the upper castes. In this sense it is continuous with the politics of Hinduness. Subaltern theory, which is a component of postcolonial theory, studied (on its prominent instances) the 'failure' of the modern legal system to accommodate the caste obligations of the upper caste housewife—for example the criminalisation of 'sati'. This explains the conflicting perspectives that upper castes and lower castes have on English, modern constitution, the sciences, and even on the colonial era. That is, the lower castes perceive these terms as having overcome the items of old values—Sanskrit, dharma shastras, rituals—on which the hierarchy was dependent, while post-colonial theorists today teach with nostalgia the devotional writings of the pre-colonial era.

Gandhi's path marks have been following us, be it in electoral issues (Hindu, Hindi, Cow), academic praxis (post-colonialism and subaltern theory), or our 'tolerance' towards the invariant of the subcontinent. The present crisis in politics is nothing but the realisation that the Hindu-Hindi model cannot mask the inhumanity of an arrangement wherein the upper caste minority controls all socio-political spheres and through them the lower caste majority. But another epoch in politics has already begun. Horace said of crossing dangerous waters, 'Those who have dared to begin are already half done'.

Gandhi, the thinker, will still lead another posthumous life. We failed to attend to the other dimensions of his works all these years due to the services and hospices that his name could provide for the stasis. Gandhi was one of the most acute thinkers of nihilism and the first to bring it in contiguity with politics. His critique of 'civilisation' took the form of perpetual negation: of the city, technology, and mobility to a minimal living quieter than the night. Gandhi expressed the tremors of thought before man's great creations—industries, transportation and communication systems, 'newspapers at the touch of a button'. Today, these tremors articulate each warning about climate catastrophes and the generalised guilt we feel at every pleasure, desire and invention.[9]

9

ASSEMBLIES OF FREEDOM

TESTING THE CONSTITUTION

The constitution of India asserts that it is a republic that is guided by the principles of egalitarianism, liberty, justice, socialism, and secularism. The national project is assumed to be the creation of a democratic egalitarian society. But in reality, the upper caste supremacist control of state institutions and wealth has prevented the free democratic development of India into such a society. Dwivedi and Mohan show that the very constitutional promises are often betrayed using other constitutional provisions, a process in which they implicate all the institutions of the state including the judiciary. They argue their case by citing the father of the Indian constitution, Dr B. R. Ambedkar, constitutional judgments, and philosophical principles. The challenge or the test proposed by Dwivedi and Mohan is that the most fundamental of the freedoms of any constitution is the freedom of assembly, which can correct the course of the decadent political class betraying the constitutional values, and they urge people to assemble freely and exercise that freedom guaranteed by the constitution. When we read this text together with 'Democracy and Revolution', two realities are opened up. Assemblies of freedom are the real criteria of democracies and that these assemblies have a revolutionary power. It is one of those texts where if a few details are changed it could apply to any democracy in the 'west'.

> Thus so long as the name of freedom was respected and only its actual realization prevented, of course in a legal way, the constitutional existence of liberty remained intact, inviolate, however mortal the blows dealt to its existence in actual life.
>
> —Karl Marx, *The Eighteenth Brumaire of Louis Bonaparte*

What is the state of health of the Indian union? Is it wounded, 'eroding', breaking down, breaking up, 'backsliding', critical? How can we know whether we are still living in a constitutional democratic system constituted by our consent? Is there a constitution of India still?

These are the questions for which we should take responsibility and act in politics according to the ratio between the answers received and what they reveal about the future of India. These essential questions cannot be answered through the newer glib phrases borrowed from international media such as 'erosion' and 'backsliding' which are meant as 'all the perfumes of...'.

We can check the liveliness of our constitutional democracy only by testing the constitution through thoughtful political acts. Of these tests, the most important ones for this situation are the *freedoms of association and assembly*. Further, if these freedoms are opposed by the upper caste supremacist militias, or the police which is at times indistinguishable from such militias,[1] we should urgently seek the opinion of the judiciary—*Are we will still a constitutional democracy, your honours?*

As the physicians of democracy we administer these tests while granting our assent to constitutional democracy. Without the manifestation of such tests of freedoms the constitution is a crumbling parchment written in an indecipherable script.

Who is opposed to constitutional democracy?

Today there effectively is no freedom of association and assembly, especially for the lower caste majority position in India. At the same time, the RSS (National Self-Service Corp), the supremacist organisation of the minority upper castes (less than 10 per cent of the population of India), and its (conveniently disavowable) offshoots are at liberty to violate all constitutional and international norms to take out armed processions, attack mosques and churches.[2] We should consider the differences in the political lines of demarcation between the associations and the assemblies of the lower caste majority and of the upper caste minority.

The most recent hate campaign of the RSS *mafia famiglia* began in the Nuh district of the northern state of Haryana in July 2023 against Muslims. If we perceive it and speak of it the way the *mafia famiglia* wants us to, in terms of 'Hindu majority' versus 'Muslim minority', we will be morally responsible for the crimes against humanity which await us in a future of India. Most conflicts, political and of other kinds, including the events in Nuh are concerned with prolonging the caste ordered society. The mafia-like organisations of VHP (World Hindu Society) and Bajrang Dal,[3] involved in the worst events of terror in India, were created to counter lower caste assertion and to prevent 'caste wars' of the kind witnessed in Bihar and Gujarat in the last century.

In Haryana, the BJP (Bharatiya Janata Party, the political arm of the RSS) has been facing the anger of the Jat community. The now historic farmers' protest of 2020–21 was organised predominantly by the Jat farmers of several states, including Haryana, against the farm bills introduced by the union government.[4] It has the rare reputation of succeeding against the government as the farm laws were repealed. These associations and assemblies of the farmers were criminalised by the BJP, and by the end of it over 750 farmers died.[5]

From January 2023, the wrestlers' protest which saw the assembly of national athletes alleging sexual harassment against a prominent BJP member of parliament and 'strong man' were suppressed several times using the police and the media, even after receiving international condemnation. These ongoing protests too are led by the Jat community as 'Most of the female wresters who have accused Bhushan Singh of sexual assault and harassment are Jats'.[6]

The BJP in Haryana is also struggling to contain the conflict between the upper caste Rajput leaders of their party and the Gurjar community over the contestation of the caste of a ninth-century ruler.[7] All these divisions of caste never provided a favourable ground to the BJP and other upper caste political organisations in modern India's history. Such contestations will again raise new, towering figures of lower caste politics as Kanshi Ram, Mayawati, and Lalu Prasad Yadav had been in the past.

The organisational *mafia famiglia* often countered such situations through pogroms against Muslims, Christians, and Sikhs. In Nuh too, it has been observed that 'Hindu consolidation may paper over such cracks'[8] among castes and it requires directing mobs and media towards Muslims, while the judiciary watches, without yet watching over.

The constitutional sense of association

The International Covenant on Civil and Political Rights[9] finds in the rights to associate and assemble the fundamental political right which is essential for all people 'in shaping their societies'. These rights constitute 'the very foundation of a system of participatory governance based on democracy, human rights, the rule of law and pluralism.' Article 20 of the Universal Declaration of Human Rights states that 'Everyone has the right to freedom of peaceful assembly and association' and 'No one may be compelled to belong to an association'.[10] The Indian constitution under Article 19(1) (c) guarantees freedom of 'association or unions' with a few restrictions which are public order, decency, and the sovereignty of India. We should note that it is the people who are 'sovereign' and that 'a judicial decision or order which violates a fundamental right is void'.[11]

Freedom of association founds the meaning of life through the sharing and creation of new meanings and powers. It is most commonly the freedom, and the power, to form organisations including political parties. Freedom of association is also the power which grounds our freedom to love, to create languages, to marry, to educate each other, to convert to religions and form communes among friends. Caste order is explicitly opposed to freedom of association and it has been subverting the constitution. B. R. Ambedkar gave the clearest explanation in *Annihilation of Caste*:

> What is your ideal society if you do not want caste is a question that is bound to be asked of you. If you ask me, my ideal would be a society based on *Liberty, Equality* and *Fraternity*. And why not? What objection can there be to Fraternity? I cannot imagine any. An ideal society should be mobile, should be full of channels for conveying a change taking place in one part to other parts. In an ideal society there should be many interests consciously communicated and shared. There should be varied and free points of contact with other modes of association. In other words, there must be social endosmosis. This is fraternity, which is only another name for democracy. Democracy is not merely a form of Government. It is primarily a mode of associated living, of conjoint communicated experience. It is essentially an attitude of respect and reverence towards fellowmen.

Caste order and its ethos prevents the people of the lower caste majority and other religious groups (especially the lower caste majority of those groups) from associating with one another through love, living in shared neighbourhoods, sitting on the same table, studying in the same class rooms, presiding on judgment in the courts of India, in the parliament, and in the media. There are new laws, with unpronounceable Hindi names, which are opposed[12] to the right to associate freely and they are the bad omen for the more evil transformations of the state after the 2024 national elections.

Today, the restrictions on freedom of association are often imposed by the media and the *mafia famiglia* of the RSS. The state too is clearly intervening in the domain of religious freedoms, especially the freedom to associate with any religion and the negative freedom to dissociate from religions. This is a the subversion of the constitution. For understanding negative freedoms the iconic example is the religious conversion of B. R. Ambedkar, who did not wish to associate with the 'Hindu' order and hence chose Buddhism in a mass religious conversion event on October 14, 1956.

The 22 vows[13] taken by the father of the constitution of India at that mass conversion event say much about the conflict between the constitution of India and upper caste supremacism which directs itself as the interest of the state. We must recall three of the vows:

A) I believe in the equality of men.

B) I will try to establish equality.

C) I renounce Hinduism[14] *which is harmful to humanity and hinders the progress and development of humanity because it is based on inequality, and adopt Buddhism as self-religion.*

Both A and B are consistent with the constitution of India, while C points to the serious threat posed by upper caste supremacism to the constitution of India. These threats are becoming more alarming as the caste order is surreptitiously introduced into the education system,[15] in the name of encouraging 'traditional' crafts and jobs.

Nearly all religious groupings and many political parties of India are in violation of the freedoms of the constitution, as can be seen in recent incidents where the freedoms of expression and association appeared in conflict with religions. A lower caste leader of the AAP and a former minster of the government of Delhi, Rajendra Pal Gautam, had converted to Buddhism in October 2022 in a mass conversion event 'where hundreds of people denounced Hinduism and adopted Buddhism'.[16] After several 'legal complaints' by the BJP and the refusal of the AAP leadership to defend him amidst reports that 'chief minister Arvind Kejriwal "is extremely displeased" with Gautam', Mr Gautam had to resign from his ministerial position.[17]

The real restrictions to freedom of association are imposed through the brutality of mafia organisations springing often under the paramilitary organisation of the RSS, an organisation banned thrice since 1947 for operating against the constitution.[18] These restrictions are supported and aided by the police and other state institutions, and occasionally by the judiciary, which indicates that an upper caste supremacist 'state machinery' is about to wriggle out of the chrysalis of the Indian constitution.

Of all kinds of associations that are being challenged and suppressed, the most alarming and revealing suppressions are of the associations which oppose the caste order to lead towards a society assuring *Justice, Liberty and Equality* which are the promises of the constitution. That is, these three values are both the principles, understood as ground, and the *telos* understood as *that towards which* all the activities specified by constitution should strive.

Who are the ones unable to associate and assemble

On 20 August 2023, a collection of organisations called *We20* met in Delhi's 'HKS Surjeet Bhawan, which is owned by the Communist Party of India (Marxist).'[19] The We20 organisation's declaration 'People and Nature over Profits for a Just, Inclusive, Transparent and Equitable Future' should be most welcome.[20] However, the police denied them permission to gather through an irrational statement—'non availability of the vital information pertaining to the gathering, visitors etc. which is needed as per oredor (sic) of the Hon'ble High Court of Delhi...[permission for] program is hereby rejected'.

In 2018, scholars, activists, academics, former judges, and people from all walks of life gathered to commemorate the 200th anniversary of the victory of a lower caste army over a Brahmin kingdom in Maharashtra. Then the worst violations of human rights, international law, and the constitution of India were unleashed in order to imprison many who participated in these events and some who did not.[21] The evidence was found to have been planted on to the computer of an accused and the statements of this spurious evidence are ludicrous and juvenile.[22]

The slow judicial process in this case and the death of Father Stan Swami in prison[23] serve as intimidation and warning to all those who seek an egalitarian polity from the point of view of the lower caste majority position. Those who speak, associate, and assemble from this position are considered 'anti-national' by the Brahminical minority position, as asserted by the Akhil Bharatiya Brahmin Mahasangh (All India Brahmin Congress).[24] But this is not so from the point of view of the constitution of India, not yet.

Soon, negative freedom of association may appear as it did in Nazi Germany, everyone may be made an automatic member of the RSS. Before that comes about, we should breath life back into the constitution through the exercise of the rights guaranteed by the constitution.

The fitness test of the constitution

The health of the constitution must be tested on the streets and in the halls of justice, and these tests are the responsibility of everyone, not just the lawyers and activists. We should gather over a cup of coffee under an idea whenever possible. We should form newer associations in the mode of weekend clubs to educate one another about the political history of India, mourn its present, and draft its future. We should associate and share books, articles and other resources so that we become the egalitarian gathering of an effervescent power opposing an evanescent force composed of barely literate goons and clowns. We should also visit those neighbourhoods within our neighbourhoods which are kept apart under caste and religious apartheids. Above all, associate in the greatest of numbers for egalitarianism as such.

These acts will be policed, mobbed, terrorised with the connivance of some office bearers of the institutions of the constitution of India and by the cowards who walk the streets in large numbers to terrify everyone in the name of a recently invented religion.[25] The RSS, as we have known them in the history of the anti-colonial movement and since 1947 are cowards who operate in the dark, in the safety of the crowds or, today, in the security offered by the high ranking police men.[26]

Therefore, we should freely assemble in the open in order to open politics again as the quest for freedom; bearing moral courage and the creative power of lamentation within; and must return again and again in greater numbers festively and peacefully so that we become the *kinesis* of freedom ourselves.

While assembling and gathering we should study the judgment of the two-judge bench of Chief Justice Prashant Kumar Mishra and Justice D.V.S.S. Somayajulu of the high court of Andra Pradesh in May 2023:

> historically, culturally and politically, the tradition of public meetings, processions, assemblies etc., on streets, highways etc., have been recognized in this country. These meetings, processions etc., constitute an important facet of our political life. The freedom struggle is replete with examples of processions,

> dharnas, satyagrahas etc., conducted on the roads which lead to India's tryst with destiny on 15.08.1947.[27]

The constitutional court acted according to the principles and the *telos* (the goals) of the constitution and against the trespass on it by the executive. Further, the judgment gives an argument for the rights to associate and to assemble: *since the constitution is itself a product of free associations and assemblies, it cannot be used to suppress these rights.*

The constitution itself says that these articles of freedom have been put in place 'to protect these rights against State action'. If there are restrictions and challenges, including the criminal mobs directed by the upper caste supremacist organisations or the police then one must test the constitution's health at the courts. These judicial tests may be disappointing. Romila Thapar[28] and others moved the Supreme Court with a public interest litigation questioning the arrests of activists and academics in the Bhima Koregaon case and sought an independent enquiry into the events. Her plea was dismissed by the Supreme Court.[29]

It is only through the ratios discovered between the free associations and the assemblies for an egalitarian world, and the opposition to these actions by the *mafia famiglia* and the state institutions that we can diagnose the health of the Indian union. In the same way, the ratio of the outcomes of the petitions placed before the judiciary and the guarantees of the constitution alone can tell us of the salubriousness or otherwise of the institutions of the constitution. Or help us gauge the length of the time that the present fascistic political situation has borrowed from the deferred revolution of the lower caste majority for an egalitarian world.

10

LOOMING OBJECTS AND THE ANCESTRAL MODEL OF HISTORIOGRAPHY

For the French translation of the essay 'The Hindu Hoax: How the Upper Castes Invented a Hindu Majority', which was prepared and edited by me, Mohan and Dwivedi composed this additional theoretical essay on historiography. It was to show the systematic movement and revolutionary force underneath their historical interventions. It proposes a new philosophy of history in terms of the concepts of the system they developed in *Gandhi and Philosophy*. This text is also a development of the themes present in Mohan's writings on history and historiography. It is perhaps the most technical article in this anthology, a philosophical text in the classical sense. It divides historiographical styles into two. The common style of historiography based on a 'common ancestor' (a concept developed by Dwivedi and Mohan with reference to an observation I had made in my commemorative text on Jean-Luc Nancy). This model presupposes an identity, either of a people or of a culture, and it is called the ancestral model of historiography. In contrast, they propose an anastatic model of historiography which does not rely on any 'common ancestor', identity, or racialised people. The anastatic model is revolutionary. It bastardises histories, and shows histories to

> be constantly a mixture. They also make a distinction between two kinds of historical objects, looming objects and ersatz objects. Looming object is a concept developed from nautical history. These are objects and concepts which are closer to the comprehending law, in the particular sense that removing or adding a looming object can transform a whole world. One needs to think of the contemporary world without computer networks or ancient history without ships.
>
> Religion and racism are the two salient looming objects which must be understood as such in order to understand how, when, and why what appears as religion across time is in fact new arrangements. In the case of 'Hindu' new arrangements have served as means to conserve the old end of the oldest racism of caste.

We are not historians. But we have been writing the history which remains shunned by the historians of India. It is the history of the political aspirations of the real demographic majority of India, the people oppressed for three millennia by the racialised system of caste order. The text 'The Hindu Hoax' contains, implicitly, a criticism of the historiographical silence among Indian historians. Histories are written by the victors, this is a common place understanding which hides more than what it reveals. History is the explanation of the question *why a society is constituted in that particular way, and why it should continue to be in that way*; and, it is written by those who hold power in order to regularise the social order and prolong it interminably. In India, all histories are upper caste histories, many of which often do not ever mention the lower castes who are the demographic majority. The wider world too views India through the popularised versions of upper caste historiography. In fact, many 'European' interests in Indian societies and historiographies work alongside the upper caste interests in such a way that a kind of internal colonisation—the upper caste minority colonising the lower caste majority—is enabled by an external political and epistemic colonisation. That is, the 'white man' too has been at work in invisibilizing and silencing the lower caste majority of India, which is especially alarming in recent years.

What remains implicit in each history needs to be articulated so that what could follow from it can be comprehended. It is also necessary to draw out the principles behind historiographical tasks of this kind to ensure that the rest of the world too may not carry on the 'days like any other days' beneath historiographical silences in their distinct forms. The phrase 'days like any other days' often appears in fiction, only to be followed by 'except it wasn't'. That is, something interesting or critical takes place when the resemblance between one day and the other days is broken. A day when one says 'except it wasn't' comes to be of political importance only when that day constitutes another beginning which promises freedoms to a people who had been denied freedoms for ages. Historiography has a role to play in breaking the regularities and orders of days, so long as it is theoretically distinguished from the historical perspectives of the oppressor. *A day unlike any other* is the promise of the great leaders and intellectuals of the lower caste majority; this promise guides the text 'The Hindu Hoax'.

The field of history

History is a science of its own kind, irreducible to the norms of other sciences, and the only other discipline with which we may entertain its analogies is biology. History emerged in the seventeenth century alongside the concern with the 'comprehension of the whole which the seventeenth century employs and expects';[1] only since then did it appear as a specialisation which deserved theoretical attention, and such attention would take the eighteenth century and onwards through at least Kant, Hegel, and Marx when the principles of history began to be articulated and contested. Philosophers entered history at the level of concepts and ideas, and the objectivity of history. When we have a system of objectivity, an object can be recognised in an objective field. For example, without the objective field of epidemiology the objects of infection, contact, vector, R0 cannot be recognised or be traced along the objective field. It is not too different with history: Without the field of political theory, a history of politics would appear confused.

The history of politics in a region presupposes a certain objective field constituted by political components in relation;[2] the components include territory, the state, society, institutions of the constitution as the components of the state (such as the judiciary and the parliament), those institutions which are defined constitutionally without enjoying a componential relation with the state (such as societies and clubs), demography, the norms of citizenship, wars, obligations outside the territory such as treaties. A historian may often trace the developments of one object in a field, presupposing one or the other specific grouping of components for that field. In the history of an object, we also find the histories of components and the different epochs of these components in relations. For example, a historical description of the works of the painter Andrea del Sarto may presuppose the theoretical field—or the strata of seeing—of the Italian renaissance.

Everything in a political system, as with any other system, is identified as components in articulations with other components. That which comprehends the components in their relations (according to componential laws) is never itself a component. For this reason, Plato would warn that one must not try to understand a language in terms of a component (στοιχεῖον), such as only the nouns, or verbs, or grammar. That which comprehends a language is inexpressible as a term within that language—*the comprehending law of a system of components is not itself a component*. In the ancient world this understanding extended to political systems. For example, the Platonic state is comprehended by justice, which is not a tangible component. However, often the game of power is to set a component as the *comprehending law*,[3] and this game merely leads to stasis. When a group which identifies itself either through a self-racialisation or theologisation seeks to be the comprehending law of a political system, we come to the all too familiar phenomena such as Hindu fascism, Taliban, Nazism, Islamic state, and Christian theocratic imperialism. There are other ways into stasis including the financial aspect of an economy determining the componential relations of a system towards its self-interest and dominance; it is still stasis when the military or militaristic programs, which are the components of a political system, seize the whole system to become its comprehending law as witnessed in China, Pakistan, and Myanmar. In India, the stasis is three millennia old: The upper caste minority—less than 10 per cent of the population—interprets itself as the comprehending law of the society and sees its dominance as the only end acceptable in politics. The enduring success of the upper caste minority, across centuries, lay in their cleverness to present their self-interests as the only matter of interest—the only objective field of history—to all those who conquered the subcontinent and those who took historical interests in the subcontinent. As a result, the objectivity and the objective field of the archaeology and history of the subcontinent has been centred on the upper caste thematics of 'Aryan', 'Vedas', Sanskrit texts, and myths of dominance of the 'Aryans' over the older populations of the subcontinent such as found in the Brahmanical Sanksrit epic 'Ramayana'.

Without an account of the objective field, and the other fields with which it has relations, no object can be traced.[4] For example, in the history of the object *ship*, Richard Woodman gives accounts of the fields of religion, astronomy, folktales, geography, and economics. Moreover, to show the long era of human excursions over waters, he introduces archaeology, 'Homo erectus was probably capable of transporting himself across water before 200,000 BC'.[5] Further, when one speaks of ships one must also speak of ports. Not all cities maintain the same relation to their ports. As we find with Aristotle, the distance from the port to the city is determined according to the calculus of epidemics and other vices: the city should not be so far from the port that transportation to and from the ships become costly, and at the same time the city should not be so close to the port that diseases and unwelcome cultures invade the city. Then, so long as water bodies are present, the object of ship can gather nearly everything in order to determine the regularities and the componential laws, and to affect the comprehending law of the region under consideration. Not all objects have the same power to gather nearly everything. For example, if we were to write the history of the blast furnace in the state of Ohio, it could tell us something about the field of European migration into America, the cannon balls, the civil war, the working class in America and the appearance of the condemnable term 'white trash'. At the same time, the history of the uses of the metal iron can gather nearly everything, from the formation of stars to the wars of most ages.

The divisions of historiography

At this point, we need to make a distinction between two kinds of objects of historiography, which will be found necessary to gather what is at stake in the histories of religions, races, and their often deliberately confusing mixtures. Beyond the consideration of vital necessities, there are objects and functions which determine the very form of comprehending laws of systems in their histories, that is, those objects and functions which remain *components in resonance* across epochs or the changes in the comprehending laws. These objects such as ships, taxation, agriculture, writing, racisms, religions, armies, the accountant, misogyny, horses are capable of gathering towards themselves nearly everything which were the concerns of their dominant epochs. Such objects move into other epochs with ease like a family heirloom while resisting changes to their internal regularities. For example, the ceremonies of state power continue like a transmitted heirloom from the mythic, ancient, theological epochs, and into the modern world. They are the objects of frequent use, a regularity which cannot be discarded without exchange with another comprehending law, and for that reason *they loom over* most relations among the components. We mark the objects which determine the direction of the comprehending law as *looming objects*. Since we discussed the example of the ship, it is notable that the term 'loom' emerged as a nautical term in the sixteenth century to describe the apparent slow motion of ships along the horizon. When we go further back into etymological speculations, it is probable that 'loom' could have meant tools of frequent use. The *looming object* can cause a change in the *comprehending laws* of society as much when it enters as when it exits a society. When horses and chariots were mated together it changed the landscape of west Asian steppe region, and then much of the land below it, which has been called the 'Indo-Aryan' invasions. These regions—the Asian Mediterranean, much of what later came to be called Europe, and the north-west of the Indian subcontinent—experienced the destruction of older cultures, peoples, and even ancient memories, which changed the comprehending laws of the ancient world. Between the region called 'Middle East' or 'West Asia' and the north-western subcontinent, civilisational systems such as the Elamite were destroyed. In the subcontinent, the memories of the destructions of civilisations and then the subjugations of the local populations through the denigrate-dominate function[6] are retained in the texts of the Brahmin social codes from 1500 BC and in other upper caste myths; today this memory still orders the society as the oppressive caste order and prevents politics. In the Americas, when colonisers arrived, the steel axe was introduced into the South American societies and destroyed the tribal order and social customs. Colonial artefacts and even the very presence of bodies from elsewhere led to genocides of peoples and cultures in the Americas. We should not forget on this occasion that the catholic priests in the Americas deliberately destroyed the great civilisational archives of the earliest inhabitants of the Americas, rendering them without memories. In contrast, colonial rule in India had a mostly liberating effect on the lower caste people as compared to the previous epochs of rulers who had come from elsewhere, including the armies of Alexander and the Turks. This was due to the introduction of the system of rational legal order open to the lower caste majority, the colonial military which provided education to the children of lower caste soldiers, and most importantly the right to use public roads and transportation to the lower caste people.

The objects and functions which do not determine the comprehending law can be marked as *ersatz objects*. Ersatz objects lie on the other side of looming objects and they are occasionally found to be dispensable, such as the calculus of military units as replaceable by other military units. Ersatz objects often perform functions which are exchangeable, as in the history of writing which retains the writing function with different componential relations even today, including the diversity of scripts, grammar, and the materials through which writing is accomplished. The componential relations between bulls, carts, and agriculture were found dispensable in most parts of the world. When tomato was introduced to the rest of the world from South America, it was used in exchange for previous objects for the souring function in most kitchens. Our concern is with two kinds of *looming objects* and their relations—*religion and racism*.

Of looming objects: religion and racism

History of religion takes a special place in the history of objects for three reasons. First, it makes assumptions about the meaning of a particular religion according to the political investments in that history, and in this regard, it implicitly invokes the racialisation of a people. For example, following the hoax of the 'clash of civilisation' theses, which were soon followed by the illegal wars launched by America and Britain in the region they called 'the Middle East', we found the appearance of new histories of Islam which were founded on Islamophobia. Secondly, histories of religions often stake a claim on the totality of an epoch; that is, such theologised histories see in the heavens of departed eras the reflected outline of a quest for a divine essence on earth through which all things came to have significance in that past. This is an experience still closer to the 'western' world, for George Bush killed millions of people in Iraq and Afghanistan because his god told him to do so.[7] Thirdly, histories of religions gather the variations of religions from time to time and from place to place by assuming that the meaning of 'religion' is understood and this is how the apparitions of 'common ancestors' arise.[8] The best example of this was the antisemitic attempt in the eighteenth century to trace all European culture and religions, especially Christianity, to the 'Aryan' ancestor. In biology, the 'common ancestor' is a term with a logical reality which need not correspond to a real life form in the past, and instead, it indicates the range of variations from out which a particular line of descent is possible. The 'common ancestor' has been deployed as the *Idea of religion*, to which most religions are then shown to conform or from which they are shown to deviate, and the exceptions that are in evidence all around are then forced into lineages as the effect of contingencies and are categorised as 'nuances'.

The classical model of history conserves the 'common ancestor' in its endeavours. The myth of the 'Greek exception' in modern history projected on to the 'ancient Greeks' the wishes and anxieties of a listless will which constructed the modern northern 'European'; that is, something like 'Europe' was constituted through the projection of a common ancestor, from which 'Europe' derived a depth of time—the depth of a vague ancient origin—and therefore, an eventually racializable identity. At a certain moment from the nineteenth century, this common ancestor wavered between 'Indo-Aryan' and 'Ancient Greeks', as exemplified by the texts of Nietzsche. That is, the 'common ancestor' wavered between a model of ancestral 'Ancient Greeks' and European progenies or ancestral 'Indo-Aryans' and European progenies. While the 'ancient Greek' myth[9] dominates (for better today) the imagined past of 'Europe', the myths of the 'Indo-Aryan' kind remains active through the underground participations with global Nazi-inspired organisations leading often to the RSS in India.

It is through the circularity of definitions—'the ancient Greeks were us and we are now the ancient Greeks'—and the circulation of 'a narrowly European outlook'[10] that 'Europe' meditates on itself. This circularity which circulates the intangible vapour of 'the European' can be found foremost in Hegel's art history and Heidegger's narrative of the history of metaphysics. That is, the birth of the northern 'European' was in the land towards the south and in a people who did not call themselves Greek. These so-called Greeks never had anything to do with the northern 'Europeans'. Before the exercises in circular self-definitions of the latter, the former—who were more than and less than what goes by 'Greeks'—had exchanged loves, strifes, concepts, words, and divinities with the peoples who were contiguous with them, including the Africans and those who were called the 'orientals' until the early twentieth century. In fact, there was a geographical quadrant among the people of the Mediterranean on the basis of the complex concept of 'health'—'The first, health—this is a necessity: cities which lie towards the east and are blown upon by winds coming from the east, are the healthiest; next in healthiness are those which are sheltered from the north wind'.[11]

If there is a Greek exception it is this: The ancient cultures of the 'Asia minor' belong to everyone, for they left no claimants behind. The gift of the ancient people of the Mediterranean is in their very disappearance, and the curse of the ancient people who called themselves 'Aryan' is the very persistence of this self-designation in history. Indeed, from this understanding of an ancient bastard people of the Mediterranean it is possible to conceive other Europes.

The ancestral model of historiography

Then, we can discern two opposing currents in historiography. One of these can be called the history of the common ancestor, *the ancestral model of historiography*, which we encountered above in the construction of Greeks. The *ancestral model of history* is often the apologetics for the prolongation of stasis. Opposed to the ancestral model is the *anastatic model of historiography*, which has no references to a common ancestor, but instead, it seeks to end the reign of the common ancestors and the domineering ethno-spirits. Anastatic historiography brings to an end the delirium of 'days like any other'; it breaks open the ceremonial orders of the 'ancestors'. The ancestral model presupposes a certain exception, a sudden birth with little to correspond to an umbilical cord. The object or the period may have remained entirely unaware of this designation, as with the ancient Greeks who did not know that they were 'the Greek exception' giving birth to a project named Europe which was distant in space and time. Even worse and literally pernicious is the case where an ancient people displayed a certain self-designation as 'Aryan' and systematized the denigration of the other, which they conserved through rituals and texts through the ages. This is an 'ancestor' who had killed and continues to kill peoples in different corners of the world, especially in India. That is, the so-called ancient Greeks could always be home for everyone through discerning historiographies which can establish relations between them and the peoples of 'west Asia', Afghanistan, Ghana and Timbuktu, or anywhere in the world. It is a world that remains open to an account of mixtures and bastardisations, since those who lived in the ancient Mediterranean left behind no ethno-political progenies.

In contrast, when the 'Aryan' doctrine is repeated it establishes the worst tendencies of racialised oppression through the maintenance of purities. Indeed, it was repeated many times in the recent past.[12] The ancestral model of historiography conserves the image of the common ancestor across all the changes it encounters by treating the bastards among the common ancestors (the so-called Greeks were the cultural bastards of Egyptians, Sumerians, Afghans, and those who came from Ghana and Timbuktu among other locations of Africa) through the narrative tools of 'nuances' and the logic of exceptions and contingencies. That is, whenever things and events do not fit the common ancestor—such things are plenty—they are adjusted to the margins of historiography through the excuse that these are merely the exceptions. The ancestral model of history in most cases tells a tale of declines, and its politics projects the will to restore the ancient glory, such as 'make America great *again*'. For example, the classical model of art sees art as a decline from the classical harmonious era. Or, at other times, the ancestral models perceive in history everything conjuring to reanimate the corpse of the 'common ancestor' and bring it back to the present in spectacular instantiations.[13] Both these tendencies are present in the invention of Europe through the 'common ancestors' of 'Greeks' and 'Aryans', and equally in the invention of 'Hinduism' which was taking place in India. Indeed, the resources shared by these two developments, the partnerships between the European philologists and the upper caste scholars (mostly Brahmin), and the endorsement of these developments with a self-interest—the interest of the denigrate-dominate function of all supremacisms—by European intellectuals is well known.[14] The most famous example remains of Romain Rolland who celebrated the leaders of this 'Aryan' revival from India in France.

We are all too familiar with this model in the recent histories: particularly in the nineteenth century in the return of the 'Aryan doctrines' and at same time of the Greeks, and often in a mixture which treats the two as 'one' or 'one people', as can be found in the texts of Nietzsche. Such a model of mixture is founded on the very 'common ancestor' concept of 'Indo-European'. The other instance is the highly influential ancestral model of Heidegger, which perceived history as the 'history of the occident'. The 'history of the occident' itself was, for Heidegger, the process of the decline of the essence of the Greek exception. However, when considering the oblivion of the thought of Being, Heidegger thought it ambiguously as an accomplishment in German philosophy of the 'Greek' essence. As though the 'Greek' opening into the thought of Being arrived at the understanding of the telos, the limit, the end, of metaphysics through German philosophy, and as though Heidegger's were the final ears to receive the relays of the 'common ancestor'.[15] The historiographies of the 'Hindu' account for the survival of a certain 'Aryan' self-designation into the modern forms of political institutions in India. They often celebrate the self-affirmation of the 'Arya' which subordinates all morals and norms, for example by deploying the theory of 'dharma', that is, the doctrine that any and all means are necessary to perpetuate racialising domination over the majority people of India.

Religion and the laws of history

When the components of the state—the army, the traders, the landowners, the slaves, the philosophers, the rulers, the law makers—are unable to produce regularly articulated relations with each other, when there is no comprehending law which gathers the components, we find *anomia*. Anomia is not the absence of the law-making institutions and the law enforcing components, but the absence of a theoretical ground which comprehends the institutions of the law and other components. For example, the events known as 'Paris, May '68' showed that the legal institutions were still functioning during the occupation of the university campuses, but the relation between the legal components on the one hand and the universities and the unions on the other hand were held together no longer—they came to be disjointed limbs[16] in search of a body, or they came to act as if they were each a body. For the ancients, another way into crisis was through *stasis*, which occurred when one or more components of the state attempted to be the comprehending law: When the tradesmen tried to align the activities of the state to suit their interests, or, when the military men tried to divert all the resources of the state towards their enhancements and to lead them towards wars. Stasis, then, is our most familiar evil today. In the ancient and modern world, we do find that religion, a component, sought to be the comprehending law. Religion sought to give the definitive names to everything, or it enforced new significations for all that there was; and it encoded, decoded, and recoded all activities. It did not always succeed, as can be seen in the emergence of *qanūn* (laws) and *adab* (customs) in large parts of mediterannean, west, central and south Asia as secular legislations which religious *Shari'a* law could never subordinate. Nevertheless, the histories of long durations are written often, and sometimes inadvertently, as the changes in the comprehending laws of a religion. This is evident in the descriptions of the long durations of the theocratic empires and the theologised empires of the world; and further in the appraisal of certain aspects of the cultures of the past which goes by the titles of 'Hindu mathematics' and 'Islamic science'. Or, in the contemporary fact that the planets and the heavens in general are encoded by 'Europeanised' gods of 'Indo-Aryan' origins, which assumes that 'god' is gazing at the law-bound gods of the lower realm from the great beyond, away from the reach of any technical or mathematical eye. We are still not out of this era, as can be seen in the struggles that women face across the world to be released from the theologised social fields, as in the denial of reproductive rights in America to women and of female education in Afghanistan. In India, the directive to theologise politics appeared in the mainstream through Gandhi, who sought to interpret India as 'Hindu' for both Indians and his audience in Europe and America. It appeared as the anxious upper caste response to the emergence of Dalit politics for the accomplishment of freedom, equality, solidarity and democracy in the true sense.

11

DEMOCRACY AND REVOLUTION

This text by Shaj Mohan was composed for publication in an Indian newspaper. However, the conditions imposed by media, in turn, due to the conditions imposed on them by the government and the mafia organisations, required that democracy itself was not a preferred subject anymore. As is often the case, the article was put in circulation among friends and colleagues. This article is a philosophical discussion of democracy and its relation to revolution with minimal technicalities and references. At the same time it is not an accessible text one finds on a news website. The basic thesis is this: Democracy is legitimate only when it creates conditions for freedoms, creates new forms of freedoms and shares them with everyone. When democracies take a turn for the worse they need corrective measures from the people, which is the responsibility of the people. The corrective measure should not be a mere overthrow of a government but a creation of a better democracy which is generous and compassionate to everyone. Previously, Mohan had called it 'the redemption of democracy'.

Democracy, *Revolution*, these are imperatives which imply each other. These are imperatives without imperators, without empires.

Ideally we should follow these declarations through a critique of the concept of democracy beginning from the Greek model of democracy. This model was founded on the principle of free deliberations which occasionally drew the questions of transcendence (Plato) into the existence of the many in the polis. We should also critically approach the threats to democracy in the very name of democracy in the capitalistic model. In this model, the freedom of the market now stands in surrender before the growing absolute monopolistic exploitation which is in the process of discarding democracy, like the pulled skin of an animal, for a new form of totalitarian system adequate to absolute monopolies and monopsonies. The urgency of this situation, of the deliberate destruction of the institutions of democracy and the constitution in India, and the need to not let this imperative (which is also a wail for freedom) be kept in the vaults of books that not many read anymore, demands of us that we draw out the principles of both *democracy* and *revolution* with minimal references and allusions.

This means, we should think of the meaning of democracy and the constituting components of it urgently. In India, democracy is founded on the constitutional promise to deliver an egalitarian and just society where all are equal participants in the making of decisions; or tautologically speaking, it is founded in the production of the future, and not in the excavation of the artifice of a past, which would be our burial ground—the choice offered by Modi, 'Shamshan ya Kabristan'[1]—being prepared by the upper caste supremacist organisations.

The *telos*[2] of democracy is not an impossibility nor an unattainable ideality. It is rather simple: the care for the freedom that is realisable through togetherness in this moment. The very conception of an ideal or an Idea of democracy betrays the reality of the world which develops as the unprecedented and unexpected orders of events; in other words, for each and every event reason must be given sufficiently, without lazily borrowing that reason from another order of events which we find in the political games of equivalences. If one posits the Idea of democracy, it will always be the totalitarianism of the containment of the variations that are the worlds. The realisation that there is no *Idea of democracy* is what prompted Plato to oppose it. In other words, democracies are opposed to Platonisms.

There is the theological conception of freedom, which is related to the absolute tyranny of the One, under which falls the concept of god. That is, a transcendence which imposes and regulates order and disorder according to itself in the world. The rigidity of the One is imitated by the totalitarianisms of history. As opposed to the theological conception, democratic freedom is the freedom to mend and to amend. Democratic freedom is kind and generous, and theological freedom is imposing and overbearing. Philosophically, and therefore politically, freedom is given by the arrangement of the components of a particular here and now.

Then, that which is not founded on the principle of transcendence, on the outside of the world or of the super-sensible, is still with a foundation. This foundation is given in the reality of the developments of newer components and relations that the world—the so called inanimate, animate, and technologised worlds—unfolds as freedoms, that there are always newer orders of freedoms created within the world. Democracy is founded on the commitment to realise the freedom which is this: the power of each moment for the sake of the *demos*, that is *people without exception*.

There is a reason in democracy and it demands that its processes are not deployed in order to destroy the possibility of democracy, or to betray the freedoms of a given arrangement of the components of the world. If critique is the science which determines the reasons, according to which conditions are obtained and sustained for the existence of something, democracy is more than critique. That is, democracy gives reasons for its conditions and, according to reasons produces and sustains the conditions for its existence with the responsibility that without democracy there is no room for critique. Critique presupposes democracy, and this is the Kantian thesis; in his political writings Kant expressed the angst of the philosopher who realised that for the praxis of critique a politics which is analogous to democracy was necessary.

The phrase 'imperfect democracy' to describe India in this context is wrong. Democracy is the actual practice guided by and leading towards the telos of democracy. For this, reason each moment of the democratic process has the responsibility to ensure that these very processes are not subverted to destroy a democracy and to lead it away from the democratic principle, as happened with Weimar Germany. In India, what is taking place is the betrayal of freedom for the majority lower caste people, for the retention of the 'height' of the minority upper castes over the whole of society. In this betrayal, the upper caste minority themselves are experiencing the depletion of freedom and peace.

We often assume that history creates freedoms, as in the theologised notion that history has been reducing the hypophysical quantity of violence.[3] History does not increase freedom, although history makes us experience an increase or decrease of a quantity because it is still a theologised form of thought grounded in the One—the world as the egg which will never hatch for it is contained under the orders of the One. In reality, freedoms are to be measured only here and now for two reasons. The freedoms of those who were dead and gone cannot be lived by those who are here now. The arrangements of events and objects which make up this world have the potential for a different order of freedom compared to those of ages gone by. It is for the same reason that it is immoral to tell someone suffering from poverty in a 'first world' country to look at the lives of those who live in the squalid conditions of a poor country, such as most of India. Poverty is a function of the lack of power given in a particular arrangement of the world.

In the common-place thought, revolutions are opposed to democracy. Philosophers, from Kant to Simone Weil, have cautioned us about revolutions, often correctly. However, revolutions have also founded democracies. There is a tradition that raised revolutions to the redemptive power of existence in philosophy. On the other hand, there is a peculiar poverty in the history of philosophy to conceive democracy democratically, that is, to conceive it anew, to give kinesis to it again and again, for each here and now. This poverty of philosophy is understandable since philosophy itself was concerned most of the time with transcendence. For this reason it took the last century for democracy to find its great philosopher, Jean-Luc Nancy, who found the founding principle of democracy in the 'being-with' of all things. That is, nothing is ever by itself, we are always with someone, with something. The 'with' is that which guides and is guarded by democracy from the tyranny of forms, such as the 'Hindu' form, or the 'French' form, or the Stalinist form. For Nancy, there is a 'truth of democracy' which is that democracy 'is not a political form at all, or else, at the very least, it is not *first of all* a political form'.[4]

Revolution is correctly opposed to democracy when it is either an instrument to overthrow a government for some particular interest, or is guided by the thought of the One to found an order which is not grounded in the here and now. The latter was the case with the communist revolutions and we know of their effects as their rulers came to think of themselves as transcending the people, into the position of the One—the One who makes everyone one people.

Then, should we retain the word revolution? We should, since it is as polyvalent a word as any other word, and it signifies the defiance of authority, so long as those who defy it are the people who seek freedom. Further, revolution should be qualified and distinguished through the guidance of another concept, *anastasis*.

Democracy demands revolution from out of its very principles. When democracies are seized by those who create order in the image of either god, gods, caste, race, force, avarice, or the One, then the democratic principle calls for revolutions to restore democracy. To sit and wait for something miraculous to appear to set things aright is moral turpitude in a democratic people. The only revolutionary principle is democratic, to restore democracy, to create the conditions for the exploration of and the sharing of freedoms given by a here and now. This latter principle is properly clled *anastasis*,[5] that is to come over *stasis*.

There are democracies in stasis across the world and they demand anastasis such that hierarchies are discarded; such that the ruins made by the seizure of the One are gathered in a generous embrace of revolution and are raised again as something else, something other than the past; the anastases of democracies are therefore the only redemption for our kind.

In India, such a revolution will be the annihilation of caste and the raising of the lower caste people across religions up to the stages, podiums, theatres, courts, and libraries to which they were forced to bow down to. In India, anastasis will be the creation of a democratic reality of the sharing of freedom by people without exception. The imminence of the revolution of democracy in India can now be felt like bass notes ringing in the distance, no matter where you are.

12

THE FUTILITY OF 'RESISTANCE', THE NECESSITY OF REVOLUTION

This text appeared in *The Wire* and was republished in an international newspaper, *World Crunch*, under a altered title: 'Beyond Resistance: What India Needs Now Is A Revolution'. I have maintain the original title. The article exposes the limits and the dangers of the concept of 'resistance' in politics, and contrasts it with revolution.

It was written in the context of extreme insensitivity shown by the police and the judiciary towards human lives. In February 2020, there was a protest held in the south Indian city of Bangalore (now Bengaluru) and there a young woman named Amulya Leona shouted slogans for the well-being of both India and Pakistan, something that is not against the law. However, she was soon harassed by a mob and was arrested for sedition and 'promoting enmity between different groups and imputations, assertions prejudicial to national integration'. Leona is known for her speeches which insist on the principle that love for a country does not imply hatred for another country. She is an internationalist.

Mohan's text shows neither outrage nor anxiety. Instead, it is a calm and measured assessment of the realities of politics in

India. It concisely performs the task of a philosopher in politics by separating the concepts which disable political action from those concepts which empower fruitful political engagement. It clearly discards 'resistance' as a category from twenty-first-century politics. It educates more than it agitates, even when it directs our thoughts once again to revolution.

We are apparently resisting right now, in India against citizenship laws and procedures, in Hong Kong against the fugitive offender's amendment bill, and across the world against border controls. But is it enough? In political theories, resistance came to be the most popular concept since the passive resistance model of M.K. Gandhi showed success and the romance of the European resistance to Nazi occupation became well-known through literature. Today we use 'resistance' to designate nearly every political activity, or activism, with an ethical claim. In fact, we assume that all the good people are resisters.

In a metaphysical sense, resistance is at least as fundamental as existence. These two terms came from the same etymological root '*sistere*', meaning 'to take a stand'. Interpretation of things on the basis of 'existence' would imply that all things stand indifferently 'out there'. But when we interpret the world through resistance, it shows that all things stand against each other, or resist each other, in being.

When something slows another thing down, or at the limit, halts the progress of another thing we say that *there is resistance*. This kind of resistance is very useful, for it performs a work or a function. When the flow of electricity is resisted by the filament of a light bulb it creates heat and light. Or when the tires of an automobile enjoy friction with the road we can manoeuvre it, accelerate it, and apply the brakes effectively. Now we can see that resistance is found within a system—electric or mechanical—and performs various functions in it.

In politics, we should investigate if our resistance is performing a work for someone else, a work that we did not intend, and is thus going well against our ethical claim. In the familiar example of factory workers resisting, we can see the way resistance often plays out. The factory management increases work hours and reduces wages as a part of cost reduction measures. The workers go on strike, resisting the factory management. Eventually there are negotiations, at the end of which the workers settle for a marginal increase in wage without any change in the increased work hours.

As we know, inflation eats into the value of currencies every day which means that the factory would not lose much by way of increased wages. But the increase in work hours surely adds to the profit for the management. That is, economism as resistance leaves that system qualitatively unchanged, and at best functions as a regulator slowing and hastening the innate tendencies of the system.

In the above example, resistance appears analogous to the militaristic notion of defending a terrain. That is, when something that we perceive as malicious approaches the objects, institutions, and terrain we created, we resist it. To give a contemporary example, we are today talking about resistance on behalf of the values of the constitution of India, which we must note is conceptually different from the Republic of India. The republic is a promise we make to each other that we will strive together to realise certain values—socialism, egalitarianism, secularism, climate security, destruction of the caste system, intolerance to racism and patriarchy.

In world politics as well as in India, the reality of all political systems might be that they are tending towards the critical limits of their innate possibilities—through dismantling of the universities; leaving workers without pensions; reducing the health care benefits to the people; privatisation of the police and the military; and corporate surveillance displacing 'intelligence gathering'.

We should take note of a certain fact of the last few decades: Politics has been played on the basis of the co-ordinates of 'left' and 'right', where the line between the two has been drawn invariably by the 'right'. The notion of 'centrism' then implies that a resister takes the space previously occupied by the right, which has now shifted to a position farther rightward. In India in recent years, we have started resisting the Hindu right's version of fascism with a 'resistant nationalism'—by waving the national flag at all times, ensuring that Muslim protesters sing 'Vande Mataram' despite its obvious religious imagery, and politicians of the opposition visiting temples and reciting religious prayers at press conferences.

But something repugnant took place on Thursday. A young woman, Amulya Leona, chanted slogans and wrote posts for the well-being of all countries and she was booked for sedition. This took place at a resistance event organised under the banner 'save the constitution' and some of the organisers took offence at this internationalist young woman. Often those who lag behind in moving towards the ever right-shifting 'centre' (always drawn by the right) are 'thrown under the bus'.

Resistance often results in the resisters resembling the opponent—'The creatures outside looked from pig to man, and from man to pig, and from pig to man again; but already it was impossible to say which was which'.[1]

The romance of resistance

The romance of resistance lies in the social illusion it provides with the noise of action, which is never political action, nor transformative participation. Instead, resistance often lets political systems reach the limits of their innate tendencies to the point of death while regulating their decay. Therefore, resistance creates heroes who knowingly regulate the innate tendencies of the system while seeming to be opposed to it. The classic example is the union leader who takes a cut from the workers and the factory owners. *Resistance can be good business.*

The most popular interpretation of resistance is 'civil disobedience' which presumes that the natural duty of a human being is to obey. When the circumstances are not ideal we are supposed to make the exception and disobey under the condition that everything is 'civil'. In this case, 'civil' refers to the kind of relation between the agents of the state—the ministers, judges, and the police—and those who disobey; that is, the agents of the state remain obedient to the law and human rights conventions, and the protestors obey all laws except the one they choose to disobey.

For example, a crowd seeking to disobey the law against 'freedom of organisation' is expected to obey all laws except that one. The difficulty today with this notion of 'civil disobedience' lies entirely in its premise of universal obedience. As we have argued, even the struggle against the CAA (Citizenship Amendment Act) requires disobedience of not just the unjust law and its associated processes such as the NRC (National Register of Citizens) and NPR (National Population Register) but also disobedience of the rules of caste oppression. Unless it tends towards universal disobedience—of all norms, codes, rules, constructs that keep the oppressive system intact—'civil disobedience' will eventually dissipate.

The liberal superstition

Concepts like 'civil disobedience' and even 'non-violence', which we recognise under resistance, work well in an idealised liberal state in which persuasion on the basis of moral hegemony changes the course of history for 'the good'. The trouble is that liberalism is founded on the superstition that all possibilities are equal in value and that they can co-exist in politics. As Martin Buber tried to explain to Gandhi, we know that the Jewish people and the Nazi state could not co-exist.

The difference between resistance and what we can call 'revolution' for the time being can be explained through the encounter between M.K. Gandhi and P.C. Joshi in 1944. Joshi was the first general secretary of the Communist Party of India. Gandhi the resister feared the approach of 'western civilisation' through colonial rule, which for him, reached the ultimate limit at the point when it began to transform the 'eternal' caste order of Indian society, which he called 'Hindu'. Gandhi spoke of the feared ultimate event during a conversation with Sardar Patel at Yervada jail in 1932—'the untouchable hooligans will make common cause with Muslim hooligans and kill *caste Hindus*'. *(emphasis added)*

In this case, Gandhi was being a 'bourgeois thinker' in the sense in which Wittgenstein used the term—'he thought with the aim of clearing up the affairs of some particular community'.[2] Wittgenstein had opposed the 'bourgeois thinker' with the philosopher who must be indifferent to the interests of communities, because the philosopher is concerned with the very meaning of 'interest' and 'common'.

P.C. Joshi was involved in the project of 'people's struggle' to bring an egalitarian society, to create something new rather than resisting changes to the old. Gandhi, who had a limited conception of the people as 'caste Hindus', found it curious and asked Joshi who these people were. Joshi responded: 'People in people's war means *all peoples the world over without exception*'.

This '*without exception*' implies that 'people' is not just the sum of all men and women but the sum of all the possible inclinations and all the impossible desires of humankind. This drive for the infinite which we find in Joshi is something that confounded Gandhi but which is an essential for change. For this moment, then, revolution implies this: We must go beyond 'resistance' to struggle for people, without exception.

13

FROM PROTESTING THE CAA TO EMBRACING THE DALIT-BAHUJAN POSITION ON CITIZENSHIP

In December 2019, the Modi led government of India passed an unprecedented Citizenship (Amendment) Act, 2019 (CAA). It was the very first legal step in India's history to not confer citizenship in the name of religion, that is it clearly excluded Muslims. Indirectly, this also targeted the Dalit-Bahujan or the lower caste majority. For example, a proposed National Register of Citizens (NRC) required the people to submit documents to establish their citizenship, which is impossible for millions of lower caste people in India who traditionally did not have the right to own land in several parts of the country. Dwivedi and Mohan wrote that the 'real majority has less access to the legal system, state welfare policies, and participation in shaping the commitments of the state, and they are therefore merely "formal citizens", citizens only in name, citizens living already in camp like conditions in the slums and ghettoes; and, forced to die in the sewer lines cleaning the shit of society'. Protests erupted in all parts of India and quickly many died, and many more would die later. In Delhi, a place close to the Jamia Milia Islamia University became a centre of protests, sit ins, and debates. This was also the place that was attacked by

> the upper caste supremacists and the police. Arrests, pogroms and an atmosphere of total terror followed. It was precisely in this context that Dwivedi and Mohan wrote, 'In the Indian context, revolution has only one sense, the end of the caste system, and "Citizen" has only one sense, the people of the state who have shed caste and racism.'

We are protesting. But we are not here to avenge the ashes and the cadavers of the various ancients.[1] It is not our concern whether the Scythians, Parthians, 'Aryans' and Mughals were invaders or not. It matters little who invaded first. Instead, what must matter in this moment is that those of us who are here—alive and concerned for the freedom, equality, and the meaningful future of all in this land—must be able to reason. We do not need to play the roles of the ghosts of the past to gain the approbation (or disdain) of our 'elders'.[2]

In these protests, tens of people have already been killed, many more maimed, and hundreds arrested by the police. This volatile situation might soon lead to riots and worse; one can see more than the auguries in the social media hate campaigns. It can also lead to civil 'conflicts' as several ministers, state functionaries, and Hindu leaders have been urging the 'public' to crush the protestors. We do know that when a state instigates mobs against its own people such an event is not called 'riot' but genocide.

But we the protestors are not able, yet, to define a horizon for ourselves other than the minimal duty of 'protecting the constitution'. After rehearsing the familiar, we have to let the real horizon of India's politics come towards us such that we ourselves become the chrysalis of the new.

The confidence that many people of India had in their formal status as citizens has been destroyed by three government measures in 2019—the initiation of the National Register of Citizens (NRC), the Citizenship (Amendment) Act (CAA), and the construction of massive detention camps.[3]

The NRC is the procedure to verify documents—the particularities of which have been kept mysterious by the government—in order to parse through the people to identify 'legal citizens'. The CAA defines which 'refugees' can be given citizenship. The CAA excludes Muslim refugees from Afghanistan, Pakistan, and Bangladesh, and also the Tamils who have been living in India after fleeing the genocide in Sri Lanka.

The misdiagnosis of the protests

Since 15 December, thousands of students, activists and ordinary people are out on the streets every day in every city. They have been brutally crushed by the police of the states ruled by the BJP. The BJP and Sangh parivar through their public statements and internal propaganda are projecting the CAA as a *Muslim minority* problem. Unfortunately, many media reports and some liberal critics of the government also see the official agenda as especially problematic for Muslims, and that the 'Hindu majority' is safe.

In fact, there is no such thing as a 'Hindu majority'. The 'Hindu majority' was invented in the early twentieth century to suppress the fact that the 'upper' castes are not more than 10 per cent of the population while the 'lower' castes are 90 per cent and are the real majority of India. The former has been oppressing the latter for millennia, and this system is the worst and most enduring form of oppression known in history. The false majority, 'Hindu', was then given an enemy, the Muslims, which resulted in the partition of India and in pogroms against the Muslims since then. The transfer of power from the British colonial rulers to Indian 'upper' caste rulers was facilitated by this notion of the 'Hindu majority'.

There are 'lower' castes among Christians, Muslims, and Sikhs as well. Therefore, the CAA and NRC will bring acute suffering to the real majority population of India—the 'lower' caste people and Dalits (the oppressed) in *all* religions. This *real majority* has less access to the legal system, state welfare policies, and participation in shaping the commitments of the state, and they are therefore merely 'formal citizens', citizens only in name, citizens living already in camp-like conditions in the slums and ghettoes; and, forced to die in the sewer lines cleaning the shit of society.

Hence, the unfolding events are witness to something which we must begin to recognise before the subcontinent is once again seized by a genocidal paroxysm. This 'something' is the limit expression of the implicit logic that has animated Indian society through the past 3000 years right up to today: it is the conservation of the caste order, which now can no longer conserve itself. In these unprecedented and vulgar excesses of the repressive use of all the institutions of the state against the protestors we should recognise the panic in Hindutva organisations that they are aware that these are the final days of the ancient social order. It means that we should also be concerned that the worst is yet to come.

Possible politics beyond all communalisms

The most vital aspect of this ancient social logic is that caste is the only category recognised in all strata of life. Each caste group—Brahmin at the top and Dalit at the bottom—is strictly endogamous in matters of sex, marriage, politics, culture, and residential areas. The 'upper' castes continue to control all the spheres life—politics, academia, media, economy. It reflects how the condition of the 'lower' caste majority has been maintained by the masking principle called 'Hindu'. Decolonisation has not brought freedom to them but only to the 'upper' castes. Even today the 'lower' castes do not have the right to earn a living, equality before the law, and freedom to love, to speak their point of view, and in some cases to appear in public. Persecution of religious minorities, such as the massacre of Christians in Kandhamal, Odisha, are deeply related to caste, since the lowest castes often seek refuge in Christianity, Buddhism or Islam for relief.

The national parties and a section of the media and academia have secured the consensus to terminate all analysis at 'Hindu-Muslim' so as to turn the attention away from the surging criticisms of lower caste intellectuals and their political struggles against the oppressive caste social order. The political processes have cultivated tensions and periodic bloody conflagrations between 'Hindus' and Muslims. Post-colonialists and subalternists continue to limit our gaze only to the evils of the 'West' and 'colonialism', while 'recovering the pride' in 'upper' caste ways of life.[4] The upper caste establishment wears many cunning masks such as 'Hindu spirituality', 'Hindutva', and 'Indic culture'.

The prolonged agony of the religious minorities can be ended in an instant through the rejection of the 'Hindu majority' invention and the destruction of the caste order. But the 'upper' castes who speak of 'Indian secularism' refuse to relent. They fear that this will bring an end to the *false problem*. For the Hindu nationalist government, Chandra Shekhar Aazad[5] and the Bhim Army's protests since 15 December in which the majority 'lower' castes take the political centre stage in order to protect the religious minorities is anathema.

In recent years, intellectuals (such as Suraj Yengde, J. Reghu, Kancha Ilaiah Shepherd, Hartosh Sigh Bal[6] and others) and organisations (*Dalit Camera*, *Round Table India*, Bhim Army[7]) have made the 'common cause' of freedom across religions. They are also gathering a younger generation of 'upper' caste students and intellectuals as friends of the 'Dalit-Bahujan position' in politics. The Dalit position is furthest from Gandhi's theologisation of politics. The Dalit-Bahujan position is characterised by 'fleshly love' as opposed to 'spiritual kinship', reason as opposed to 'religious feelings', courage as opposed to 'surrendering to karma', invention as opposed to caste traditions, and above all freedom as opposed to the destiny of 'caste dharma'. Through the Dalit-Bahujan position, the 'lower' castes of all religions have been searching for real citizenship in recent decades.

This moment can take India into chaos and darkness if the false majority ('Hindu') and the false problem (Hindu vs Muslim) are not rejected by the 'upper' caste elites. But this can also be the event in which India will finally find the meaning of citizenship. The little tremors from Bhima Koregaon,[8] the incident of the Ravidas temple in Tughlakabad and the April 2018 anti-caste protests should be sufficient indicators for the wise amongst our 'elders' that steadily the end of the upper caste establishment is walking across the subcontinent.

In the Indian context, revolution has only one sense, the end of the caste system, and 'Citizen' has only one sense, the people of the state who have shed caste and racism. Azad has presented the complete picture of this moment: 'India's Muslims are only an excuse. Modi govt also wants to take away Bahujans' power with CAA & NRC.' For this, he is under arrest and there are concerns for his safety. This unfolding moment must not be squandered for another transfer of power to a 'Hindu lite' coalition. Instead we must seize this unfolding and let ourselves be seized by it such that there is finally freedom.

14

THE CURRENT PROTESTS IN INDIA ARE A TRAINING GROUND FOR A BREAK WITH THE PAST

The protests against the CAA and NRC saw unusually strong participation of students from the lower caste majority who were asserting their position in the middle of the struggle by raising the blue flag of Ambedkarite movements. The seas of blue flags can be see through a simple image search on the internet for that period. The most defining and the last glorious moments of these protests were those of the lower caste majority leader, the charismatic Chandrashekhar Azad 'Ravan' protesting outside a police station, then disappearing, reappearing elsewhere, and finally making a speech before an ocean of people from inside the Jama Masjid in Old Delhi. Perhaps it is one of the most powerful images of twenty-first-century politics anywhere in the world.

These moments were also disconcerting for an upper caste owned public sphere. Postcolonial and other such conservative academic currents in India were questioning the protest movement. Dwivedi and Mohan defended the movement and Chandrashekhar Azad Ravan in the way philosophers do. First, by distinguishing the protests from a political campaign which seeks only the relatively tolerable outcome, and also from revolution—'The protest events in India are more than

> a campaign and, so far, less than revolutionary.' Secondly, they point to the necessity for political movements to learn from each of the distant corners of the world and be inventive. Third, by embracing the lower caste majority position, which concerns as they say the very rules of the game of politics in India, that is, the caste ordering of society, 'Unless we are prepared to question the rules of the game, chants of freedom can become a mere campish performance'.

The moment seizing India is something unprecedented and as yet unnamable. The protests across the land against the Citizenship (Amendment) Act (CAA), the National Register of Citizens (NRC), and the National Population Register (NPR) exceed the mere demand for the repeal of laws as they gather differing interests—anti-caste, atheists, religious, communist, liberal—into a legion which is beginning to conjure unknown possibilities for politics in the subcontinent. This actuality is exciting and at the same time confounding. For the first time in a long while, an epochal—and to that extent generational—divide is clearly apparent in the midst of these events.

In a recent article for *The Wire*, Partha Chatterjee has drawn attention to the indeterminateness of these events.[1] He expresses anguish at *the unknown* guiding these, according to him, leaderless and spontaneous protests. 'Where will this amazing burst of youthful passion, bravery and creativity lead us?' he asks, pointing to the failure of recent protest events—from Occupy and Arab Spring to Hong Kong—across the world to realise anything concrete like electing a liberal version of the very political order against which they protested. He believes the essence of Hindu nationalism lies in its totalising and homogenising character, and proposes the federalist reorganisation of formal politics. Though Chatterjee does not say so, his analysis even suggests that a return to the era of regional satraps—which leaves the caste based social order intact—would be a step forward.

It is obvious that Chatterjee, who has the historian's intuition, can see the developments more clearly than most of us. Yet, what makes something apparent or visible to a historian is determined by the conceptual atmosphere in which he or she breathes.[2] Only if we move aside his frames of reference can we conceive the political possibilities of these protests.

Neither anarchy nor failure

To begin with, one is surprised by Chatterjee's comparison of the highly possible tragic outcome of the Hong Kong protests with the Indian protests. Indian protestors are learning lessons from Hong Kong while being aware that the Hong Kong protestors are isolated from the Chinese mainland. In India, the protests are seizing the 'mainland' while Hindutva is appearing each day to be the island.

Chatterjee offers the Arab Spring and Occupy as cautionary tales against youthful protests for the reason that they were followed by the installation of conservative regimes. For example, after half a decade of protests against the rich 1 per cent in the United States, Trump was installed in the White House. However, none of these protests were about a change of guard in the existing political order. When people protest against the rich 1 per cent controlling the very political process, they are not aiming to substitute one electoral supplicant of the 1 per cent—say Bush for Obama. Rather, all these protests have been witnesses of the transformations of the global political order in the twenty-first century, and they have been opposing these very orders instead of merely seeking 'regime changes'.

Even, the achievement of 'May 68' was not the election of a Left-leaning government, which was in fact followed by a conservative government, but of instituting a new power of perception and thoughtfulness towards all political processes.[3] As the philosopher Jean-Luc Nancy explained in *The Truth of Democracy*, 'What preceded 68 and gave it its fundamental condition of possibility [was] a scarcely visible but insistent disappointment, the nagging sense that we had never recovered ... democracy.'[4]

The protests raging through India are not yet a political movement as the anti-dam movement was. But neither are they a chaos erupting through mass hysteria in the manner of most of the events under the title 'Anna Hazare'.[5] To make sense of this we have to note the difference between a political movement and a campaign. While campaigns such as 'Swadeshi' or the 'anti-war movement' seek explicit outcomes, a political movement seeks to change the way politics itself is conceived and practiced while leaving some fundamental conditions such as the head of the king, the name of the god, or the constitution unchanged. Political movements are at once conservative and transformative. The protest events in India are more than a campaign and, so far, less than revolutionary. Revolution in the Indian context is the destruction of the caste order, which is incompatible with any notion of 'azadi', 'viduthalai', or 'freedom'.[6]

Protests are training grounds

Global protest movements like Occupy have also been training grounds in many ways. Due to differing social, institutional and tactical factors in their respective contexts, all the protests did not have the same outcome—Tunisia was different from Egypt. Nevertheless, protests contract energies, conviction, and organizational strategies from previous and distant as well as contemporary and neighbouring political movements. Further, they anticipate, often more accurately than political observers, the transformations of institutions. The anti-austerity protestors in Greece created communities which shared services and labour in a world in which governments are withdrawing from caring for the people. Certain currents of *Nuit Debout* in France constituted free universities when public universities are being dismantled. Alongside the Occupy movement in the US, 'do it yourself' communities sprang up.

In India too—from the birth of the Ambedkar-Periyar Study Circle in IIT Madras[7] and 'Pinjra Tod' (break the shackles movement)[8], which began in Jamia University with girls breaking their hostel curfew rules—students and young activists across the country have begun a training programme. The protests against the NRC are in fact the resonance effect of the Ambedkarite anti-caste movements, the new feminist movements, and new intellectual currents which sprang within the Ambedkar-Periyar-Phule movements. They draw inspiration from and are also a part of the international protest movement.

The very language of protests has changed from manifestos to that of memes. Emily Apter shows how the meme language of politics perpetually makes a distance from the objects opposed by it—'Memic caricature has the capacity to stigmatise its targeted subject, but it also traces the outlines of the abuse of power, etching its occurrence on historical memory, transmitting it epigenetically as historical form and idea'.[9]

The new conditions

In all these ways the amorphous character of these protests, despite the attempts by several political actors to leverage positions[10] within them, continues to develop into a scale which Chatterjee has compared to the national movement. However, apart from the scale, everything else is different here. We are not in the midst of political events which were possible only under the post-war conditions of the twentieth century—of constitutional democratic arrangements which were production processes of long duration, predictable movement of population, climatic stability and more. The very first step towards understanding the sense of the protests in India and in other corners of the world is recognising that the twentieth century conditions of political institutions—and hence of politics as we understood it—have been changing rapidly through technological transformations and the migration of people, without an orientation as yet. Then, it follows that the political movements these changes have inducted too are without orientation.

Chatterjee characterises the protest events with a view to direct their forces for 'the Good' which he finds in 'true federalism'. But, the term 'federal' itself is no longer definable in twentieth-century terms. For example, the Goods and Services Tax conceived by the Congress-led government and implemented by Modi—which Chatterjee says disturbs 'federalism' in India—is part of an international adjustment. The steps taken from the UPA government onwards are part of the same international adjustment which includes the 'liberalisation' of universities; making surveillance precise and hence a control instrument through biometric data and other features; increased militarisation of the police; and, the normalisation of the security state which has discarded the notion of citizen and in its place sees only potential combatants. All these transformations have reasons which will take longer to attend to.

For new rules of the game

In India, something similar is indeed happening. Let us call it the 10 per cent protest: Indian society remains divided between the 10 per cent 'upper' castes and 90 per cent Bahujans. Its fundamental inequality is determined by caste (across religions), according to which both wealth and privileges are distributed. The fact that these protests are animated in most instances by the widespread appearance of icons of the majority lower caste movements for the first time—Ambedkar, Periyar, Savitri Phule, Sahodaran Ayyappan,[11] Rohith Vemula—should indicate that this moment is not the senseless expenditure of the youth of their 'spontaneous energy'. The participation of organisations such as the Bhim Army and the more recent Alliance Against CAA-NRC-NPR[12] cannot be erased from the scene.

The distinction between these protests and everything else we have witnessed since the 'regime change' instituted through the Anna Hazare protests is its emerging rejection of the false problem in Indian politics which was a part of the freedom struggle and has grown in salience ever since. This is the invention of the idea of a 'Hindu majority' in order to mask and contain the Bahujan struggles which had begun from the late nineteenth century. The *false majority* required a *false problem* to stage its politics, and the 'Hindu-majority'-versus-religious-minorities became that false problem. The present BJP regime is the limit expression of this false problem.

From the provenance of lower caste politics through the post-Mandal era politics, the Congress party lost the ability to protect upper caste interests,[13] which led to the rise of the BJP. Neither the Congress nor any other party will be able to deliver the interests of the 10 per cent any longer in these times of increasing awareness and mobilisation of anti-caste political and student movements. The NRC and other oppressive measures and the protests against them should be understood as the beginning of an epochal transformation in the subcontinent.

The risk of the 'theatre' model

However, it is important to heed some of the advice of those like Chatterjee, who have lived through and observed many political movements. One of the cautions is that one must not have an innocence or pretence to innocence in politics. As Milan Kundera found, it is nearly impossible—without metaphysical instrumentations—to distinguish between innocence and ignorance.[14] All gatherings of people, once they become regular, are arranged by some interest or the other. People do not appear spontaneously day after day, which is something that the Manmohan Singh government learnt the hard way during the Anna Hazare movement.[15] The present protests, although they are too large and dispersed to manage, could, in fact, be managed and this is a risk the protestors should be aware of.[16]

For example, these protests imitate the theatre of war model adopted, since the Anna Hazare movement and JNU-2016, in Shaheen Bagh. That is, a small space in the national capital comes to be the theatre of action and is then nationally projected through various media to affect opinion. This is risky given the possibility of manipulation of small spaces, and also, in this instance, unnecessary since there are massive protest events happening across India each day.

Further, the protestors should overcome the consternation of those who seek outcomes within the familiar models of politics. Instead, these events should be seized as the training grounds for the transformative possibilties which India surrendered for so little during the independence movement. We do know what we want, as we keep chanting freedom. Then, it is also time to get intimate with it; freedom comes to be only when it is shared equally—without the divisions, whether of 1 per cent or of 10 per cent.

Here, it is important to read the constitution of the Indian Union, not as senseless mantra, but critically. While deploying the constitution and the nationalist paraphernalia as precautions, we must be aware of what Pritam Singh called 'The Hindu Bias'[17] in the constitution. The preamble of the constitution promises what the republic will deliver—secularism, socialism, egalitarianism, and justice to all. However, Article 25 is concerned with the welfare of

'Hindus'. The directive principles include 'cow protection' which is a tool to oppress religious minorities and all Bahujans. It includes the proposal to develop 'Hindi', the recently invented 'Hindu' language as Alok Rai has shown,[18] which the constitution urges us to develop by drawing vocabulary from Sanskrit, which is Brahminical. These are also some of the risks in retreating to a 'federalism' within the constitution. Unless we are prepared to question the rules of the game, chants of freedom can become a mere campish performance.

Most of the well-known intellectuals from India are batchmates of Salim Sinai of Rushdie's *Midnight's Children*, born with the transfer of power. This generation nearly totally controls speech, theoretical frameworks and publications. Therefore, we do not yet know what is 'Young India' unless one starts talking to the youth. When you speak to a crowd of young people you will hear that the false majority—'Hindu' masking the oppression of the majority Bahujans—and the false problem—the opposition between 'Hindu majority' and the religious minorities—is disappearing. There is a boredom with the past, which is creating space for the new in India.

15

THE OBSCENITY OF TRUTH

ARREST THE ANTI-FASCIST!

This article appeared after the arrests of intellectuals, academics and activists in India for their participation in or connection to the commemoration of the Battle of Bhima Koregaon. The battle took place in 1818 in what is today the state of Maharashtra. A lower caste army liberated a region ruled by the Brahmins, a rare event in India's history, causing long lasting shame to the Brahmins and the upper castes. For the lower caste people this moment was always a promise to themselves, that they can liberate themselves from the racialised enslavement of caste. In 2018, as in previous years, the battle was commemorated by millions. The people congregating for the celebration were attacked by the police and upper caste supremacists. Many died and many were arrested. The evidence in some cases were their personal libraries which had such incendiary texts as *War and Peace* by Leo Tolstoy. In some other cases, the police claimed that they were practicing the crime of anti-fascism. A shorter version of this text was published in the French newspaper *Libération* on 5 September 2018.

In India, and certainly everywhere else, activists are fond of the motto 'speak truth to power'. This motto implies that power is afraid of what is called truth and it crumbles when faced with truth. But what happens when power speaks the whole truth and nothing but the truth? When power speaks the truth, speech itself would wear Columbian neckties and politics would become a whited sepulchre. The criticalisation of speaking-the-truth has been reached in India, which makes the clamour about post-truth redundant.

On 28 August the police in the Indian Union raided the homes of five activists, confiscated their computers and mobile phones, forced them to give up the passwords to their email accounts, and took many of them into custody. These are Anand Teltumbde (academic and Dalit intellectual), Sudha Bharadwaj (academic and lawyer), Varavara Rao (retired professor and poet), Arun Ferreira (human rights lawyer), Vernon Gonsalves (academic and writer), and Gautam Navalakha (writer, journalist, and human rights activist).

So far, the clearest allegation by the police against these individuals is that they are part of 'an anti-Fascist front' made up of Dalits, tribals and Muslims that is striving to weaken the government led by the Hindu nationalist Mr Modi.[1] The police are certainly implying that the central government is fascist and that being anti-fascist is a crime. Further, the police has accused the arrested intellectuals of 'reading so many books' and 'spoiling students'. The police has also alleged that these activists are working with the Dalits and the tribal people towards their political mobilization and that they had a role in the commemoration on 1 January 2018 of a Dalit victory against a Brahmin Kingdom in central India. All the calamitous developments have something to do with this 200-year-old battle as we will find. The Supreme Court has since, unjustly, placed all these activists under house arrest.[2] More arrests are going to follow soon, according to the police.

The beginnings of Hindu fascism

All of this might be very difficult to understand, especially the uncanny moment when a state proudly declares that it is Fascist and that being anti-Fascist is a crime against the state. However, the persecution of intellectuals will begin to make sense if one recalls that the Nazis called modern art 'degenerate' and their book burnings 'festivals'. Still, a little background is required to understand the calamities unfolding in India for which it is important to begin with the meanings of 'Hindu' and 'Hindu nationalists', and then visit the meaning of 'speaking to truth to power'.

The BJP (Bharatiya Janata Party, founded in 1980) which rules India is the political front of the most powerful non-governmental organization, the RSS (national self-server's corp, founded in 1925). The RSS believes that India should be the nation led by the upper castes, especially the Brahmins. Throughout its history, the RSS was headed by Brahmins, except for a few years in the 1990s by Rajendra Singh who was a Kshatriya (the upper caste associated with warriors). The RSS had its beginnings in British administered central India, the region today known as 'Maharashtra'. Here in 1818, the kingdom of the Brahmin 'Peshwas' was defeated by an army made up of Dalits and the British forces, which was a rare moment. Since 1850, the British administration introduced legal measures, such as the caste disabilities removal act,[3] which along with employment in the army, provided the conditions for the lower castes to seek equality and dignity through education. The upper castes found both the memory of this humiliating defeat and the unprecedented demands for equal rights from the Dalits a direct challenge to their millennia old dominance over the social order.

This phase is one of the origins of 'Hindu nationalism'. The other phase consists of the invention of the religion 'Hindu'[4] by the upper castes in the aftermath of the census operations of the British administration from the 1870s. The census revealed the upper caste population to be a demographic minority and this threatened their dominance in the imminent era of democracies. The religion 'Hindu' was thus meant to encompass all castes while still maintaining caste distinctions and the dominance of the upper castes in society. Gandhi played an important role in the creation of the 'Hindu' religion. He convinced the lower castes that gaining entry into upper caste temples and a limited participation in their religious rituals was a sufficient price to pay for the acceptance of this new religion.

The creation of Hindu religion and the 'Hinduness' politics (of a state totally controlled by the upper castes) made the RSS the 'voice' of the upper castes. However, this new religion also placed certain restrictions on it. The upper castes could not always enter into public conflicts with the lower castes for it would destroy the charade of this new 'religion for all castes'. Instead, they directed their animosity towards the Muslims and the Christians, terming them 'the outsiders' or 'the Semitic races' while quietly continuing the oppression of the Dalits and tribals.

The RSS is a product of the descent-based caste logic (one of the oldest forms of racism) reinforced by the biologised racism of early twentieth century. It had friendly transactions with Nazism and Italian fascism. This friendship with Nazism continues even today. In fact, in Mr Modi's home state of Gujarat text books have described Hitler as an exemplar. It will be important to quote from it:

> Hitler lent dignity and prestige to the German government within a short time by establishing a strong administrative set up. He created the vast state of Greater Germany. He adopted the policy of opposition towards the Jewish people and advocated the supremacy of the German race.[5]

Following upon this legacy, today India is the most important hub of far right movements from around the world.[6]

The political emergence of the RSS and the beginnings of a Hindu state

The BJP came to political prominence in 1992, following the demolition of a sixteenth-century mosque and the subsequent pogroms. Mr Modi, who is the prime minister of the BJP led government came to national importance in 2002, riding on the events known as 'Gujarat riots' which killed about 2,000 Muslims in the state where he was the chief minister at that time. In 2008, hundreds of poor Christians were killed by Hindu terrorist groups:

> The media records stories of dismemberment, men buried alive and attackers wearing a victim's intestines like a garland. Mobs

> raped and molested a reported 40 women and girls, including the rape of a young Hindu dalit girl, because her uncle had converted to Christianity.[7]

The electoral victory of the BJP in 2014 which allowed them to form the national government was preceded by a pogrom in 2013 known as 'Muzaffarnagar riots'.

The RSS and other Hindu nationalist organisations under its aegis are able to rule only when mass murders take place. That is, the thin idea of 'a nation governed by the upper castes' is difficult to defend with words, and hence these 'Hinduness' organisations have a severe phobia of anything intellectual and literary. Since 2013, three rationalist philosophers have been shot dead and a prominent journalist was assassinated outside her home in 2017. Hindu nationalist organisations have been behind these killings as well. More recently, an important student leader Umar Khalid was shot at in public by Hindu nationalists who moonlight as 'cow protectors' (mostly killing those who eat beef). Khalid narrowly escaped as the gun failed to fire.

Since Mr Modi came to power, a new model of killings began. This involves radicalizing politically unaffiliated people into the 'Hinduness' programme using national television, newspapers, social media, and Whatsapp. This propaganda targets the upper castes and incites them with visions of an imminent threat to their existence from the Dalits, Muslims, and Christians. The feeling of 'victimhood' and impending 'existential threat' are then directed to the activities of 'cow protection', guarding of 'our women's honour', and 'defence of Hinduness'. The terrorism of the cow protection militias has killed at least (statistics of pogroms and killings are highly contested in India) 30 people since 2014 when Mr Modi (and the RSS) came to power, and most of the victims, who are either Dalits or Muslims, were lynched in public. The difference between the radicalization strategies of ISIS and 'Hinduness' nationalism is that the state, which is governed by the BJP, steadily protects the killers and takes legal action against the killed and their families. As we write this a young man was lynched by 'cow protection' terrorists.[8]

The illusion of independence

There is a long history of the legal protection enjoyed by the upper castes when it comes to the killing of Dalits and the religious 'minorities' in India. But we have to keep in mind that India names one of the portions of the Indian subcontinent, which was created as a single territory, politically consolidated, and administered by the British colonial administration. On 15 August 1947 the British administration initiated the 'transfer of power' of one of the divisions of 'British India' to an upper caste administration while King George the 6th remained the head of state. It was on 26 January 1950 that the transfer of power was completed and the constitution of India came to define the state. 'Independence' was in reality the strategic transfer of power and the paraphernalia of a modern state into the hands of the upper castes under whom the tribals, Dalits, and other lower castes remain subjugated, which is illuminated by the fact that India has never had a Dalit prime minister.

Many lower caste and Dalit political leaders, including Dr B. R. Ambedkar, have refused to accept this ambiguous sense of 'independence'. Dr Ambedkar, the principal architect of the new constitution, called it a 'delusion'.

The growing resistance of the Dalit thinkers and political activists to 'Hinduness' and 'independence' is causing panic within the RSS and other 'Hindu' organisations. This is evidenced by a sequence of events. The first wave of repression by the present Hindu right government started in 2015 when they banned the Ambedkar Periyar Study Circle (a forum created by Dalit students for political discussions) of IIT (Indian Institute of Technology) Madras. In the same year in Hyderabad Central University, Dalit students were punished extra-legally for protesting against the death penalty, for screening political documentaries, and for supporting autonomy for Kashmir. Dalit and tribal students in India often rely on the scholarships provided by the state and the hostel rooms to study and also to support their families. The withdrawal of the scholarship and the hostel room resulted in the suicide of a Dalit student leader Rohith Vemula in 2016.[9]

Following Vemula's 'institutional murder', the Dalit and lower caste students in JNU (Jawaharlal Nehru University) initiated protests, which provoked the sharpest reaction from the Hindu nationalist government and eventually some of the student leaders were arrested. However, the student organisations, academics, and intellectuals who protested this incident converted it into a debate on good versus bad nationalism. These nationalism debates were compiled into a book whose introduction admits that the teach-in had 'glaring absences...Did the inaugural moment of the JNU struggle, Afzal Guru and the Kashmir issue, retreat into the background? Was the somewhat muted engagement with the Dalit struggle at Hyderabad Central University also not a sign of failure?'

In 2014, an organisation named Bhim Army for the education, equal rights and dignity of Dalits was founded by Chandrashekhar Azad Ravan to oppose the state-supported oppression of Dalits by the upper castes. Mr Ravan was arrested under the National Security Act in 2017 and he has not been released since. This gesture was to clearly demonstrate to the Dalits and the lower castes that the Indian state is for the upper castes, or that it is already a 'Hindu state'.[10]

However, these setbacks notwithstanding, several Dalit organisations gathered and commemorated the 200th anniversary of their victory against a Brahmin kingdom in 2018. The celebrations outraged the Hinduness political organisations and soon arrests were made using undemocratic provisions. These arrests were followed by more lynching of Dalits across India.

Power speaks truth

Parallel to these killings across India, the 'saffron-isation' of education (using school and university syllabi for Hinduness propaganda) has been taking place, which is destroying higher educational institutions. These gestures have the sanction of 'postcolonial theory' which too seeks to restore nativist wisdom and caste laws to their ancient prominence. These 'Hinduness' educational programs include experimental research on the divine and medicinal properties of cow urine, the recovery of ancient medical technologies which created the elephant-headed god Ganesha (a god with the head of an elephant and the body of a boy), the aviation technologies of the ancient subcontinent which allowed the gods to fly around, the celebration of the 'evidence' for wireless telecommunications in ancient times (namely, that nobody has been able to find any wiring systems during archeological digs), and establishing India as the origin of all civilisations in the world.

However, Mr Modi has also been speaking the truth from out of the great power he enjoys. A first for an Indian politician, Modi declared during his election campaign that he was 'a Hindu nationalist'. Ministers of Mr Modi's government have called Dalits 'dogs'. Now, the police has stated that the central government is Fascist and being anti-fascist is a crime against the state. Further, the police have declared that the political association of the Dalits, tribals and the religious minorities is a threat to the Indian state. These episodes of 'truth telling' have made many political commentators express their admiration that 'after all we know what they stand for, unlike most other political parties'.

Our political systems are haunted by the ratio between 'truth' and power. The separation of those who speak truths (the good citizens) from those who are afraid of the truths (those in power) ensures the very appearance of both power and truth as political categories. This ratio founds our desire to 'speak truth to power', because in electoral democracies certain truths can have consequences for those in power. In other words, truth makes sense only as that speech which brings consequences.

There are several ways in which this ratio of truth and power can be made redundant. When a state practices absolute surveillance on its citizens all conducts come to be transparent and true before an opaque state. The effect would be indistinguishable from a Gandhian state where all citizens would live their lives out in the open.

But the case which concerns us today is of a government that openly speaks the truth about its corruptions, Fascist intentions and electoral expectations, leaving its people nothing to speak. In India those in power do not feel the need to worry about electoral consequences, or they already experience total power. With great power comes least consequence, and this is the obscenity of truth, which should be the cause of the greatest alarm.

16

FREEDOM FIRST
MANIFESTO

In 2017, cultural freedoms were being trampled across India. Novelists were being attacked, cinema was entering into self-censorship, works of art could no longer be displayed, and academic writings were also under watch. At this moment, Dwivedi and Mohan with several intellectuals initiated a project of maintaining the freedom of ideas and arts in quieter private domains through the creation of diffuse communities which could keep the light going. At the same time it was also a preparation for the very manifestation of freedom. The manifesto is a text which is now applicable to the whole world as we are together entering into darker and unknown terrains of new variants of far right parties, fascisms, neo-Nazisms invading political and social spaces everywhere.

Individual freedom and human rights are under threat in many parts of the world, including India, United States, Hungary, Poland, Turkey and China. This is evident in the statement 'America First'. 'Nationalism first', 'religion first', 'race first', 'sentiments first', 'markets first' and 'cow first' are versions of this statement which are suppressing freedoms and the rights of individuals. Through such statements, the organised minorities of oppressors are able to terrorise the vast free thinking humanity.

This is possible because this word, 'Freedom', was appropriated by neoliberalism as a brand name and a war cry; it was surrendered in the name of securitisation and the permanent global war; freedom has come to be a militarised term in many states, including India where its translations as 'Azadi' in Urdu and 'Viduthalai' in Tamil have invited punitive measures from the state; and the free thinking people have not organised to defend and expand their freedoms.

'Freedom First!' is envisaged as a movement of free thinking individuals to organise and to demonstrate our basic human rights, freedoms and expressions of love. The hard-won idea of human rights and freedoms sustained many a struggle and undergirded international laws and constitutions. It was assumed that politics takes place under the validating condition of freedoms and human rights, even in those places where their violations continued to take place, including caste discrimination, racism, and gender discrimination. That is, the availability of freedoms and human rights as the end and the ground of politics let their absence and violations be manifest. However, freedoms and human rights have been taken for granted like a jade in a vault which is not needed in our everyday life. Should we wonder if it is still there in that vault? Not only are they not universally available to all people, but they are also progressively eroding wherever they did obtain.

Today this condition provided by the rights to free speech, to life and liberty, to cultural expressions, to love, to non-normative sexuality has been undermined. This condition, which is enshrined in international law and in the constitutions, is itself in need of rescue. Unless we insist on these freedoms and rights by demonstrating them, they will soon become redundant before the law itself.

It may seem a strange idea to demonstrate the very freedoms guaranteed by international law and human rights. Even today we would not think of sneezing, eating, and loving as a political acts. And yet, eating a certain food and loving outside one's religion, caste, gender norms and race are already being curtailed through illegitimate (that is, contravening freedoms and human rights) legal measures and force.

Freedom First! is a protest movement that is made up of collective, continuous, simultaneous acts of freedom that anyone, anywhere can commit. Through these acts of freedom we shall make a positive exercise of them rather than wait for their disappearance to hold a 'Freedom's wake'. Freedom First! is a call to all to break through the borders and 'big, fat, beautiful walls' of nationalisms, fascisms, languages, religions, skin colours, gender norms, market tyrannies, passports and war hysterias.

These acts can include fighting censorship by distributing, displaying, and performing restricted and banned literature and works of art; inventing and expressing forms of love; expressing the freedom to wear clothing without being subjected to anyone's code; inventing ways to practice or not to practice religions, including the invention of new religions or multiple religious conversions; persistently challenging the restrictions to freedoms through legal means and practicing non-cooperation with unjust laws.

The goal of Freedom First! is to instantiate the already existing freedoms and rights, to display them in public, and through this display to strengthen our constitutional and democratic institutions. It is not meant to be an organisation since 'Freedom First' defines humanity itself. The title 'Freedom First!' is more like the title of a book still being written or a cinema in the making. This movement is the creative intervention of each one of us. This movement and its protest strategies should be relayed everywhere and the lessons learned from each instance of protest should be gathered under the title 'Freedom First!' as a common work in progress of humanity. It is also a test of the state of humanity to explore its own freedoms and rights in this way, and an interminable experiment to discover new freedoms.

17

THE TERROR THAT IS MAN

Within months of taking power, the Modi government and the RSS-led organisations in India began forceful conversions of Christians and Muslims into 'Hinduism'. This soon became a regularity with frequent disruption of society, and the use of legal institutions, media, and the police to create an atmosphere of permanent uncertainty and fear. The political investment of the 'Hindu right' in the forced conversions of Christians and Muslims has been unsatisfactorily explained as a show of might by 'Hindu majoritarianism'. As the following texts show, this picture is devious and subtly cooperates with the upper caste supremacist organisations led by the RSS.

The anthology shows that the real majority of India are the lower caste people who are more than 90 per cent and the upper castes who control academia, judiciary, parliament and the RSS are a minority of less than 10 per cent. The fear of all upper castes in India is at three levels: the fear of being exposed statistically and politically as a minority; and on the other, the fear of mixtures with the lower caste majority who had been kept outside the upper caste temples, the temples of education and bureaucratic spheres, cultural domain including cinema; and the fear of the possibility that one day the lower caste majority may come to power. This is essential to understand India and its academic and political discourses. Religious conversions—to Christianity, Islam, and Buddhism—had been a way for the lower caste majority to escape the extreme forms of caste oppression, to some extent. For example, conversion to Christianity opened education to many lower caste communities, and gave everyone a new freedom to merely walk on public roads. The fear of the upper caste minority, even those who appear to western audiences to be 'liberal', is that such mass conversions can expose 'Hindu'as a false majority, and can transform the politics of India in new directions.

This text was written by Mohan in the context of the extreme terror created by the 'Ghar Wapasi' or 'return home' campaign initiated by the RSS controlled organisations, in which many died. It was published in translation in Malayalam in an anthology against these events created by J. Reghu and published by D. C. Books in 2015. The text is philosophical and, at the same time, does not presuppose the knowledge of any philosophical tradition. It creates a new meaning of 'conversion', which is consistent with the philosophical system of Dwivedi and Mohan. The usual weight attached to 'conversion' in Indian society as a fearful and extraordinary act is opened to new senses, including the transition into genders, nationalities, cultural groups, fashions, and life styles. The terms 'conversion' and 'containment' refer implicitly to their concepts of homology, analogy, polynomia and functional isolation which the reader will encounter directly later in this anthology. The appendix of concepts can also be consulted.

> *Manifold is the un-homely, yet nothing is more un-homely than man.*
>
> —Sophocles

The middle of the previous century is understood to be the termination of all kinds of containments of man, having witnessed the worst containment in the Concentration Camps. This termination resulted from a crisis that is both philosophical and political: what is the de-termination of man such that he is not the contained? A summary of this scenario is found in a trivial understanding of

Foucault's statements concerning 'the end of man' (*The Order of Things*) and Derrida's deconstruction of the notion of 'the end' in his essay 'Ends of Man' (*Margins of Philosophy*).

As a result of the exigencies of the philosophical and the political, the concept of the state located itself, in the 'occidental domain', away from the containers. The State would no longer claim to be the clergy and the sovereign of containers such as race and religion. Instead, the State demanded only the right to primary containment—first Indian and then Muslim, first British then White, first Spanish then Basque. The list, the differences, the classification and the management of all the other containers—religion, caste, language, race, public, private—were left up to the new clerics, the new academic disciplines and the NGOs. If all containers were opened up then everything should have flooded out and mixed to form a substance of a new world of people; rather, a substantiality for the interminable formation of people. This new people-substance should have dissolved the traces of all the containers, the way science-fiction often imagines the future to be. It should have left for us tales which are the negative of memories, that is, taboos, or myths. For example, the tales that we received about incest from the ancients, the tales of cannibalism in fairy tales, the tales of the world's resistance to Nazism.

However, we do know that this is not the case. The Camp, terrifyingly, is becoming a vague ancient memory even though it came into the active consideration of everyone only in the 1960s. As the Camp compares itself each day to the camps sprouting everywhere—the Palestinian camp, Moquoble camp, Chinese labour camps, Muzaffarnagar camp, Guantanamo Bay camp, the containers in which people are shipped—the moral force it once exercised appears to be in decline. This decline of the moral force of the Holocaust also indicates that the politics which led to it is permissible again. There is a distinction between each of these recent camps in relation to the states which have instituted them.

For instance, the Muzaffarnagar camps in India remain outside the domain of legality in the sense of a common place: 'a puppy being run over by a car'[1] is not a matter of law. While we are less than certain about our moral and political responses to the camps in India and the Middle East, we are so certain about most of the camps in the West, including the refugee camps. There is constant questioning of the legitimacy of the Guantanamo Bay Camp by leading intellectuals and the western media. We are in agreement that the shipment of people in containers is outright illegal, even if the many people held in them might have opted to be there.

However, from the point of view of the people who are the current residents of all these camps, without regard to the colonial/post-colonial axis, the difference is only a matter of degrees. Are all containments of man the same? Is the membership of a man in a communist organisation the same as his conversion into Islam? Is the membership of a woman into the activist group *Femen* the same as her conversion into a Christian Consecrated Virgin? Is the conversion of a woman into an actress the same as her conversion into a mercenary? All these questions of containments, camps, conversions and baptisms are global, and also questions of globalisation. But there is something unique to the Indian problem of 're-conversion'.

The change of a person from one containment to the next is conversion. Although in India, by conversion we mean the movement of a man from the Hindu religious containment into something unreal. When a man gains in wealth he is converted into a member of the conspicuous sphere of spending which in turn converts him into an upper class; when a man fails to pay back a loan he is converted into a criminal; when an upper caste woman marries a lower caste man she is converted into a shameful object; when a woman kisses a woman in public she is converted into an obscenity. There are many baptisms of men, many more than there are men. This plenitude of baptisms is the sign of the pure convertibility of the human-substance. The fact that when the word 'conversion' is spoken in India what is heard is 'a Hindu man has been converted into a non-Hindu' tells us enough about the essence of man in India. First, man is not purely convertible in India. There is only one baptism of men in India which is his birth into his caste order and caste is the most codified form of racism.

Now, the question *is there a man that is not purely convertible or a man that is not the effervescence of infinite baptisms* should remind us of Hegel's thoughts on man in India—'what is the essence of man-substance in India?' Or 'is there a man-substance in India?'[2] The weight of this question should not be set aside using the simple machine of postcolonial theory; further, Hegel's questions concerning the meaning of religion ought to make us ask again what really is religion for us, here, right now. Only then can we re-articulate, in an articulation of the human that is new, what is implied in the 're' of re-conversion and 'home' in the command 'return home!' Second, religion in any generous consideration should be defined as the practice of faith. Having a faith in something or someone is a convertible event; that is, faith moves a man from one containment into another. When the faith is broken a man moves on to the practice of another faith. When a faith is boring a man changes it to make life a little interesting. However, what this command 'return home!' makes clear is that being Hindu is not a matter of faith at all. It is rather of birth, blood, race. Then, the problematic of religious conversion is not universal, since even after a change of religion the Indian retains his position in the caste order, and hence we have untouchable Christians and untouchable Hindus and untouchable Buddhists—*be you Jew or Greek* of St. Paul means little in India. But then, is the offer of a conversion into the Universal, the ideal envelop of a single containment, possible elsewhere?

The assumption in the command 'return home!' is of a kind of betrayal—that those men who converted have betrayed their home, the home which set rooms on the basis of racial lines and assigned them distinct labours which are castes. At the same time, this command reminds the men that those who strayed have never lost their essence which keeps them as the men of their home: their racial lines are not erasable and they carry them visibly no matter which new homes they find to hide in. Hence, they are allowed the chance of a return. This sense of a betrayal, of straying far from home, is a feature common to the other 'time-pass' or entertainment that we call 'honour killings'.[3] The essence of the woman is to keep herself in the containment of her caste home. Her change of home is decided according to the caste laws of the home. The betrayal by the woman of the domestic caste laws by loving the men and women of her choice is the dishonour of the home. This betrayal and its taint can be removed, and the home purified, by blood alone. This game of impurities, accumulating into the pure and their sanguine purification, is inherent to the Hindu socio-political system. What would the 'Hindu' socio-political system be without this game? What would India be without this game?

Gandhi acknowledged time and again that he was opposed to a legal abolition of caste since there can be *no Hinduism without caste*. The refusal to think of an Indian subcontinent without the games of purification is the effect of the conception of man in India. The essence of Man, as we found, is the infinite convertibility across the containers that are always more than there are men. The political fight waged today for the right to kiss in public as an expression of love and the fight against the closure of conversion (through the command 'return home!' and the legal measures proposed to prevent conversions) are meant to keep the essence of man as a practical condition available to all men in India—the fight to bring the essence of man to all men or to render man unhomely. Derrida's questions in 'Ends of Man' concern the name of this being that is unhomely: man or overman? Even though Foucault was opposed to a certain kind of teleology, of perfection or an actualisation without remainder, he set an end for man—a substance capable of enduring the terror of his unhomeliness, such that 'man would be erased, like a face drawn in sand at the edge of the sea'.

The purely convertible substance that man is grounds all politics. But the actual practice of politics is distinct from this ground. Then, we have two different kinds of politics—a politics for access to the essence of man and, opposed to it, a politics to condemn men to a particular container. Each political unit of the latter kind fights for a certain containment of men. Either this fight is waged by posing as the sentinels of a containment—such as Nazism fighting for the right to maintain the purity of Aryan blood; or by posing as the scaffolding for a future containment—such as the Indian nationalist movement which proposed to liberate men into one single containment, that is, of being an Indian. The command 'return home!' states that there are containments of men that are not convertible. The inconvertibility is birth, bloodlines, genetics. Since those who converted to Christian and Muslim faith were of the Indian subcontinent they are condemned to be Hindus forever. Rather, their conversion is not real. Their 're-conversion' too is not a real conversion, but an illusion, maya. It is their obedience to the command 'return home'. That is, man is not convertible in India. The converted are currently being led from the unreal into the real—from the maya of the pure convertibility of men into the brahman of inconvertible condemnation. It is not difficult to see that the really real that is understood here is not religion, but racial lineage; the politics of birth, blood, and soil.

The notion that man is inconvertible in 'the Hindu geographic region', that his containments are immutable within the caste order, and that his deviations from the containments are measureable and punishable, resembles the Nuremberg laws very much. But the millennia old laws of containment have gained an extra legal force which a recent invention such as the Nuremberg laws could not have access to. We have come to accept that electoral politics in India (and soon everywhere else) is the game of creating immutable containers that arrest the conversions of men. Rather, the politics of the subcontinent is defined as the terror before the essence of man as the most unhomely. In this peculiar sense the question 'what is man' is alive in India. As these inconvertible men fight for their rights to be inconvertible, the decisions that concern everything else are held away from men. We must note here that the herding of the unhomely into a determinate home defines fascism.

Not all conversions are the same, as we have seen. The conversion of a man through the baptism of an automobile collision is permanent. Even if he comes through alive out of critical care he would not be the same; either he would be less capable than what he was or more. The conversion of a girl programmer into a hacker activist through the baptism of anonymity is reversible. The conversion of a group of men into a new ethnic group through the baptism of sex and centuries is irreversible. Then, there are conversions that are impossible. The conversion of a Nigerian into a Hindu Brahmin; the conversion of a Shia girl into a Sunni cleric; the conversion of a man of the Church of South India into a man of the Mar Thoma Church;[4] the conversion of any woman into the Sabari Mala temple priest in Kerala. There are no baptisms for these conversions. Then, the politics for the access to the essence of man must be the production of as yet unknown baptisms. There are more baptisms for man than there are men. It is not an easy task to invent new baptisms. The great conversions were effected by the labour of the invented baptisms. Great baptisms were also revolutionary: the conversion of Siddhartha into Buddha, the conversion of nature into mathematics by Galileo, the conversion of the foundations of mathematics into computing machinery by Turing,[5] the conversion of God into Truth by Gandhi.

As we can see, men are converted not merely by the conversion of their faith. In fact, man-substances are converted into revolutionary contagions when a thought is converted into another in the case of the Buddha, a containment of matter is exchanged for another in the case of Galileo, or when a problem is converted into a technology. The invention of new baptisms is again evident around us—Anonymous, FEMEN, synthetic biology, Pussy Riot, Kiss of Love movement in Kerala, bionics. But is the essence of man available to all men for these baptisms to form new contagions? This is perhaps the question that would find it difficult to travel in a dinghy and cross the border into the terrain of postcolonial theory where historic (a very inconvertible sense of history) containments of men are held away from the possible contagions; that is, postcolonial theory and the protection of the interests of 'nativeness' are not easy to distinguish from one another. To bring the man-substance into a practical condition for all men today would require the formation of a Conversionist International since the national and nativeness are opposed to the essence of man.

18

THE HOAX OF THE CAVE

This text was published just when the BJP led by Modi had won a second term to govern from the centre of the Indian union. He had created a theatrical gesture of sitting in a cave in meditative postures while getting clicked by busy camera men. For several of us, this text caused a worry for the safety of its authors the moment it appeared, since Modi had won the elections by a new record. It is defiant and aggressive. It is also deeply philosophical with an ease characteristic of Dwivedi and Mohan.

The text examines Modi and the RSS as creators of hoaxes and at the same time as the objects which have importance only due to the hoaxes they create. Politically and morally this article asks everyone to be responsible, in a way similar to Hannah Arendt: as they write, 'A hoax in politics takes many men to invent and sustain, for politics is the responsibility of the many'.

The concept of 'hoax' is important in the works of the authors as can be seen in the title of the long essay 'Hindu Hoax' that they would go on to publish with J. Reghu in 2021. But this concern appears by way of an interest in Truth. Philosophers are concerned with the meaning of truth and the truth of meaning. Mohan had previously written about the relation between secrecy and truth, where he showed that if something is held in secrecy, it will be perceived as the truth even when it is not true,

> and will do so in proportion to the difficulties in revealing that secret.[1] What matters in politics is that which is presented and perceived as truth, something we now know in this period of crisis about propaganda, fake news, and fake videos.[2]

Hoaxes are the most interesting of phenomena from the point of view of truth. They often serve to restore a feeling of truth as the hoax itself is made to unravel.

Consider, for example, 'the 1995 miracle' of Ganesha idols drinking milk—which is similar to the weeping Virgin Mary hoaxes.[3] From the 'Hindu milk miracle' alone we learn something important about hoaxes. Depending on their provenance, they can send a country, an academic discipline, or global political orders into a state of stupor until the hoax is revealed to be one. If the 'milk miracle' lasted for months, the 'Piltdown man' hoax lasted for decades in biology.

The term 'hoax' itself has an air of *hoaxiness* to it. It is likely that it came from the phrase 'hocus pocus' which magicians used to utter before creating *something out of nothing*, such as a rabbit from a hat; transforming an object into something else, such as a kerchief into a bird; or, making something disappear, such as a coin.

The phrase 'hocus pocus' may have come from the symbolic yet magical act, referred to by the Latin phrase '*hoc est enim corpus meum*', which means 'this is my body'. Christ said 'Take; this is my body' while breaking bread with his apostles according to Mark 14:22. Today, the Catholic priest utters 'hoc est enim corpus meum' in order to turn the host into sacrament.

Now, this act of consecrating a value into an object is not peculiar to the Catholic religion as it can be found in the act of making an idol in temples and also in the offerings made to the idols across religions in the subcontinent. Such consecrations exist outside religion too. In general, these consecrations of value can be called *hypophysics*.[4]

But we are concerned with a particular hypophysical act—that of perpetrating hoaxes. Consider 'the Piltdown man hoax'. In 1912, the amateur archaeologist Charles Dawson found the remains of an early human which he said was the link between modern humans and apes. Later, this archaeological 'sample' was found to be a carefully organised aggregate of the remains of orangutans and humans. This hoax succeeded in deflecting the course of physical anthropology for a while.

There are academic hoaxes, of which the most popular is the 'Sokal affair' in which the physicist Alan Sokal wrote a paper about physics in the style of 'postmodern literary criticism', which was nonsensical from the point of view of physics, and Sokal succeeded in publishing it in the journal *Social Text*. But there are two hoax essays which are more interesting for us today.

Michel Foucault is the philosopher of power in the tradition of Nietzsche, Weber and Arendt. He found that nobody came forward to write an entry on him in an important encyclopaedia—*The Dictionary of Philosophers*—and he took it upon himself to write one under the name 'Maurice Florence'. The essay named 'Foucault' written by Florence began with the clause 'To the extent that Foucault fits into the philosophical tradition …'[5] and continued without a moment of satirical distance.

On the other hand, something more interesting happened in India in 1937 when a hoax was pulled off by Jawaharlal Nehru. Nehru, who would become the first prime minister of the Dominion of India in 1947 and later of the Indian Union in 1950, had by 1937 been a third term president of the Indian National Congress and his popularity was already at a peak. Nehru found it quite troublesome that his own popularity could contribute to a hypophysical projection of a value-in-itself to the personality of 'Nehru', which could then be used to train the people of the subcontinent further into the cultic politics undertaken by Gandhi. As we know, the gestures of violating the rules of asceticism in public were undertaken by Nehru throughout his career, including smoking cigarettes, of which Gandhi disapproved.

Nehru's essay under the pseudonym 'Chanakya' appeared in the *Modern Review*, published from Calcutta, and it was titled 'Rashtrapati' or the 'husband of the state'.[6] It begins with a description of the cultic popularity of Nehru—'There is a great procession and tens of thousands of persons surround his car and cheer him in an ecstasy of abandonment. He stands on the seat of the car, balancing himself rather well, straight and seemingly tall, like a god, serene and unmoved by the seething multitude.' Soon 'Chanakya' poses the question whether all that were a hoax, 'Is all this natural or the carefully thought out trickery of the public man?'

Following the suggestion of a hoax at work, 'Chanakya' has a warning: 'A little twist and Jawaharlal might turn a dictator sweeping aside the paraphernalia of a slow-moving democracy. He might still use the language and slogans of democracy and socialism, but we all know how fascism has fattened on this language and then cast it away as useless lumber.' The essay concludes: 'His conceit is already formidable. It must be checked. We want no Caesars.'

This hoax of an essay by Nehru is a complex text. There are a few remarks to be made about it before we come to the hoax of our times. Nehru's 'husband of the state' makes allusions to Nietzsche and Weber, and the essay is situated between the publication of Weber's *Politics as a Vocation* in 1919 and Adorno's *Authoritarian Personality* in 1950, which deal with cultic forms of power.

Weber had found something *hypophysical* in the cultic form of power—that the people witnessed in the very being of the leader the values which they held to be the highest. That is, the cultic authoritarian is consecrated with value to the point that he *is* that value, which can be called *hypophysical power*. For example, in the phrases 'Gandhi *is* Mahatma', 'de Gaul *is* France', 'India *is* Indira', 'RSS *is* India' and so on, a certain value comes to be the very individual, or the organisation as in the case of the RSS. Weber found that there are two distinct forms which are a requisite to construct hypophysical power, *the magician and the gang leader*—'the two figures of the magician and the prophet on the one hand, and in the elected war lord, the gang leader and condottiere on the other hand'.[7]

In that case, the maximum of hypophysical power will be obtained by the individual who is both the magician who can generate hoaxes and the gang leader who can terrorise through destruction. There are only a few figures in modern political history who could conjoin these figures into a monstrous form. The magician-gangster in these limited cases from history appears to lead to a particular outcome of total devastation.

Do we have something like this at hand today?[8] The hoaxer and the gang leader in one? Let us look at a few instances of his magic. The magician has managed to switch the responsibility for climate crisis from capitalism to old age and a general frailty of mankind—*we feel too hot and too cold because we are too weak*. He managed to find the equivalent of the crude oil of West Asia in the sewer canals of India—the gas in the sewer, he said, can be extracted with a pipe and it can be lit to make tea.[9] He brought Alexander to Bihar to give the latter a proper drubbing.[10] He invented a new post-graduate degree called 'Entire Political Science'[11] of which he remains the sole awardee. He has invented and installed radars in Pakistan which are blind to airplanes when it rains.[12] There is much more, and we know that the magical prowess of the parent, RSS, far exceeds those of the prodigal son.[13]

Of course, one must not forget the *magical gang leader* under whose watch over a thousand Muslims 'vanished' without a name for their 'vanishing' (pogrom, genocide, mass murder) in 2002.[14] Since 2014, the nameless 'vanishing' of Dalits, Muslims, intellectuals, Right to Information activists, the mysterious threat suffered by the Supreme Court judges, the rendering of thousands of poor people across India poorer through the still nameless 'vanishing' of currency notes.[15]

There is a peculiar difficulty to think through in this case. What we just described as magical acts could be both a way to the relieving experience of truth or the way into a deeper hoax. The unravelling of a hoax is in the comic relief—'see, he doesn't get what the radar is about!' At the same time it presages our further descent into the enduring appeal of a permanent hoax which has become 'the essence of India'—'the ancient Indian values manifesting from time to time in the magical bodies of the avatars'.

There is no easy way to decide between these two options in politics, in India and everywhere else. Rather we must look for *another way* while contemplating this image—there is an oversized man (*56 inches to be precise*[16]) in a cave swaddled in saffron robes posing for the cameras in a stance of catatonic freeze. Frozen men in mountain caves are consecrated with divinity in the myths of the subcontinent. This image, as with all images, captures the mode of capturing as well; that is the mode in which an image is generated is registered in the very image.

This particular image of the large man in the cave comes in a series of images. In one of them, a cameraman crouching obsequiously at the feet of the overbearing saffron subject and pointing at the face making the pose was caught by another camera which was focused on the same subject from behind. The latter image which reveals the making of the image is important. It shows that a hoax in politics takes many men to invent and sustain, for politics is the responsibility of the many.

Further, is this man the whole of the hoax? Is it the robe? Is it the stone idols who are legal persons in the juridical system?[17] Is it the media? Is it in our myths which are continuous with our present? Is it our histories?

How did we arrive at the hoax of the cave? Was it through the hoax of corruption (as the present dispensation has not seriously prosecuted cases against anyone) worth mythic proportions of money? Or was it through the anti-corruption hoax (as we are yet to see a people's anti-corruption bill) set up by the RSS and Anna Hazare?[18]

These questions matter one way or another to people across the world and the way around these questions and puzzles is to adopt a view towards all arrangements of power as hoaxes, behind which there are always more. Rather, the appearance of truth in politics is the worst hoax of them all. The German philosopher Kant approached political institutions as though they were hoaxes in a network. He conceived reason as the power which allowed men to expose the hoaxes of institutions. The ability to live without dependency on either *the truths of the hoax* or *the hoax of truth* was called the maturity of mankind, or enlightenment. At the same time, Kant saw in reason a responsibility which corresponded to its power to expose the hoaxes. This responsibility was tasked with finding a community of reason, where everyone would be mature enough to be free of hoaxes, which would ideally remove the hypophysical forms of power to the museum of politics.

19

SEX AND POST-COLONIAL FAMILY VALUES

In October 2017, a student published a crowd-sourced list of prominent Indian academics who were suspected of sexually harassing their students. This was the first prominent (and perhaps the only) moment of the #MeToo movement in India. However, upper caste academics with postcolonialist and subaltern theory credentials from institutions including JNU, which had suppressed the lower caste students' protest momentum in 2016, joined to defend the important figures of upper caste academia. The list included several prominent postcolonial and subaltern historians. Dwivedi and Mohan's text is an examination of two problematics: first, the theoretical, juridical and technological grounds from which the relation between sex and consent have been evolving, and here they give a stark warning; second, the upper caste character of and control of feminist movements in India, which they show is being broken through by lower caste feminist movements. It is an important reading for feminists as it makes a new demand to feminism: 'You are already a gathering in the form of a conch shell from which the matter of the world is murmuring its invitation to create an animal which can relieve the human.'

Do I contradict myself?
Very well then I contradict myself; (I am large, I contain multitudes.)

—Walt Whitman

Raya Sarkar has brought us a List, setting the creeds and schools in abeyance, and we will not understand what *They* did until it has all been done. This list comes in the epoch of the leaks[1]—'Unlike societies in the 1970s, our social body is defined by leaks; everything leaks, from surveillance tapes, wire taps, nudity on a remote beach, books, music, medicinal drugs and lives'. It comes also in the epoch of new technologies of sex. In this, the list should not surprise us.

All we need to know about the list for now is that it is a 'crowd-sourced list naming alleged sexual harassers in academia'.[2] Further, some of the names in the list are the leaders of postcolonial theory which also determines the most dominant feminism in India. The list liberates women from the terror of men and the demand for submission to the postcolonial norms in academia. In this, the list reveals the criticalised state of feminism.

All we need to know for now is that Raya Sarkar is *They* since we do not give a damn about what anyone was born as. This *They* is not Whitman's multitudes but something different which indicates the passion for the future which—this time it is of everything—is already here. They and their list are showing us something beyond sex, death, and the little fascisms in the name of 'the left'.

Criticalised feminism and its necessary line of descent

The list has elicited bitter responses, and more lists have appeared. These incoherent sounds of a broken internal milieu—the Lists, casteism, more and more pronouns, territorial shouts, threats, curses—are the only ones a criticalised movement can make, like the tattered skin of an old drum. These paranoid gestures—checking the locks, tough postures out of a vacant power, camping into caste ghettos, territorial markings, dirt wars—are all that an organism in a foreign milieu can make. This is Feminism at its critical limits or the birthing moments of critical feminism.

Critique is the activity of passing something—an organism, a system, a society—through a sieve to find the distinct powers within it, and then to find the limits of these powers. Critical is, in mathematical terms, the point at which a curve changes direction, either up or down. We know too well that when the hospital tells us that 'he is in a critical condition' he will not return from this state the way he was earlier; he may come back either as better or as worse, but never the same.

Critique was at home in the concept of 'Feminism' since its beginning. This beginning came too late in the history of the concepts of politics, even later than racism. The division of people into men and women in a hierarchy, determined by the concept patriarchy—of which we still have not understood everything—was to be opposed. The opposing concept which would reverse the hierarchy was named 'Feminism', and it was destined to remain in a relation of dependency with patriarchy.

Feminism made the division in people explicit and made us aware of the hierarchy which held men superior to women. It soon became an epistemology, the science of how we come to know some things to be what they are. Feminist epistemology allowed us to see the investment of male enabling values in most human institutions and even in our language. As feminism was brought into contact with anti-racist epistemology it was forced to see that feminism was predominantly a white people's theory with their point of view of the world. This meant that if white women were in charge of 'due process' they could be trusted to be first white and then women. That the division between people into black and white is more powerful than the division between men and women. This forced a division in the feminist process into white and black feminism, so that white women will not speak for and sell the voices of black women. This is also the moment at which what is called identity politics entered feminist politics.

This gesture of a division was imitated by postcolonial theory. Postcolonial feminism was necessitated by the understanding that first-world women were first first-world and then women. Now, postcolonial feminists spoke for postcolonial women. These divisions were also about taking territories and concentrating power. Power is the ability to decide how people should or should not behave, to make the laws which define regular behaviours, to negotiate between men and women, to speak for the many and to be symbols of cool activities. Postcolonial theory and postcolonial feminism too concentrated power in the hands of a few women in the subcontinent. They held that universal human rights, class struggle and progressive institutions were in truth invested with first-world enabling values. Postcolonial epistemology aimed to expose the continuation of colonial ways of seeing and speaking about the third-world people even after formal decolonisation. It aimed to let these people speak for themselves in a non-universal language, through non-European epistemic categories. It aimed to let these people speak from out of their own histories and traditions.

But, it is evident that all postcolonial women do not have the same epistemology and power. Muslim women are not in the same position as Hindu women. Dalit women (the pejorative term 'subaltern', like the term 'harijan', should be rejected) do not have the powers upper caste women have. South Indian women are not equal to North Indian women. Women of the north east are not as visible as the women of the north west. It was clear from the history of the feminist process thus far that it ought to yield to more divisions—Islamic feminism, upper caste feminism, Dalit feminism, Dravidian feminism.

However, of these divisions the one between upper caste and lower caste feminism is more significant since caste is the determinant of all relations in the subcontinent. Caste is the codified racism which defines the social order in the subcontinent. It might be objected that racism is a colonial construct, but we too can object saying that after all caste inspired racism and the construction of 'race' greatly. Casteism refers to the discriminative, eliminative and oppressive racist practices of the 'upper castes' against the 'lower castes'. It cannot ever designate the lower castes since the upper castes are the creators and the regulators of caste laws historically. In symmetry, postcolonial theorists cannot be called colonialists by the colonialists.

In the story of the modern style of politics in the subcontinent starting with the anti-colonial struggle that resulted in the Union of India, the upper castes spoke on behalf of lower castes and have held power. This trend continues in postcolonial theory and feminist struggle in the subcontinent too. The argument should come as no surprise to postcolonial feminists that like first-world women who are first first-world, upper caste women are first upper caste. And that postcolonial epistemology suppresses the anti-caste consciousness and struggle which sees tradition, nation and postcolonialism differently.

Now, Raya Sarkar's list has brought this division into something which must be addressed and it has also forced the barely contained casteism in the academic and the public spaces to become visible. Like the divisions between white and black feminisms, and that between first-world and postcolonial feminisms, the apparent division between 'upper caste' and 'lower caste' feminism too is about more than feminism.

Sex, death and 'due process'

There are two primary accusations against Raya Sarkar: *They are* destroying the unity of the feminist movement and that *They are* violating the norms established by 'due process' and possibly endangering men who are likely innocent.

In the societies of the subcontinent, women were expected to commit suicide to protect their honour/modesty/shame before a sexual crime was to occur or after the crime. Legend[3] and Bollywood[4] maintained this expectation. We see this relation between sex and death extending to men who have been accused of sexual misconduct and harassment too as in the recent case of the activist Khurshid Anwar's media trial or a kind of listing, and suicide.[5] There have been other such incidents in India[6] and elsewhere[7] before Raya Sarkar appeared on the scene. Raya Sarkar in a few statements and the list indicates that the intention is to be liberated from this power held over sex and death.

Prominent feminists such as V Geetha[8] and Priyamvada Gopal[9] have commented on the insufficiency of 'due process' in most situations. That the list was irresponsible was refuted by Karuna Nundy who equated this gesture with civil disobedience. It is likely that there will be more lists until all of us are included in them, then animals and plants, and even stones. Lists should not make anyone kill themselves. They are meant as a map for navigation as Nehmat Kaur points out.[10]

When a man accused of stabbing another does not have to kill himself and the woman who was stabbed does not find it necessary to kill herself in order to protect her 'honour' it appears that harassment, molestation, and crime with the adjective 'sex' point towards death. Perhaps, this is the power invested in sex, in the nomenclature of sex offences, its policing and trial, that it is a matter of life and death. It is important to think about the history of the separation of sex from one domain into another; for example, from the domain of caste laws which decide who can have sexual relations to the biological domain and eugenics. This isolation of sex from other relations of power has a history.

Eroticism and technologies of sex

The technical determination of sex in order to separate it from reproduction began early with contraceptives in the ancient worlds of Egypt and Greece. The effective separation of sex from reproduction became possible only in the twentieth century with the industrial production of contraceptives and their political deployment by Margaret Sanger, and it gained the possibility of art, as anticipated by the works of the Marquis de Sade. This recent separation allowed the power over sex to change hands from family and religion to social organisations and the state. The separation of sex from reproduction was soon followed by the separation of gender from birth through technological assignment of gender.

In the recent decades, gender has become a technologically assignable physical condition which can eventually be more than man, woman and in-between. We do not yet know the possibilities involved in gene editing. Gender can be given as yet unknown regularities by those who are creative. Gender can be an art.

With Viagra and the related developments, sex as an art has been separated from sexual desire. There are already devices of remote sexual engagement, including long distance kissing devices[11] and hence the possibility of contactless sex. Soon implantable devices, 3D printed body parts, also for sexual art, will be industrially produced. The 'Future of Sex Report' authored by Jenna Owsianik and Ross Dawson claimed that by 2024 'people will be able to be anybody with anybody'.[12]

Corresponding to these developments, technologized policing of sexual activities to prevent crimes is available. One of the difficult problems of philosophy, the meaning of consent and will, is being solved through consent apps such as We-Consent.[13] Even these apps may not resolve the problems entirely as they can also be coercive in enforcing what had been agreed before commencing sex. The recording of sexual acts being made mandatory is not entirely unimaginable in this era of continuous surveillance. However, it is already possible to separate a sexual crime such as rape from legality through the invention of sex robots with variable settings for resistance.[14]

Corresponding to the increase in penal and political attention on sexual activities the possibility of sex without human to human contact is increasing. It is conceivable that soon humans will not be able to engage in human to human sexual contact without the concern about one kind or the other of sexual offence being committed at least accidentally. It is perhaps not a terrible development that ours could be one of the last generations to experience human to human contact and practice the already too dangerous act called sex.

A politics of love and affirmation

Harassment inside institutions takes not only sexual but equally other forms which also remain shrouded in complicit silence. Both are made possible by the power of social status that regulates people's interaction. Students and research scholars are forced to perform menial domestic chores and even unacknowledged research work for teachers. Research directions and publications which are counter to the established norms are suppressed through cliques. There are as yet no guidelines and no 'due process' to redress this exploitation that also occurs on caste lines within institutions. It must concern us that a charge regarding sexual harassment seems so legible while the charge regarding caste discrimination remains questionable.

The tone and the reactions from traditionalist feminists to the list are disturbing and threatening. There are lists given of what Raya Sarkar and her friends are or are not—Dalit, queer, American, Indian, Hindu fascist agent, liar, a hoax. These intimidating gestures are aimed at the young men and women of all castes and religions who are anti-caste seeking new possibilities in politics. They further reveal the politics of sex and death.

The reactions against the list are also fascist in their language, *if you are not with us you are with evil*. This, ironically, is similar to the language of 'anti-national' used by the Hindu right for anyone who opposes it. A wave of repression by this Hindu right government started in IIT Madras against the Ambedkar Periyar Study Circle. It reached Hyderabad where Dalit students were attacked for protesting the death penalty to Yakub Memon and the disruption of the screening of *Muzaffar Nagar Baqi Hai*, and for supporting autonomy for Kashmir. The Pune Film Institute was next. Then, Dalit students in JNU celebrated 'Mahishasura Martyrdom Day', which provoked the sharpest reaction from the then HRD minister, but, all this receded before the nationalism debates in JNU. These were compiled into a book whose introduction admits that the teach-in had 'glaring absences ... of themes from the north-east, the minority communities of India ... too little discussion of the virulent communalist and divisive legacies of which we are heir. Did the inaugural moment of the JNU struggle, Afzal Guru and the Kashmir issue, retreat into the background? Was the somewhat muted engagement with the Dalit struggle at Hyderabad Central University also not a sign of failure?'.[15]

The JNU protests brought intelligent and articulate voices from the left in Shehla Rashid Shora, Umar Khalid, and Kanhaiya Kumar. Perhaps the voices and concerns which were eclipsed by 'JNU protests' are rising again.

Raya Sarkar has been insinuated by many including Partha Chatterjee and Nivedita Menon to have been working for the Hindu right by targeting the academics of the left and destroying the possibility of defeating the Hindu right. However, Menon herself, the leading opponent of the list, has spoken ambivalently with respect to the Hindu Right. Defending herself before the Hindu Right, she opposed Hindutva to Hinduism and wrote, 'Hinduism as a heterogeneous set of religious practices, that have cultural roots and deep meaning, which I respect as I do all religious practices'.[16] In the same essay, Menon accused the Hindu Right of not showing sufficient respect for 'the views' of Savarkar who coined the term Hindutva, which she opposes: 'That Savarkar in fact was opposed to caste discrimination but modern day Hindutvavaadis don't read him or respect his views'. One feels certain terror imagining a time in which all the 'views' of Savarkar are realised, which includes his idea of national pride, 'To keep up the purity of the nation and its culture, Germany shocked the world by her purging the country of the semitic races—the Jews. National pride at its highest has been manifested here.'[17]

What is troublesome about these remarks is that both Hindu religion, temple entry movements and Hindu right politics were invented at the same moment in reaction to colonial census circulars in the last century which would have otherwise reduced the upper castes of India into a religious minority. It is pertinent that we should not distinguish between Hinduism, casteism and Hindutva-vaad which are all to be annihilated.

Inspite of all the viciousness in the air, there is also the generosity of a revolutionary embrace in this event of the list. In moments of disruption such as this it is possible to imagine and invent new forms of politics, alliances, responses, responsibilities. If Raya Sarkar—it should not matter who they are or what castes they are or whether they are—and their friends who are already charting new directions choose to, they could also create futures which are based on love which disobeys the laws of caste, religion and class. They could begin the schooling—which descends from the ancient Greek *scholē*, which meant leisurely creation—in loving, seeking forgiveness, forgiving, wooing, accepting rejections, consoling one another in sorrow, caring. It should never take an oppositional stand to Menon and what her generation has consolidated and represents.

Instead, there is room for everyone in this world to create new alliances to dissolve identities; to take new territories of thought;

gift each other new ideas of togetherness; to give birth to what is more than nations and passports; create systems and epistemologies which remain open to reason; experiment in language to make poems which send love across languages; through care make skins permeable to *let in pains and joys of all*—Dalit, Kashmiri, Adivasi, American, Feline, White, Canine, Bahujan, Gymnosperms, Black, Stones, Pakistani, Forests.

In this era of technological explosion all of you are—you know who you are—already worlds away from the fantasies of postcolonial gossips riding their bullock carts calling out to 'the subalterns' to get out of the way. You are already a gathering in the form of a conch shell from which the matter of the world is murmuring its invitation to create an animal which can relieve the human. You are also suffering the weight of unprecedented crises which are descending.

20

OUR WANDERING SENSES: ...
FOR THE JOURNALISTS OF THE WORLD

This text was written during the pandemic while Jean-Luc Nancy, Divya Dwivedi and Shaj Mohan were engaged in the historic debate with Giorgio Agamben and others about the meaning of life, the relation between science and politics, and virology.[1] 'Our Wandering Senses' was written for the creation of a new journal in India by a gathering of journalists, artists, and academics when many media houses were surrendering to the ruling party and the government. It is an éloge to the journalists of the world who wander restlessly on our behalf, often risking their lives. The text had been in circulation since then among the other unpublished writings on the pandemic situation by Dwivedi and Mohan. It remains extremely relevant today, including in India, Palestine,[2] and France where journalists face, incomparable, yet similar constraints in working for the people.

Those who are reading these words are most likely the ones who are practicing isolation. This isolation is merely to prevent the overwhelming of the health care system, as we do not yet have cures of any kind for this strain of coronavirus. But there is a world out there, no longer available to our senses, which is turning into new and distinct species, depending on the regional conditions: In Hungary, Orban has finally sat on his throne; in the United States, the state is a competition amongst its organs; in India, the final pretenses to a parliamentary democracy are being discarded; a catastrophic famine is underway in most parts of the world, and potential geo-political conflicts are developing.

These global conditions and the regional speciations from out of them are much older than this coronavirus. But we have to attend to something imminent—our eyes and ears are slowly being excised, especially in India. In the past two hundred years, we have been accustomed to seeing the distances of the world with conviction through reporters and journalists. Many decades ago we would unfold the newspaper to confirm 'yes, the world is still out there'. Then, it became the turning of the knob of the radio, pressing the remote control of the television, and now clicks and touches on browsers and applications. The journalists have been our wandering senses in the epoch whose ideal—that is, *the necessary pretense*—had been 'principled parliamentary democracy', which has been coming to a close at least since the 1980s. The expansion of the world into everyone's world through education, travel, and migrations, was held together by these wandering senses. At this point we must caution that this term does not apply to the anchors of rancour and the scavengers of death who sneer from the television screens.

One can still hear the adages of the kind '*you must go out and see for yourself*'. But how much of anything can one individual see? For example, the knowledge of the destruction of the vast forest lands and tribal communities in India cannot be witnessed by one individual, rather we have come to bear witness to it through the sacrifices of many journalists. In the middle of this pandemic, it is not within the power of most of us to read the accumulating scientific literature, but we receive it mediated by the journalists. In that sense, the journalists have always performed a certain selection, which, however, has never been up to their individual wisdoms but came about through another process. The journalists, in their negotiations with various powers—the state, the industries, the militias—shared that which was determined as the optimal concern; that is, the point at which the diverse concerns of society met with the concerns which it can afford to attend to. In other words, journalists were never the conduits of the totality of truths, but the negotiators of the concerns of the 'people' with respect to the arrangements of power which determined these very people as citizens (democracies) or as subjects (the bewildering continuation of monarchies) or as refugees.

There is something properly evil in these negotiations with the powers which forces the journalists to turn a blind eye on each occasion in which relevance is obtained. Negotiation of relevance is at the same time the property of every sense organ. That is, a sense such as the eye is not only restricted to light but to the visible spectrum, from which it further selects according to 'relevance'. The journalists began to lose the power to determine relevance at first through the birth of media corporations and then through the very withdrawal—owing to wars, fiscal decisions of states, trade laws, surveillance laws—of the terms of negotiation available to democratic processes. Then, the ability to join the negotiations with the various powers we referred to earlier, and to determine 'optimal concerns,' is no longer with the journalists. But they are continuing for just a little longer like the warriors who are bereft of their milieu in Kurosawa's cinema. Something literal can be witnessed in India where once celebrated journalists have been wandering the nearly empty streets without great media houses behind them to report the conditions of the left-over lives of Muslim workers, the poor peasants, and the migrants.

These wandering senses of 'us' who are in isolation do not have the protection, or at least the *pretend* protection, of the institutions of democracy anymore—let us not pretend anymore that the press councils, the courts, the human rights bodies, and the states have been attentive to the concern of journalists. In fact, it is the participatory pretense of journalists which has allowed these very institutions to continue. When one does not have the power to negotiate, each negotiation is a onesided game of death, or playing a suicidal Ronin, as we have been finding with the death of journalists and RTI (Right to Information Act) activists in the past decade in India. We should care to note in this moment of the pandemic that health care workers have been under attack in the middle of the pandemic in many parts of the world, especially in India. There have been digital voices demanding protection for them and now through a new law the health care workers have a measure of safety in India.

But for the journalists, telling the story of the pandemic has been another story. They had to contest the Islamophobia which was overriding the Indian government's response to the pandemic. Many journalists have already contracted Covid-19. A suffering which began a long time ago has been aggravated when they have themselves been made invisible from the people through curfew and come under attack from the authorities. Since the curfews came in place, several journalists have been charged under draconian laws for the crime of reporting the facts; for showing the poverty and caste discrimination which defines India; an editor was summoned to attend a court far away from his home which would have forced him to violate the curfew laws; a columnist with health problems was arrested; and a photographer in Kashmir was charged under terrorism laws. As an aside, we must note that India was far ahead of Drakon with its caste-protecting law codes, and for that reason the appropriate 'Indic' term for draconian laws might be 'Brahminical laws'.

Those who once negotiated with the ruling powers to determine 'relevance' for us are no more relevant themselves so far as the powers of our time are concerned. It does not mean that this vocation—of the negotiation of relevance—is at its end. Rather, the people of this vocation must themselves discard the ideals—the necessary pretenses—of a milieu which had long departed. We can only suggest something of a new strategy here for another beginning, such that *our wandering senses* are restored appropriately for this nascent and challenging milieu. The journalists, irrespective of nationalities, should form a council with the people irrespective of nationalities, and report the world as it is today, without nationalities. As we know 'Special Drawing Right' (SDR), Goods and Services Tax (GST), surveillance companies, offshore banking, multinational corporations, Bill Gates, coronavirus and 'hydroxychloroquine' have no nationality. It is time for our senses to wander the world together for the sake each of its corners.

21

'HE HAS LIT A FUNERAL PYRE IN EVERYONE'S HOME'

Dwivedi and Mohan had been among the prominent philosophical voices in the world responding to the pandemic. Here Mohan answers the question of the meaning of being a philosopher in the middle of the pandemic in India where nearly five million people died due to Covid according to estimates.

The text takes its title from the lamentations of a poor woman named Neena in the crematorium. Mohan shows here that this speech was the essential poetry of the *Moiroloi* (the genre of mourning which curses and crushes). He distinguishes it from the praise poetry practiced by the Brahmins: 'This is what a philosophy must do—be seized by *Moiroloi*, holding itself out to the edge of stasis in order to be received by anastasis, that which overcomes the stasis'.

Dear Kamran Baradaran,
Your question is complex—'what does it mean to be a philosopher in the middle of a pandemic in India'.

Philosopher has no adjective—national, linguistic, and even of schools. In your question 'the pan' or 'the whole' of the 'pandemic' (what has befallen the whole) speaks of that which exceeds adjectives such as national boundaries. However, 'the pan' exists as that which is found as the varying swaying silhouette of all the individual existences.

The extraordinary calamity that is unfolding in India is due mainly to the political conditions of Hindu fascism which is letting the coronavirus ravage through millions. It is a project reliant on the invention of Hindu religion. Hindu religion masks the fact that the real majority of the subcontinent are the lower caste people, the 90 per cent, and the 10 per cent minority of upper castes have been oppressing the former for millennia. To ensure upper caste rule, Muslims and other religious minorities were invented as the enemies of the 'Hindu nation'. RSS (National Self-server's Corp) is the parent organisation of this government in India, and they are enabled in projecting the hoax of a 'Hindu majoritarianism' by the media which is owned by the upper castes. Therefore, even in the middle of this calamity the scale of the sufferings of millions is hidden away by the media; we get our news from international media. They must hide it because for the sustenance of the Hindu hoax the RSS and Modi cannot show that they are causing misery to the majority; misery must be reserved as a spectacle for the religious minorities.

Here, the fascist cronies who have now been made gods, but of a lesser stature than Modi, are profiteering from the sickness and deaths of the poor; and we will soon have new coronavirus billionaires in India. There are people selling living breath for hundreds of thousands of rupees here. At this very moment Modi is continuing the construction of a coffin-shaped prime ministerial palace for himself in violation of Delhi's lockdown rules which is costing billions of dollars. As the poet of this calamity, a grieving poor woman named Neena, said of Modi, '*He has lit funeral pyres in everyone's home*'.[1] Then it is appropriate that Modi will soon address India from his new *coffin palace*!

This is the ground from which philosophy speaks the voice of the pan right now. Since parking lots, parks, pedestrian ways and animal burial grounds are now cremation grounds and cemeteries here, the voice of the pan speaks from the ground of millions of deaths, a *megadeath ground*. In this moment, philosophy takes the ancient aesthetic form of the lament—the *Moiroloi*, the lamenting of that which disposes us.

There was a time when *Moiroloi* in the Mediterranean region was perceived as the art of women who helplessly expressed all the realities which were hidden by men in power when wars and calamities ripped open these hoaxes and veils of power. However, this freedom was possible then only in the circle of time opened by deaths and destruction. On the other hand, men who lamented were mocked by poets as those 'liquified' by sorrow into femininity. Homer was embarrassed by Achilles when his warrior-being was liquified by the news of the death of Patroclus and he lamented in great sorrow. That is, *Moiroloi* seizes a body made rigid and blinded by heroic masculinity into something liquid which is able to enter the hidden corners of the veils of power. Even if it could eventually destroy everything, *Moiroloi* shows us the future from the edges of the end.

This new *Moiroloi* of India has something to say for the whole world. You know that in the subcontinent, only Brahmins were allowed to think and write, and they did only that, ensuring that their writings not only did not disturb the social order of caste oppression but fortified it with magical and mystical pronouncements. This Brahminical style is akin to the masculine poetry which opposed itself to *Moiroloi,* which was *praise poetry*. The Indian subcontinent had always been the land of praise poets.

But today philosophy everywhere risks being abducted away from politics into praise poetry, in which case it cannot be philosophy. It exists as the reception of the 'exalted ones' who merely think thoughts about thoughts, which will create something resembling what India is right now by abandoning the polis for the collegium of Brahmins.

So, to answer your question again—To be a philosopher anywhere now means this: to be an ambulance driver, a primary school teacher in a village, a carrier of the dead, recipient of the beatings of the fascists, agitator, the agonist of unnamable sorrow which snatches the soul away from the call of the dead to mourn for them because there are worse days still ahead. Then this is what a philosophy must do—be seized by *Moiroloi*, holding itself out to the edge of *stasis* in order to be received by *anastasis*, that which overcomes the stasis.

Wishing you the best
Shaj Mohan

22

A GREAT INTOLERANCE

By 2019 the public sphere of India had already accepted the total dominance of upper caste supremacism which continue to be called 'Hindu nationalism'. There were gestures of meek demands or requests which appeared to pass for debate, an atmosphere of pleading with the upper caste supremacist organisations for a little tolerance for culture and values. This text, published in the *Outlook* magazine, only two days after 'Courage to Begin', analyses the relation between tolerance and intolerance in politics. It is a philosophical reflection with a certain underlying complexity that is masked by its humour. With indirect references to Bergson, Kant, and Francisco J. Varela among others, it provides a novel affirmative account of the journey of Ulysses. The argument is something like this: if something is destructive for the very system which is tolerant of that destructive force, then it should not be tolerated. This is a revolutionary thesis which is valid for all liberalist justifications of far right actions everywhere. The far right and fascist movements everywhere are working hard to destroy the liberal or tolerant state. Dwivedi and Mohan call for a great intolerance towards such forces.

The mass and majesty of this world, all
That carries weight and always weighs the same
– 'Achilles's shield', W. H. Auden

The meaning of dissent is implicated in the meaning of tolerance. We dissent when something is intolerable—'*I just can't take this anymore . . . enough is enough*'. No one has the power of infinite tolerance. The liberal doctrine of politics expects these two concepts, dissent and tolerance, to lead parallel lives such that they never encounter one another. But it is imperative that we introduce them to one another through the theological lessons of M. K. Gandhi.

Gandhi allows us to ask if it is necessary to assent to and obey all that passes for 'Law'. Is it our obligation to receive all that the rulers give us: imprisonment (Yervada jail), illegal occupation (of India), banning of books (of *Hind Swaraj*), mass murder (Jallianwala Bagh), and economic catastrophes (the Bengal famine)? Gandhi had something of an answer, 'But there come occasions, generally rare, when he considers certain laws to be so unjust as to render obedience to them a dishonour; he then openly and civilly breaks them and quietly suffers the penalty for their breach'.

The term dissent denotes in our everyday use, especially today, the act whereby we publicly express disagreement or shock over something illegitimate implemented by the government, or blatant acts of political crime tolerated by the legal system. The asperity of the present can be seen in the slogans we raise these days and the responses they are met with: 'not in my name' with 'who are you?'; 'I wasn't there' with 'so what?'; 'take back my awards' with 'where is the rest of you?' We must not forget that three rationalist philosophers and a journalist were assassinated in recent years in the same way that M. K. Gandhi was assassinated by a Hindu nationalist conspiracy in 1948; *death looms over dissent and tolerance*.

Infinite suffering is death

Dissent is possible only when something is capable of receiving or feeling some other thing. One must be able to receive sound in order to say that 'it is too loud', or see light to say that 'it is too bright'.

One must be able to *assent* to the very thing up to a certain degree in order to *dissent* from it at another degree. The ability to receive the world and respond to it is called *sentience*.

Sentience is the power in the living to feel and inhabit a certain range of the world. The sentience of animals can be observed in the way they move into or away from the gradations of heat; the ectotherms such as turtles are cold and slow in the mornings, and they seek the sun. If a living being suffers more than the tolerable range, it would perish. Increase in suffering is terminated by death such that *there is never something like absolute tolerance*. A rock on the other hand receives everything without movement and complaint, in the same way that a cadaver surrenders to the surroundings. Living is *assenting* and *dissenting* in every moment to what is received from the world as sensations. This explains why there is no such thing as absolute dissent either. If we dissent from everything it would be suicide, the way the philosopher Simone Weil died of hunger through her dissent from the world. *Absolute dissent and absolute tolerance both find death*.[1] Here we must depart from Gandhi who said, 'There is no time-limit for a Satyagrahi nor is there a limit to his capacity for suffering.'

Tolerance, understood as the limits of the sentience of the living, shows us the range of the world—its heat, poisons, pressure, hardness, sharpness—over which something is able to live. These ranges vary from animal to animal, and from human to human. The range of sound waves that a bat is able to receive is different from the range of the human ear. The super-rich can withstand environmental disasters more than the poor, which makes the former more tolerant of environmental changes.

We can already see that *dissent is a function of tolerance*, and that at the level of sensations as tolerance increases dissent decreases. Tolerance can be altered and regulated through external means. This is what we do when we cook our food and thus externalise digestion. Gandhi experimented with the limits of digestion without external means when he consumed raw food over long periods and learned that the range of food sources available to us decreased as a result. A system of tolerance, such as winter clothes and internal heating, makes the world bearable for those who can afford it. In a way, it has been the work of the human species in all these millennia to make the world more and more bearable in order that we become Atlas himself. The name 'Atlas' meant 'to endure suffering', which comes from the Greek 'ἔτλην' meaning *to tolerate*, and from which the Latin 'tolero' and 'tolerance' itself descend.

Absolute dissent is death

Everything we found so far refers to the survival of the living at what can be called the biological level. However, politics is never the matter of mere survival; if one finds oneself in the survivalist nightmares of dictatorships and camps, where each thought and action must be considered in its possible relation to death, then one is already embalmed in the cadaver of politics. Assassinations and genocides eliminate not just the people they kill, but also, through the inception of fear in the survivors, they kill the possibility of any fight. In other words, if a few words spoken—'*this law is a crime*'—can kill, then politics has already died.

Politics begins with the expulsion of the fear of death when we come together to form institutional means and fight for freedoms. There had always been men who had less to fear and more to inspire it. Politics, ideally, develops an egalitarianism of fearlessness. This explains why those who would like to inspire fear destroy the political institutions first. The creation and implementation of an idea, such as the internet, is impossible in the condition where all men are afraid of death. In fact, a shared life of ideas which creates the future—the sciences, metaphysics, poetry, bionics, calculus, human rights—is possible only on the condition that politics remains at work.

Then, politics relies on a different kind of sentience which is made possible through the expulsion of the fear of death. It is founded on the creation and maintenance of the conditions under which one is able to give and receive ideas—*a world made up of the sentience of thought*. Sentience of thought sets its own limits through thoughts alone, and not through the conditions of biological nature. The intolerance we feel towards those legislations and state actions which, though they do not affect our own wellbeing, do harm some others, is founded on the sentience of thought; we feel these thoughts occurring in someone else's mind as unjust, uncouth, repulsive. By dissenting in such instances, as Gandhi said, 'The dignity of man requires obedience to a higher law.'

There are ranges over which bearable and unbearable thoughts are distributed just as there are ranges for tolerable sensations. The thoughts of genocides and of the destruction of people's democratic institutions are unbearable. On the other hand, when Emily Dickinson writes 'And that is why I lay my Head / Upon this trusty word', we assent to the poeticality of this thought. Gandhi knew that thoughts can develop into worlds of technological exuberance or of murders. The sentience of thought involves the ability to learn of the range of events that thought can achieve in the world as it unfolds, therefore Gandhi said, 'We have known of murders committed by words. Therefore, just as our hands and feet should be kept under control, so should our tongue be'.

Gandhi conceived a different set of conditions to judge his own limits of tolerance for the thoughts of others. Of these conditions, the most important was the act of taking a vow. Once we set the limit of permissible thoughts, we take a vow in order to bind that limit. Gandhi had a simple definition of the vow: 'The "vow" I am thinking of is a promise made by one to oneself'. We do know that one must not break one's promises. Then, 'the vow' sets the limits of one's sentience of thought. In this regard, Gandhi practiced great intolerance when he refused to break his vows for the sake of the others. This is the lesson to learn from Gandhi, that one must be intolerant in order to protect thoughts and ideas, such as the idea of a peacefully shared world.

The liberal superstition

The liberal view is founded on the superstition of the co-existence of all possibilities in politics. Gandhi's acute awareness of this impossibility defines his political project: 'A man cannot commit both civil and criminal disobedience at the same time even as he cannot be both temperate and furious at the same time'. The superstition makes the liberals say, 'engage with everyone, even the mass murderers', which is of course due to the liberal's insentience to thought and its consequences. This superstition presupposes that the political conditions of liberalism—constitutional democracy and rule of law—are unassailable, and hence the liberal allows society to be seized by the very ideas that would destroy its foundations. Now, to explain this in terms of the natural model of sentience, it will be to suppose that a human ought to eat everything, including poison and glass crystals, and superstitiously hope to live on. The wisdom of dissent is to know which ideas can endure a relation with which other ideas.[2] We know that fascism and democracy are incompatible.

Yet, there is a way in which societies are able to entertain at their margins those very ideas which are destructive, such as aestheticized anarchy and fascism through pop culture. A system—for instance, anaesthesia to endure a surgery—is constituted in order to transiently receive something that is irrevocably harmful. In Homer's *Odyssey*, such a point comes when the encounter with the Sirens—nymphs who lure with marvellous song the passing mariners to shipwreck on their island—is imminent. The Sirens promise that whoever receives their song will be led to the things they know:

> We know all of the things that the Argive troops and the Trojans
> [...] labored and suffered;
> we know all that is on the much nourishing earth generated.

This song seeks to deliver us to the whole past once again and then forever. The thought in politics which claims the authority of the past in order to lure us into the past will lead us to certain death. Gandhi's intolerance of the past is well known: he said of traditional medicine, 'The Vaidyas do not possess the knowledge of the human body as the doctors do'.

To hear the Sirens' song just enough to know that it is incompatible with their journeying onwards, Odysseus prepares himself and his sailors into a system of tolerance. Now, the usual system of relations of a sailing vessel is that all ears are cocked to the words of the captain, all actions follow from these words and dissent from them will result in mutiny or the scuttling of the vessel. Instead, Odysseus asks the sailors to tie him to the mast so that he will hear the song but will be unable to follow the lead of the sirens.

Should I beseech you ever and give you orders to free me.
you should instead then fasten me down with additional bindings.

And he in turn must close their ears with wax, make them insentient to the song's promise and to his orders under the spell of the song, so that they can steadily row away from the alluring past, with their futures intact. The new system of tolerance has the captain tied to the mast listening to the sirens' song, the sailors deaf to his orders, and has the sirens failing to lead the vessel. This mutual binding establishes a range over which Odysseus can suffer without wreck. For the while that the sirens surround them, the mariners must *dissent* from the furious orders of their captain, so that he may himself *dissent* from the deadly song that he has minimally assented to hear. The future survives through the bond of words given by the mariners to each other.

That is, under specially constituted systems of tolerance, certain thoughts and ideas can be attended to in order to learn of the ends, or the range of events, to which they can lead; an important example is that the care with which 'Nazism' is taught in the German educational system ensures that it cultivates an awareness and repulsion of the consequences of such a thought. Then, instead of the liberal myth of tolerance given by the insentience of thought *we need to become the sentient animals of ideas, which will take great intolerance.*

INTERVIEWS

23

'IN INDIA, RELIGIOUS MINORITIES ARE PERSECUTED TO HIDE THE FACT THAT THE REAL MAJORITY ARE THE LOWER CASTES'

Divya Dwivedi, interviewed by Sophie Landrin for *Le Monde*, 3–14 February 2022

In France, Dwivedi and Mohan are known as the members of the bastard family of deconstruction; the friends and collaborators of Jean-Luc Nancy and Bernard Stiegler; and, the instigators of an absolutely necessary insurgency within philosophy to open it for the whole world. Previously, Dwivedi and Mohan have had published interactions and interviews with French media about caste oppression in India. But this interview given to *Le Monde*, which is the most mainstream centrist newspaper, created a new kind of academic interest in the problem of caste oppression and caste-based apartheid. This is the most accessible text on the 'Aryan doctrine', caste, and revolution. It is also a unique text in that Dwivedi (and Mohan), with friends who are the specialists of ancient Indian subcontinent including Romila Thapar and Charles Malamoud, maintains a careful theoretical distance from 'Indic' discourses, but here she addresses a question about the 'Vedic' people directly.

Sophie Landrin: *In an article published in the magazine 'The Caravan', you state that Hinduism dates from the beginning of the twentieth century. The Vedas, the 'revealed' foundational texts of this religion, are however very old ...*

Divya Dwivedi: Vedas were composed between 1500 BCE and 500 BCE by a people who migrated from the Eurasian Steppe region and invaded the subcontinent. They called themselves 'Arya'. They called their language too 'Arya', which is related to classical Sanskrit.[1] The religion of this population can be properly called 'Vedic'. These texts already indicate the racialised hierarchy imposed on the invaded older population of the subcontinent who are referred to as servants, slaves, and demons. That is, the caste system as simultaneously racialised and ritualised apartheid of people was meant to maintain the hegemony of the invading Vedic speaking 'Aryan' population and their descendants over the majority of the people of the subcontinent.

In this social order lasting millennia, the lower castes and the formerly untouchables were not allowed to learn the Vedas, and they were excluded from all common social, public activities as well as religious spaces like temples, and denied access to resources such as land, drinking water, roads. Simultaneously, they were confined to caste occupations inherited by birth. This allowed the upper castes to exploit the labour of the very people who were excluded from common life. It is a cruel joke to claim that this racist ideology is the religion of the very people it oppressed. It is equivalent to saying that American slavery was a consensual religious practice![2]

In fact, the lower castes, the pre-Vedic peoples and the tribes on the subcontinent have had their own rituals, gods, sacred traditions and religions.[3] What remains of these religions is being destroyed programmatically today—an ethnocide to give reality to 'Aryan' myths. From the end of eighteenth century the British colonisers were seeking one religious code for the non-Muslim and non-Christian peoples as a statistical convenience, and based on their misinterpretations they proposed that this was 'Hindu' religion. But at first the Brahmins strongly opposed it, saying that their 'Arya' religion should not be polluted by bringing the majority lower castes and minority upper castes under the same term. Only later in the early twentieth century did the upper castes realise that being an elite minority (just 10 per cent of the population) in the emerging modern political system would bring their domination to an end. They then adopted and promoted 'Hindu religion' to mask their minority status and the oldest apartheid system they had been practicing.

SL: *You compare the 'Hindu majority' to a 'hoax' manufactured by the upper castes …*

Religion is constituted when sufficiently distinct traits are identified with a definite population of adherents which appears to accept that religion. Until the twentieth century, feudal arrangement of power had ensured the dominance of the upper castes on the majority population of the subcontinent. Colonial reform disrupted this arrangement by introducing new conditions—modern education, non-traditional patterns of employment, new laws against caste-discrimination, and increasing self-rule based on proportional representation. This meant that political power would henceforth be shared by different groups based on their numbers. The colonial censuses revealed that the upper caste were a tiny minority compared to other castes and communities. Lower castes all over India had begun to challenge their oppression, criticize upper caste religious texts, and to mobilize massively. It was only then, from 1911 onwards, that upper caste leaders felt their dominance threatened, and found it necessary to invent a false majority which they could represent and lead. So, 'Hindu majority' is a hoax through which the 'leaders' of modern India asserted a religious category which would include the lower castes only in name but would maintain their segregation and exploitation. Hinduism is not a colonial invention but rather an upper caste invention made in a colonial context and by manipulating the colonial technologies like the census.

Colonial reforms were bitterly opposed by the upper castes who sought to protect their traditional power with modern means. Much of postcolonialist theory in India, which is produced mainly by upper caste scholars, continues this opposition, whereas many lower caste intellectuals welcomed the colonial disruption.

SL: *What was the role of Mahatma Gandhi (1869–1948) in this construction and in the maintenance of the caste system and caste system and the domination of the upper castes?*

M. K. Gandhi defended the caste system as the genius of the subcontinent. He insisted that the new Hindu religion was meaningless without the caste system. His Non-Violence demanded the prohibition of intermarriage and inter-dining which he saw as evil forces of miscegenation and modernity. But to understand Gandhi's role we have to also remember his phrase 'the Jews are not angels', and his words for Jewish people in 1938 when the Holocaust was imminent.[4] In an article in his newspaper Gandhi asked Jews to surrender to annihilation, saying that 'if the Jewish mind could be prepared for voluntary suffering, even the massacre I have imagined could be turned into a day of thanksgiving and joy that Jehovah had wrought deliverance for the race.'[5] We should also recall his racist attitude and actions towards the Blacks in South Africa against whom he supported the colonial government there. He demanded that 'the half-castes and Kaffirs, who are less advanced than we' should be segregated from Indian prisoners in the jails. Gandhi's anti-semitism, his racism and support of the caste system are rooted in his adherence to the 'Aryan doctrine'. He held that Indian 'Aryans' were the cousins of the European 'Aryans'. Gandhi's critique of modernity and colonialism is inseparable from his casteism and racism. In fact, we should be giving the same attention to Gandhi and the Indian caste system as has been given to Martin Heidegger, and to the racisms in Europe.

SL: *If we follow your logic, then would the nationalists in power who promote Hindutva—the ideology of a Hindu India—be motivated not by religious aims, but by the desire to maintain caste domination? How then can we understand the polarisation around minorities—Muslims and Christians—that has taken place since the BJP came to power in 2014?*

In India, pogroms against Dalits, Muslims, Christians, Sikhs, have been routinely orchestrated with tacit consent of the State even before 2014 and now it has intensified.[6] Hindu nationalists oppose conversions not out of religious competition or hatred of monotheisms, but because since the nineteenth century, lower castes and tribes have converted to Islam or Christiantiy in order to escape their caste-oppression and humiliation. Both Congress and BJP have therefore legislated against conversion, following Gandhi's opposition to conversion. Had the initial anti-caste movements not been crushed, modern India would have embarked on an egalitarian destiny. Instead, the invention of the false Hindu majority has destined the religious minorities—Muslims, Sikhs and Christians—to be cast as internal enemies. Religious polarisation is also a theatre in which the minorities are being persecuted so as to hide the real majority of India which is lower castes. A hoax in politics always has real victims. Caste persists in all religions in India but remains unaddressed as this would shift attention from religion to caste as the most important factor and problem of the subcontinent.

SL: *How do we explain the persistence of the caste system, despite the positive discrimination policies implemented for more than a century, and the urbanization and the westernization of a part of the youth?*

Ambedkar's historic agitation in 1930s for the political self-determination of Dalits was defeated by Gandhi. Instead of separate electorates to elect their own leaders as Ambedkar proposed, Dalits were forced to accept the less emancipatory policy of affirmative action, that is, 'Reservations'.[7] It applies to government jobs and educational institutions. But public sector opportunities are limited and have shrunk further since India's economic liberalization which came just when reservations were increased from 27.5 per cent to 50 per cent, thus making the policy even less effective. People who use reservations are stigmatized. The government is also diluting reservations step by step.

The caste system is a millennia-old reservation of wealth and prestige for the upper castes, it cannot be reversed by a few years of affirmative action. Upper castes who are less than 10 per cent of India's population hold 90 per cent of the positions in the private sector, in academia, media, judiciary. Our urban centres are maps of inherited inequality, poverty and humiliation. Westernisation is criticised for taking Indians away from tradition, for example, when the young people in love transgress caste-barriers. They are regularly killed to protect caste-purity. The caste system has adapted changing historical conditions to perpetuate itself. It is its own means and ends. India still awaits a real social revolution after which we could say that India is an independent country made up of free people.

24

THE WINTER OF ABSOLUTE ZERO

Shaj Mohan, inerviewed by Auwn Gurmani for *Naked Punch/ Critical Legal Thinking*, June 2020

This interview was published in June 2020 in *Naked Punch* and *Critical Legal Thinking*. The original introduction by Gurmani is retained.

There are two events in the background. The Modi led government and the upper caste supremacist organisations had crushed the anti-CAA protests through a pogrom in Delhi. There are still video recordings and photographs available on the internet which show the hate speeches by the leaders of the BJP and the complicity of the police. Guns were widely used to kill Muslims, some of whom were burned, many families were displaced out of fear for personal safety as their shops were destroyed and livelihoods lost. The perpetrators of the hate speeches and crimes roam free even today, and some continue as ministers.

At this moment, Covid19 had also arrived, and was used by the Modi government to crush protests. The Modi government's declaration of a lock-down to battle Covid was similar to his sudden announcement of 'demonetisation'. It caused panic, forced millions of people, especially migrant workers who are extremely poor and predominantly from the lower castes to move overnight in crowded transportation systems. The effects were seen later as 4.7 million died in India. Internationally, something else was unfolding. The renowned political philosopher Giorgio Agamben had written several short texts suggesting that Covid19 was not a serious problem and the precautions of governments were similar to a conspiracy of bio-power. Jean-Luc Nancy, Divya Dwivedi, and Shaj Mohan responded immediately. The texts of Dwivedi and Mohan introduced into this debate the histories of epidemics and caste, while also challenging the foundations of thinking the meaning of human life, and of politics. These texts themselves became viral. This background makes the interview interesting and important, in that it questions Mohan in two directions of the viral interest, Indian politics and international philosophy.

The silent twentieth century consensus was that philosophy was Western, which then was split into 'continental' and 'Anglo-Saxon'. In recent decades we have seen the assertive presence of non-White philosophers including Achille Mbembe, Anthony Appiah, Divya Dwivedi, and Shaj Mohan. Shaj Mohan is the philosopher who has been 'forsaken'[i] by philosophical traditions as his work is characterized by the irreverence towards both European and 'Indic' traditions. Instead, through what Robert Bernasconi called rigorous and radical interpretations, his work appropriates scientific, mathematical, technological and metaphysical resources to create new concepts for our time. Recently, Mohan has been participating in the now famous 'Coronavirus and Philosophers'[ii] debate with Agamben, Nancy, and Esposito. In these interventions the same irreverence to philosophical traditions as well as a concern with rigour and formalism can be seen. Shaj Mohan has called for a *world democracy*[1] on the basis of a radical thought of equality which he calls *the obscure experience* that is shared by everyone.

His recent book *Gandhi and Philosophy: On Theological Anti-politics*, which is co-authored with Divya Dwivedi is a work that is highly critical of Gandhi, and it has been called a breakthrough in philosophy. Gandhi is the most influential figure that we are forced to attend to when talking about the subcontinent, its intellectual and ascetic traditions, colonial past, and its politics—of 'nonviolence'—on top of that. *Gandhi and Philosophy* manifests itself as the act of thought that poses a significant threat to the intellectual, spiritual and philosophical decadence prevalent in our international theoretical praxis. For this reason Jean-Luc Nancy said in his foreword that *Gandhi and Philosophy* shows the way beyond 'hypophysics and metaphysics'.

Auwn Gurmani: *What triggered your initial interest in M. K. Gandhi? How do you place your understanding of his concepts vis-a-vis the recent scholarship on Gandhi?*

Shaj Mohan: M. K. Gandhi appeared as a non-philosophical object of special interest to philosophy, and that's the 'trigger warning'. As you know, the research and publication on Gandhi were done with Divya Dwivedi and it began when we made a presentation on Gandhi's 'Indian Home Rule' in 2006 in St Stephen's college[2] when we were students. At that time I was interested in the meaning of 'evaluation' in philosophy after Wittgenstein and Heidegger.

We discovered that the concept of 'kinesis', which Gandhi understood as 'speed', directed his critical evaluation of civilizations. Gandhi had borrowed his theory of speed and even examples from Thomas Taylor's *Fallacy of Speed*. For Taylor and Gandhi, the analysis of speed, (to put it in a dangerously simplified form for this occasion) showed that the values of things and actions changed according to the speed of their systems. For example, a pilgrimage by foot loses its value when it is undertaken using modern transportation; the presumed piety is exchanged for touristic enjoyment.

We found that Gandhi had a desire for absolute values. As you know, 'absolute zero' in thermodynamics is that temperature at which all 'kinesis' at the molecular level comes to an end, and it is theoretically impossible to obtain. Gandhi explicitly sought to reduce himself, and humanity, to the speed of zero; that is, he wanted to bring humanity to a voluntary self-sacrifice and declare 'henceforth time shall no longer be'—*a worldwide state of passive resisters creating 'the absolute zero' of politics was Gandhi's goal*. The risk we face today is precisely the attempts at the creation of an *absolute zero in politics*.

In 2007 we published a research paper on Gandhi in the *Economic and Political Weekly* after we discovered another thinking at work in Gandhi, to which we gave the name hypophysics. Hypophysics identifies 'the good value' of a thing with its 'natural state', and deviation from nature is then evil. For Taylor and Gandhi, a man taking a walk across the field adheres to the nature of his limbs which was determined by 'the Maker', but a man on a motorcycle is fleeing from his nature. Hypophysics is older than M. K. Gandhi and it is at work even now in the Gandhians and his opponents.

It is impossible to find any such given 'nature', even in what we call the 'natural world'. This problem is circumvented by most versions of hypophysics by setting up something like an *idyllic a priori*. *Idyllic a priori* are the terms and values derived from the idylls, or the desired *a posteriori* of someone or some men. All kinds of *idyllic a priori* suppress the oppressive conditions in which those idylls were possible and all idylls are derived from the experiences of privileged groups of men. For example, Gandhi found his *idyllic a priori* in the Indian villages and it corresponded to the lives of the well to do upper caste men of the village, thus suppressing the horrors of the caste order that sustains Indian villages even today. The subcontinental versions of postcolonial and subaltern studies think from the same upper caste *idyllic a priori*. Recently, in the context of the pandemic, Giorgio Agamben revealed his idyll[iii] as the small town in Europe where the churches determine man's relation to his nature, from which his *idyllic a priori* follows. In this case, it suppresses the colonial and other exploitative conditions which sustained this very *idyll*. To return to the second part of your question, most of the scholarship on Gandhi, including the criticisms, share Gandhi's *idyllic a priori*.

AG: *As much as your work is critical of Gandhi and it decenters him from his usual position of a Mahatma and a political and spiritual hero of the subcontinent, there is a cause of worry for some readers. As the political thinker J. Reghu in his review of Gandhi and Philosophy*[iv] *wrote, Gandhi has been elevated too much by this work? How would you reply to that?*

Likewise, there is a body of criticism of Gandhi's views on caste and his racial ideas. How do you view Gandhi on Caste and Race?

SM: J. Reghu is one of the most exciting political thinkers of India. Being uninterested in any consensus he is able to see the articulations of these very consensual structures which decide what can and cannot be said in public. However, I would like to think that J. Reghu had discussed some of the reasons why Gandhi became important within a philosophical project.

A philosophical interest in Gandhi is very different from the lobbying interests invested in him; the former gives us the possibility to think *the absolute zero of politics* while the latter has given us the 'Mahatma Propagandhi',[3] the man suited to sell anything. Philosophical interests cannot be determined by lobbying activities even if they have the best intentions. If someone says that we should not study the theorems of Grigori Perelman because he is against society that would make little sense.

Gandhi had created the most systematic version of hypophysics, he had drawn the most extreme consequences of an analytic of speed, and using all that he proposed the terminus for all nihilistic political projects—the voluntary self-sacrifice of mankind, or *the absolute zero of politics*. It is dangerous to avoid these insights held within Gandhi, whether by yielding to the recent model of '*don't read X or Y because we don't like their views*', or by silently passing over these insights to use the saintly icon.

Caste order is the oldest and the worst form of racist oppression in the world, and it is strange that it has endured into the twenty-first century after the end of apartheid! As you said, there have been several works critical of Gandhi's approaches towards race and caste. It began at least with B. R. Ambedkar. Today 'critical philosophy of race' is a complex discipline. The researches of Charles W. Mills, Emmanuel Eze, Robert Bernasconi and several others have deepened our understanding of the births and the speciation of racial theories; that is, *there are many racisms*.

Gandhi may have invented a new ground for racism, which is hypophysical. For him, there is something like 'natural populations'; that is, the people of the world are distributed in a 'natural environment' which is most appropriate for each of them. So long as a population remains in their 'natural state'—for example, the Dalits of the subcontinent under ritualized social oppression—there is good for him. Any inspiration to deviate from the 'natural state' would be evil. Gandhi read into Darwin a kind of moral biology according to which being moral was equal to being true to one's given 'natural' environment.

The *idyllic a priori* which conditioned Gandhi's early texts on race perfectly coincided with racialising theories of the colonial powers, especially the dominant 'Aryan supremacy doctrines', according to which, as an upper caste Indian, he was almost at the top of the racial hierarchy. Gandhi's racism had a distinctly hypophysical origin, and in practice it coincided with the common place racisms of his time. Most racial theories, if not all, refer to a certain moment in history (they are always fantasies) to assert that the perfect blend between blood and soil existed at a certain time. From it they derive a 'natural type' for some men, such that miscegenation will be the deviation for their 'own nature'; therefore, it can be said that *racism is a species of hypophysics*.

AG: *Do you think that the crisis advancing in India today, starting with the rise of Hindutva, the ever increasing oppression and violence against minorities—all such instances, as has been said repeatedly—reflect the failure of the secular model of India? Ashish Nandy said in an interview, 'I would like to believe that Gandhi has not been defeated. I am not sure about Nehru, who rejected Gandhi's idea of a self-sufficient village economy as the romantic illusion of a defeated civilization.' Would you like to contribute to this debate?*

SM: The terms of this false debate were set by the upper caste postcolonialist ethno-nationalists, and it is very difficult to distinguish between the positions of people like Nandy and the Hindu right. This false debate, which is characterized by what Simon Weil called 'intellectual leprosy', serves the function of distracting from the realities of caste oppression. Secularism never existed in India in any form because the Indian nation state was the product of the invention of 'Hindu'religion in the early twentieth century. The idea that 'Hindu'is the religion of the majority of Indians was invented to mask the fact that 90 per cent of India's population are the oppressed caste people (*Bahujan*) and that the 10 per cent upper castes control all of India's institutions and enjoy all its resources.

Indian constitution embraced this term 'Hindu', and it allowed the 'Hindu' fascist organization RSS (Rashtriya Svayamsevak Sangh) to thrive despite the assassination of M. K. Gandhi and several instances of mass murders in which it was implicated. What is horrific about the pogroms against religious minorities—Christians, Muslims, Sikhs—is that the opposition of 'Hindu'-versus-'other religions' has the singular purpose of preventing the *Bahujan* people from uniting against caste oppression. Whenever the *Bahujan* people rise up, pogroms against religious minorities begin.

AG: *You had written recently that NRC and other oppressive measures and the protests against them should be understood as the beginning of an epochal transformation in the subcontinent.*[v] *'There is a boredom with the past, which is creating space for the new in India'.*[vi] *You have also said in the context of the philosophical debates around the pandemic, 'unless we, as everyone, everywhere, understand that this world is the cobelonging equally of everyone in sharing the mysterious but absolute certainty of its persistence, and create political concepts and new institutions, this ship might become either too small or too large to set sail ever again'*[vii] *while discussing your idea of 'world democracy'.*[viii]

Are these two questions—the transformation of the subcontinent and the possibility of a world democracy—related? If yes, how is a world democracy going to be different from the other options being discussed at this time such as 'return to communism'. Can world democracy not be hegemonic?

SM: Boredom is something which triggers a yawning, the opening of a space. It is happening in India and across the world. In the Indian context, the only effective political mobilizations against the Hindu right government came from *Bahujan* movements in recent years. For that very reason, the intellectuals and the activists of the *Bahujan* people (which means the real majority as opposed to the false majority named by 'Hindu') are under extreme attack from the Hindu right and the government, because the political unity of the oppressed caste people are kicking the doors of power. This is the sense of the 'yawn' in India.

The same texts you have quoted, about the protests in India, say something about global technical and economic processes which are implemented in most nation states without any democratic consultation. For example, Goods and Services Taxes, internet protocols, privacy architectures of social media platforms, encryption standards, military robotics, automation programs which determine the way we live, think, talk to one another, organize, and learn; all these are being established outside of democracy. Meanwhile, the increasing regionalization of politics—be it ethno-nationalist or territorial or whatever—is turning the attention and involvement of the people across the world away from the development of a global techno-economic system. In India, these global processes adhere at the same time to the ancient caste order as the majority of the businesses are owned by the upper castes, particularly the *Baniya* (business caste).

There have been discussions about the 'options' of a global order in the past decade. This has been accompanied by a process of regionalization of all the people of the world into ghettos; and, the *regionality* of these regions is already being determined by the techno-economic 'hegemon'. One can expect this model to be sold as the latest in the series of 'minimum government' and 'big society', and it might be named 'self-reliant regional enclosures'.

The most important question in what I had called 'democracy of the world' is the meaning of the 'demos', or the obscure experience which makes us the 'demos'. It is too complicated to go over quickly. But we can indicate something for now. The political arrangement which makes a 'hegemon' possible is also liable to *stasis*; *stasis* is when several groups in a political arrangement strive to be the 'hegemons' and as a result the very arrangement gets *criticalised*. We can see this battle right now—between America, China, technological corporations, ethno-nationalists, postcolonial nationalists—which is making our present *stasis*. In principle, a democracy of the world will be the gathering of all the people of the world, without exception, in such a way that it comes over the present *stasis*. And for that reason, it must leave the 'hegemons' behind. We can call it *anastasis*, for now. Without this *anastasis* we will soon experience *the winter of absolute zero*.

AG: *You have been participating in the 'Coronavirus and Philosophers'*[ix] *debate with Jean-Luc Nancy, Divya Dwivedi, and Roberto Esposito. It was* *stirred by Giorgio Agamben's intervention against the state's responses to the Coronavirus pandemic. Not to mention Europe, but don't you think that in states like India and other third world countries where the police possess extraordinary power in normal circumstances, the situation, however, is different and bears semblance to what Agamben feared—the normalization of a state of exception.*

We have witnessed instances in which the police were seen whipping the general population in order to impose the lockdown, massive arrests, thousands of daily wage laborers abandoned as a result of lockdown and those who were forced to walk on foot in order to get back to their hometowns.

SM: In a way, the question already contains the answer: what could be considered 'exception' has been the norm in most parts of the world. In India, the demolition of the Babri mosque in 1992 and the pogrom against Muslims happened under what most commentators would call a 'liberal state';[4] and the mass murder of Muslims under Modi's rule in 2002 did not require the invocation of emergency powers. You mentioned the plight of migrant workers under the lockdown. But hundreds of thousands of farmers from the oppressed castes have been committing suicide since 1995, which is a genocide, and it didn't need emergency powers. So, the liberals, postcolonialists, and subalternists in the subcontinent find the theories of Agamben appealing because it lets them evade the realities of millennia old caste oppression and lead a Bollywood-like theoretical fantasy in the academies.

But, one can understand the appealing simplicity of Agamben's theories, which have their roots in the political projects of national socialist Germany, and those references we should avoid because it is not worth it. These kinds of appealing and amusing theorems are created by hiding the fallacies or the gaps in reasoning, and they are not new in philosophy. It can be found in something clever and ancient which says: *You cannot lose that which you don't have. You don't have horns. Since you haven't lost your horns you have still got horns.* The 'state' which is used as the premise in these theories of 'exception' never existed, whether in the subcontinent or elsewhere. It is a theory which has set up definitions which are not even sufficiently nominal. It is, as Leibniz would say, a 'regulae tropicae' of the 'state' which desires exceptions, or as it comes to the same thing, broken easily by exceptions. However, the pretense to a 'state' is necessary to conduct the affairs of economics, primarily. As Derrida said, in these situations *one must not pretend,* but *pretend to pretend*, which is a distinction that Agamben missed in his readings of Derrida. Further, what we are told to consider as 'exceptions' or the acts of will of some men are not really 'willing' in the Nietzschean sense. Nietzsche had warned that the state of tension which makes a thing discharge force must not be mistaken for its 'willing'. What we experience as exceptions are the world's political order in *stasis*, discharging forces.

The challenge today for a philosophical investigation into the future of politics is to find concepts which have a certain degree of reality, concepts which can explain the diverse phenomena without collapsing them into lazy analogies. We do not yet know the components which make up the world-wide political order, and much less the level which comprehends these components. We do not yet know which homological powers are being exchanged by which ones at the level of individual lives. We are still unable to determine the functions and regularities appearing through our techno-socio transactions. We can begin in this direction by moving away from the 'epoch of historicisation' and by listening to Ibn Khaldun who said that history deserves to be a branch of philosophy.[5]

[i] 'Community of the Forsaken', Divya Dwivedi and Shaj Mohan, https://antinomie.it/index.php/2020/03/12/la-comunita-degli-abbandonati/

[ii] https://www.journal-psychoanalysis.eu/coronavirus-and-philosophers/

[iii] 'What Carries Us On', http://positionswebsite.org/shaj-mohan-what-carries-us-on/

[iv] J. Reghu, 'Gandhi as Chrysalis for a New Philosophy', https://thewire.in/books/gandhi-and-philosophy-book-review

[v] 'Beyond Resistance : What India Needs Now Is A Revolution', https://worldcrunch.com/opinion-analysis/beyond-resistance-what-india-needs-now-is-a-revolution

[vi] 'The Current Protests in India are a Training Ground for a Break With the Past', https://thewire.in/rights/debate-caa-protests-training-ground

[vii] 'Our Mysterious Being', Jean-Luc Nancy and Shaj Mohan, https://thephilosophicalsalon.com/our-mysterious-being/ and 'La Corona della 'Stasis' https://antinomie.it/index.php/2020/05/09/la-corona-della-stasis/

[viii] 'The Crown of the Stasis', a short lecture https://www.youtube.com/watch?v=q-r6YjXNvwg and 'We Are In A State of Stasis', https://www.franceculture.fr/societe/shaj-mohan-nous-sommes-en-etat-de-stase

[ix] 'Coronavirus and Philosophers', https://www.journal-psychoanalysis.eu/coronavirus-and-philosophers/

25

CARGO CULT DEMOCRACY

Divya Dwivedi, Interviewed by Abhish K. Bose for *Asian Lite*, October 2022

This interview with Dwivedi became 'viral and controversial' as the interviewer remarked later because the upper caste supremacists feared that its words could 'summon the specter of anti-caste revolution.' Perhaps, it has already done that, as the responses to the interview showed the power of Dwivedi's words. According to a senior Indian journalist they led to her being 'viewed as an icon' and made evident that the '"cult of Dwivedi" often defends her with humorous responses'.

The interview clarifies the present moment of Indian politics with precise formulations, definitions, and assertions of the revolutionary thesis of Dwivedi and Mohan. The British newspaper where it was originally published had the title 'A French-style revolution alone can help India recover from its current caste stasis, says Prof Dwivedi'. But the title here is from its republication in an Iranian newspaper.

As Dwivedi began trending in social media threats and outrage followed soon after and in the international community their friends and I watched these developments with extreme concern. I drew up a petition to protect them. Patrice Maniglier, philosopher and friend of Dwivedi and Mohan, and I began collecting signatures including those of Etienne Balibar, Slavoj Žižek, Barbara Cassin, Stuart Kauffman, Antonio Negri, Judith Revel, and Hélène Nancy. The petition remains valid even now and therefore some sentences from it are notable:

> Divya Dwivedi and Shaj Mohan are among the most important philosophers in the world alive today. Their project with Jean-Luc Nancy is to find a new beginning for philosophy beyond the geo-politicised and 'racialised' histories of philosophy while acknowledging the insights of the deconstruction of philosophy undertaken by Heidegger and Derrida. Their research contributions are valuable not just to the discipline of philosophy, but also sciences and politics. Their extraordinary commitment to justice, equality, and the political freedoms of people everywhere in the world comes at a serious price. In India, where they reside, they face harassments and death threats on social media on a regular basis. These threats are significant. In recent years, while foreign intellectuals have been denied entry in India, Indian intellectuals have been jailed or assassinated.

Divya Dwivedi is a philosopher who has been a part of the philosophical tradition of deconstruction through her collaborations and close friendships with the philosophers Shaj Mohan, Bernard Stiegler, and Jean-Luc Nancy. Most of her philosophical research is in the areas of ontology, principles of history of philosophy, and narratology for which she is known internationally. She is one of the founders of the international journal *Philosophy World Democracy*. But her research into caste oppression has been constant, which includes the special issue of the Unesco journal *Review of Women Philosophers* edited by her titled 'Intellectuals, Philosophers, Women in India: Endangered Species'[1] and her numerous political essays for which she has often received threats.[2] Dwivedi, born in Allahabad (now Prayagraj), comes from a family of lawyers and politicians. Her father Rakesh Dwivedi is a senior advocate at the Supreme Court of India and her grandfather S. N. Dwivedi was a justice of the Supreme Court of India. Her mother Sunita Dwivedi is an advocate and author of historical works on Buddhist heritage, and her maternal grandfather Raj Mangal Pande was a minister for Human Resources Development at the central government. However, her political commitments and research are at a great distance from her origins as Dwivedi is critical of all political organisations, even in this interview. The interview was conducted over phone calls and emails. The text has been edited and inline references have been added wherever necessary.

Abhish Bose: *Prof. Dwivedi, thank you for joining this conversation. There is a lot of fear in India. Journalists are afraid of being raided or arrested. The opposition parties are afraid of being broken into pieces with money and intimidation. Research centres are being raided. Right to Information activists are being killed. University campuses have become quiet. What is this fear?*

Divya Dwivedi: There is extreme evil in India. All the institutions defined by the constitution of India are submitting to the call to evil, including journalism and the judiciary. The extreme manifestation of evil is when someone is being subjected to the choice between life and death. Here, life should not be understood as vegetal, merely subsisting without the concern for pain and pleasure, as we find in Agamben's conception of 'bare life'[3] which he proposed while studying the 'Muselmänner' inmates of the Nazi concentration camps. Because, when we read their own narratives of survival, we realise that even in their extreme dehumanisation and near-death state they were not solely vegetal, but actively engaged in devising some forms of escape or recovery despite their extreme weakness.[4] Moreover, life should not be understood as guided by merely epitheumea (ἐπιθυμία), which is the concern with avoidance of pain.

Instead, life is the condition in which one can experiment with the very meaning of being alive through the free creation of communities, institutions and norms. Ambedkar explained this need for free creation in *Annihilation of Caste*:

> the idea of religion is generally speaking not associated with the idea of change. But the idea of law is associated with the idea of change, and when people come to know that what is called

> religion is really law, old and archaic, they will be ready for a change, for people know and accept that law can be changed.[5]

Life in the comprehensive sense is politics itself, where the freedom to think and experience the meaning of life is secured and enhanced. Without politics, or the fight for freedoms, life approaches something akin to *coma*. In the Indian context it is the coma induced by fear into which we are collectively falling. Then, the choice being offered in India is between freedoms and death.

We do not have to reprise particular stories of persecutions through which we are being sent into the thralls of terror. We are all too familiar with the contemporary context that is being discussed here, including the imprisonment of anti-caste activists, Muslim journalists, and human rights campaigners including Teesta Setalvad who received interim bail recently.[6] There are raids happening in the offices of NGOs, think tanks, and charitable organisations. But some of these stories should be attended to in order to understand their reasons, because the prisons of India are managed by caste rules.[7] Let us remember today the academics, intellectuals, and activists who had been arrested for the commemorative event of Elgar Parishad,[8] for opposing the caste order. Of those who were arrested Father Stan Swami died in prison where he was denied access to water. Alarmingly, another Elgar Parishad activist, Vernon Gonsalves, is being denied medical care in prison.

AB: *You have been opposed to the concept of 'secularism vs Hindu majoritarianism' as the core problem of Indian politics. You had said in an interview to the French newspaper,* Le Monde,[9] *that caste is the determinant of forces in Indian society and polity. You have often written about the conflict between the norms of constitutional democracy and the caste order which governs Indian society.*[10] *Could you explain again the reasons for this minority position you have taken?*

DD: It is not a minority position! It is the position of the majority of the people of India, who are the lower caste people! At the same time it appears to be a minority position due to the dominance of the upper caste people in the public sphere. That is, if you watch Bollywood cinema or read the mainstream literature you might even think that there are no lower caste people in India, as they are invisibilised in Indian culture.

Now, I believe that the only worthy pursuit of Indian politics, as long as there is politics in India, is the destruction of the caste order. We can read the annihilation of caste as the intention of the constitution of India. Until politics in India achieves that we will remain in stasis.

But the opposite intention has dominated politics in India for the longest time, that is, the retention of the minority upper caste dominance over the whole of India. It is evident in a few facts. On the one hand, the continuing oppression of the lower caste people can be seen in the facts that 65 per cent of all crimes are committed against Dalits in India, in national media the lower caste people amount to less than 9 per cent, and Dalits and Adivasis amount to less than 9 per cent in India's elite educational institutions. At the same time, the Indian government refuses to conduct a caste census and it is holding back the existing caste census data. From the available data it is evident that the upper caste people are a minority of 10 per cent or less of the Indian population, while the lower caste people are clearly the majority. Then the majority of the cultural resources of India are reserved for the minority upper caste people. Here, we must remember that caste order exists across religions in India, including Christianity, Islam, and Sikhism.

AB: *Why is it that these facts are not apparent to most people in India? Why do you think that the logic of majoritarian versus minority is then the dominant paradigm of discussing politics in India?*

DD: The goal of the upper caste controlled institutions, including the media, is to mask these facts, that the majority of India are the lower caste people. And at the same time to prevent the consequences of recognising these facts, which is the birth of an egalitarian society in India through the seizure of power by the lower caste majority. Academics in India are fond of the idea of 'becoming-minority' which was adapted by the philosophers Deleuze and Guattari from Kafka, and this tendency is another typical instance of invisibilizing the oppressed majority people in order to forcibly maintain the fiction of 'Hindu majority'.

The false problems of Hinduism vs Hinduness, and Hindu majoritarianism vs secularism were created to prevent the appearance of egalitarianism in politics. As we know Hinduism was invented in early twentieth century to prevent the lower caste majority, who had been oppressed for millennia, from rising up to claim their rightful power of self-determination under modern constitutional democratic institutional conditions. For example, if proportional representation in parliament and the assemblies were implemented according to the wishes of Dr Ambedkar and other lower caste leaders, India would have achieved true independence much earlier.

The creation of Hinduism in the twentieth century allowed the upper castes to be the community leaders of those whom they had been oppressing and excluding from the upper caste cultural practices. The RSS (Rashtriya Swayamsevak Sangh) today effectively represents Hinduism. The RSS is the most powerful paramilitary organisation which is controlling the governments by proxy and the streets directly and it is governed by Brahmins. Here we see *the meaning of 'Hinduism'* (Hinduness or Hindutva), which is the continuation of upper caste dominance through militia under the cover of religion to adapt caste apartheid under the modern conditions of constitutional democracy and judiciary. As you know, Hartosh Bal has been drawing attention to the grave errors of maintaining this distinction for quite a while now.[11] From here onwards let me use 'Hinduness' instead of the other word, so that we shall not perpetuate this criminal distinction. For this reason Hindu versus Hinduness is a false distinction in politics. But it serves the so called liberal upper castes to keep a distance from the extreme actions of the RSS, while supporting its intentions knowingly or unknowingly. The very construction of Hinduism and through that of a Hindu majority created the partition of British India. This modern partition is necessary to cover over the ancient oppressive partition of the caste order.

AB: *It is clear that the so called far right and the left liberals both play with this distinction between Hindu and Hindutva. They are committed to a picture of India as a 'Hindu majority' country. The differences seem to be only in the conduct of such majoritarian state. What are the harmful effects of continuing in this discourse about Hindu vs Hinduness?*

DD: It is a very important question. If you look at the opinion pieces written everyday about the injustices in Indian society you will find the beginnings of the answer to your first question. Our opinion writers, who shape public opinion about politics, are all upper caste, with some exceptions such as Kancha Iliah.[12] These opinion writers never speak of caste, but only about Hindu versus Muslims, and Hindu versus Hindutva. The very discussion of caste appears to be untouchable for the liberal commentariat, as if the mention of caste is a spell that could summon the spectre of anti-caste revolution.

They remain silent about caste when the news about the killings and humiliations of lower caste people abound! A few days ago a Dalit politician was killed in Uttarakhand for marrying an upper caste. Another Dalit was killed in UP by the upper caste men who wanted his land. We have been reading about the lower caste students being humiliated or being killed from different parts of India in the past few weeks. Rates of suicides are very high among Dalit students. Five incidents of atrocities against Dalits take place every hour in India. I can go on citing incidents and evidences.

But our liberal upper caste commentariat hide behind *Hindu versus Hindutva*. The horror of this strategy can be realised through analogy. To say that the caste order is a feature of 'Hinduism' is akin to saying that slavery in America was a spiritual pact between the enslaved black people and the white slave owners.

The continuous killing and oppression of the lower caste people is a crime which is incomparable to the terrible genocides of the last century, it is much worse because it is the oldest apartheid system and the most hidden system of enslavement in the world. Further, by hiding behind a deliberately poorly formulated notion of secularism and the false distinction between Hindu and Hinduness, our polity is treating several religious groups as sacrificially expedient people. As it has been shown by the researches of Ornit Shani in *Communalism, Caste and Hindu Nationalism: The Violence in Gujarat*, religious pogroms are often preceded by caste conflicts arising from out of a surge from the lower caste people.[13] Many judicial commissions which inquired into religious pogroms have also noted this fact, that lower caste agitations and caste conflicts were made to turn suddenly into religious conflicts.

Then, there are two harmful effects, to answer your question. First, the oppression of the lower caste people is being hidden, and hence it has now acquired the character of a 'concentration camp' that is very well integrated into all the spheres of life. Second, the treatment of religious groups including Islam, Christianity and Sikhism as expedient populations which provide bloody spectacles to avert the attention from caste oppression.

AB: *What is bizarre is that it is often said by upper caste academics that colonialism fuelled and perpetuated the caste structure in order to divide and rule India. In contrast to this view, you have written with Shaj Mohan and J. Reghu that the relation between colonialism and Indian society should not be examined in a monolithic fashion from the point of view of the upper castes.*[14] *You brought attention to the remarks of the lower caste leaders, including Phule, to say that colonial experience was different for the lower caste people, who often welcomed it. Even earlier you had called the independence movement a movement for 'transfer of power' from British rulers to traditional Indian rulers, who are the upper castes. This complicates the received wisdom about colonialism. Then what is the meaning of Indian independence movement?*

DD: Mahatma Phule, Narayana Guru, and other lower caste leaders found the colonial experience to be the most liberating event of the history of the subcontinent. It was during British rule that the lower caste people gained the rights to walk the streets, to be visible in public, to gain education, to find employment of their choosing, to practice religion, and to engage in politics. Dalit visionaries and mass mobilizers like Bhagyareddy Varma, Acchutananda, and Mangoo Ram emerged in different parts of the subcontinent thanks to the colonial disruption of caste. At the same time colonialism was indeed a traumatic experience for the upper caste elites, who lost their dominance over the lower caste people to some extent. Phule, in *Ghulamgiri [Slavery]*, explained the upper caste interests in decolonisation:

> [the bhats] are afraid that if we, the shudras, really become the brothers of the English, we will condemn their wily religious books and then these bhats who are so proud of their caste will have to eat dust; the lazy idlers will not be able to gorge themselves on the food produced by the sweat of our brow.[15]

The movement for transfer of power sought to contain the effects of colonialism and to receive the power over the institutions and the territorial state created through colonialism. Therefore, the transfer of power movement cannot be called an independence movement. The independence movement is yet to take place, which will make all Indians the free and equal agents in the construction of an egalitarian polity. Independence of India is possible only through the annihilation of caste.

AB: *The Mandal Commission's recommendations paradoxically awakened the political aspirations of the lower caste people and at the same time catalysed the political consolidation of the higher castes. Could you explain the political significance of the Mandal Commission recommendations and the subsequent upper caste political mobilization through Rama temple agitation which changed the trajectory of Indian politics to the favour of BJP?*

DD: The Mandal commission's recommendation of reservation for the lower caste people is one of the clearest lines dividing politics in India on caste oppression. We can see who stands where if we look at their positions on the Mandal commission and on reservations in general, including our academics, journalists, politicians and other institutions. It should be a serious project to examine and reveal the position of our public figures on reservations. When the Mandal commission report was tabled in parliament, the political parties of India showed on which side of the caste line they stood.

Reservations are based on a few principles which acknowledge the injustices and disadvantages being suffered by the lower caste people due to the millennia-old caste oppression. Reservations are an acknowledgment of the historic crime of caste oppression, a mode of reparations, and a measure to show the state's commitment towards the annihilation of caste. As you know, economic reservation is a strategy to dilute the principle of reservation for the lower caste people by equating the economic disadvantage of some of the upper caste people with the historic oppression and humiliation suffered by the lower caste people. We should also look at the stance of political parties on economic reservation.

To come to the other part of your question, when the Mandal commission report created a Mandal movement and a surge of lower caste assertion in Indian politics for the first time, it alarmed the upper caste people. As I mentioned earlier to you, the upper caste BJP and its parent organisation, the RSS, immediately proceeded to create the worst religious polarisation in India since the partition of the territories of British India. This was the Rama temple movement. A newspaper in 1990 wrote about the Rama temple movement which led to the demolition of the Babri mosque, saying that 'Due to the aura of Ram, the demon of Reservation ran away.'

It is a remark which reveals so much about our society. First, it shows the understanding that Rama is an upper caste god who conquers the lower caste people, who are demons in the eyes of the upper castes. Of course, it should not come as a surprise when we look at ancient history where the lower caste people were referred to as Dasyu, Dasa, Asura, Chandala, Mlechchha and so on in order to dehumanise them. Further it lays bare the strategy that Hinduism is the instrument through which lower caste aspirations can be slayed, for which the religious minorities are a mere medium. We should wonder what is more sinister: That this is the reality of politics in India or that we accept this reality in our everyday life?!

The success of the BJP has to do with a singular fact. The Congress party (INC) functioned as a liberal lobbying platform for mostly various upper caste interests since its beginnings. But after the transfer of power, it was forced to accommodate lower caste interests as well to a small extent. The upper castes found that the Congress was no longer suitable to defend its interests in the face of the Mandal movement since it was not a militia comparable to the RSS. The liberal character of the Congress and its nominal commitment to the constitution of India made it inadequate to protect upper caste interests. The RSS, which was considered a malignant organisation of terror by many with liberal left sympathies, became the most viable option suddenly. We are now in the beginnings of the end of this process, which could either destroy the constitutional democratic character of India to implement direct upper caste rule through the RSS or it might criticalise India as such.

AB: *Why did Ambedkar fear that democracy will be a failed experiment in the Indian context? Is his prophetic anxiety coming true? What is the real state of democracy today in India?*

DD: In November 1949, Ambedkar marked the symbolic meaning of the date 26 January 1950 as the achievement of democracy as a political form but without a real establishment of, or even recognition of, 'social democracy' where all are equal in status and opportunity and all treat each other with the respect and fellow-feeling that this requires. Let me quote again his expression of anxiety which is, exactly as you say, prophetic: 'it is quite possible in a country like India [...] there is danger of democracy giving place to dictatorship. It is quite possible for this new born democracy to retain its form but give place to dictatorship in fact.' I can only venture an interpretation of this crucial distinction he drew, because this space of an interview is too limited to think about the politics of Dr Ambedkar.

The physicist Richard Feynman once gave an ethnographic account of a tribe in the South Seas, in order to distinguish the spirit of scientific practice from merely going through the motions or 'cargo cult science'.[16] Their islands had been used as military bases where they saw the comings and goings of airplanes ferrying precious cargo. Not being conversant with the actual workings of this phenomenon, they tried years after the war to bring back the planes by approximating the form of the activity, and so they would light the runway with fires, wear coconut shells to imitate head phones, bamboo sticks for antennae. Perhaps they hoped that airplanes would arrive if these ceremonies were performed, or maybe it was merely a new ritual without goals. These ceremonies are called the cargo cult. In India, what we have today is *cargo cult democracy*.

That is, we appear to have institutions and practices which appear to be similar to modern democratic institutions such as the parliament which does not debate the people's concerns; the judiciary which appears unconcerned with jurisprudence and justice as we found with the Babri mosque demolition case and other everyday instances; universities which teach myths in the place of the sciences and philosophy; media which either propels genocidal hysteria or functions as the propaganda arm of some or the other political party;

electoral processes hiding the supply of money to political parties. Our cargo cult democracy was anticipated by Dr Ambedkar when he called for proportional representations.

AB: *To what extent has the Congress party (Indian National Congress) been weakened by its dynastic moorings? Can the 'dynastic' element be eradicated from Indian politics, including the BJP (Bharatiya Janata Party), given that ours is a culture of patronage and tribal-minded continuities? When the BJP asserts that it will be in power for the next fifty years, is it not reincarnating the dynastic principle—party dynasty? Given that this power base is erected entirely on caste dynamics, cast in the guise of social engineering, what may we expect from the 'New India' that the BJP is unveiling today? Is 'New India' a sanitised moniker for upper caste Rashtra?*

DD: The term dynasty comes from the Greek *dunamis*, which is often translated as power and potentiality. *Dunastes* (δυνάστης) meant ruler or master. Today it means the retention of power and resources within the same family irrespective of the domain, be they the professions of academia, law, politics, business. Dynasty signifies the heritability of power and opportunities, which is also indicated by privilege. In India, upper castes in general are the real dynasts in all domains of life which matter. The RSS is the biggest conglomerate of all upper caste dynasties, it is after all called the Sangh parivar, or *the organisational mafia familiglia of the west coast.*[17] The Sangh *famiglia* now leads the ceremonies of the cargo cult democracy, as we find with the inaugurations of mountainous statues and constant changes of names of streets and cities.

But you are right, the present clamour against the dynasty of the Congress party masks the longest serving dynasty of the caste order. There is something complicated about the charge of dynasty against the Congress party. On the one hand the far right has been secerning their blood lines to accuse them of being too mixed—Muslim, Parsi, Italian, Catholic—and on the other hand they are said to be a sort of Kashmiri dynasty. Perhaps, the problem is that they are a bit too mixed to be Hindu, which means upper caste. At the same time it also shows the casteist anxiety of the Congress party which wants to show that their leader is a sacred thread-wearing Brahmin. The Congress can either accept the politics of mixtures and profess a progressive politics, or they should anxiously submit themselves to the upper caste evaluations of the RSS. But then nearly all political parties are owned by families, like family-run businesses to be inherited by their next generation.

Heritability of power and opportunity is the cultural genetic code of upper caste India, which it seeks to reproduce both genetically and culturally. I had called the concept behind such reproductions calypsology.[18] Romila Thapar had shown that India could never come out of the clan-based rule, grounded in the caste order, to create something like a modern state. In other words, India will be unable to emerge from this stasis without the equivalent of a French-style Revolution that transforms the social order and can disrupt the heritable form of power and opportunity that is caste. That is to say, it will be a social revolution, rather than another transfer of power, that alone will destroy the caste order.

FRIENDSHIPS AND SOLIDARITIES

26

THE COMPASSIONATE REVOLUTION OF SAINT STAN SWAMY (1937–2021)

Father Stan Swamy was a Jesuit priest, legal activist, human rights campaigner, and educationist who worked among the lower caste people and the tribal (Adivasi) people. In October 2020, he was arrested by the National Investigation Agency (NIA) under the draconian law Unlawful Activities (Prevention) Act (UAPA), which was strengthened by both the Congress party and the BJP together. He was arrested in connection with the celebration of the battle of Bhima Koregaon (see the note to 'The Obscenity of Truth' above). Swami's computers had been infiltrated and evidence was planted against him, as an American agency's investigation found later. Father Swamy was old and he was suffering from Parkinson's disease. In the jail, he got infected with Covid and died on 5 July 2021.

I remember that when this text was being written, Dwivedi and Mohan were still mourning for the philosopher Bernard Stiegler who died unexpectedly in August 2020. They were extremely anxious for the health of Jean-Luc Nancy who was in hospital then, and Dwivedi and Mohan were still discussing philosophical works and were planning projects with Nancy even in those final hours, knowing them to be final. Nancy passed away in August 2021. There is something of that era which is registered here and a trace of the distinct and extraordinary intensity—friendship[1]—that Dwivedi and Mohan bring to those that are friends. The text ends with the appropriation of the religious theme of redemption into the secular domain through a poetic phrase, 'the redemption of democracy'.

Father Stan Swamy, an 84-year-old Jesuit priest, died in judicial custody on Monday. He spoke sweetly of, and gazed gently at, this world. Father Swamy was already suffering from Parkinson's disease when he was arrested, and in jail he got infected with Covid. The judiciary and the National Investigative Agency (NIA), which today has the primary function of suppressing political opposition, delayed his medical care. He had to petition the courts to request a straw to drink water from (due to his Parkinson's disease), and this request too was not heeded for weeks.[2] They denied him water!

But we knew when the police began interrogating him in Jharkhand that his execution had begun.

Now, we should remember the scene of contrast. Those who committed the most vile act of terror in the history of independent India, the demolition of the sixteenth century Babri Mosque in 1992, never had to languish in custody while they were under trial. Rather, they were rewarded with cabinet ranks and other state honours—and a predictable refusal by the CBI to appeal their acquittal. Here, too, the Congress party set a precedent by rewarding all those guilty of the genocide of 1984 and not punishing those responsible for the demolition of the mosque and the pogroms which followed when they held power.[3]

India's anti-terrorism law (the Unlawful Activities (Prevention) Act as it is called) violates the fundamental principles of the constitution of India. The UAPA was made stringent by the Congress when in power. The ruling BJP later modified the laws further in order to allow the state to declare an individual as a terrorist without proper investigation, and the Congress was in favour then.[4]

However, it will not be an honest account of what happened to Father Stan Swamy nor will it be a modest tribute to him unless we understand that what killed him is still killing, imprisoning, and maiming hundreds of political activists and intellectuals in India.

In 2017, one of us (Divya Dwivedi) edited a special issue of the Unesco journal *Revue des Femme Philosophes* (*Women Philosopher's Journal*). It was titled 'Intellectuals, Philosophers, Women in India: Endangered Species', and the title anticipated these unfolding events. The issue had contributions from many intellectuals, writers, and journalists including Romila Thapar (interviewed by Siddharth Varadarajan, published by *The Wire*), Ravish Kumar, Shahid Amin, T. M. Krishna, Perumal Murugan, Hartosh Bal and Anand Teltumbde[5] who is now in prison under similar charges as Father Swamy, and is suffering from ill health. The arrests began in September 2018.[6] Then a new current of politics which brought students, the poor, workers and intellectuals together emerged in the protests against the CAA. And soon it became clear as the protests gathered strength that repression will follow.[7] It sent many young women and student activists to prison.[8]

We are reminding you here, because the 'active forgetting' that we practice today in all domains of life is the technique of cultivating calloused hearts. When we forget the crimes that have been committed, we inadvertently welcome their returns—nostalgia realised through active forgetting.[9]

The events around Father Stan Swamy's judicial murder have something to do with remembrance of an event and with the very meaning of remembrance, which is to ensure that what is remembered is the duct to something better. In January 1818, an army made up of lower caste people and British troops defeated the army of a Brahmin empire in central India in the battle of Bhima Koregaon. The humiliation of this event is at the heart of the upper caste militias which sprang up later in modern India.

The annual commemoration of this battle by the activists and intellectuals calling for equal rights is called 'Elgar Parishad'. Elgar means loudness—to remember the events of one's oppression through the victory in 1818 in a deafening clamour such that the world awakens. In 2018, the celebration march at the location of the battle, Bhima Koregaon, was brutally suppressed by the government and Hindu right-wing organisations. Soon, arrests followed, of many who spoke at the Elgar Parishad remembrance event and those who were connected with it. They were all charged under the anti-terrorism laws.

Later an independent forensic investigation by an American organisation found that the evidence was planted in the computers of the accused.[10] Today we learn that Father Swamy too was a victim of this pathetic trick whose ultimate aim has been to suppress the political awakening of the lower castes, erase their icons, intimidate their mobilisation, in short, to suppress any challenge to the idea of India as an upper caste controlled country.[11]

We can see the familiar fear and aggression of any regime of a minority of oppressors when the people they oppress arise in protest as is evident in the arrests and repressions using the muscle of the television news rooms. But the confusion for the rest of the world lies in the term 'Hindu majoritarian', which they read about in relation to the authoritarian government. They do not realise that the 'Hindu religion' as it is presented and the 'Hindu majority' associated with it are constructs of the early twentieth century to mask the fact that India is divided into the ruling oppressive minority of 10 per cent or less, essentially 'upper' caste, and the vast majority who had been living under slavery and discrimination for millennia.[12]

Today, those who deploy the word 'Hindu' in politics mean the supremacy of this caste minority. The present Hindu nationalist regime is enabled by a colluding Election Commission, judiciary and police. But the most important role is played by the big media, which is inventing demons out of the activists, intellectuals, and the poor to be slayed by the new 'Aryan' incarnations. Today, events like the commemoration of Bhima Koregaon challenge the feeling of absolute dominance enjoyed by the upper caste minority. The worry of the *upper caste supremacist* militias that India might have an egalitarian future was revealed in Sukanya Shantha's report 'Elgar Parishad: NIA Claims Arrested Accused Were Attempting to Create a "Dalit Militia"'.[13] This honesty of the upper caste militia and their workers is absent in our public sphere, which should be the cause for our greatest concerns. That is, the repressed question—the question of egalitarianism—will entomb us in this stasis.

However, as more and more lower caste activists and intellectuals are writing, speaking and organising tirelessly, in India and from 'exile' in Europe and America, the repressive efforts by the present upper caste supremacist organisations are like pouring the flowing lava back into the mouth of volcanoes.

Father Stan Swamy was also punished for his religion and his tireless efforts in helping the lower caste majority and Adivasis. The oppressed had been finding a minimum of dignity, education and community through conversions to Christianity, and also into Islam and Buddhism. In recent years, religious conversion and therefore arguments for religious freedom have been treated as crimes on par with terrorism and are now opposed by the illegal force of the militia, such as the terrorist organisation Bajrang Dal, linked to the upper caste supremacist paramilitary RSS.[14] Often, Christian priests are abused, nuns are raped, and many are killed.[15] The most notorious of these crimes took place in 1999, when an Australian missionary Graham Staines and his two young sons were burnt to death by the Bajrang Dal.[16]

It should not be forgotten that severe caste discrimination is practiced in the minority religions in India including Christianity, Islam, and Sikhism.[17] That is, egalitarianism through the annihilation of caste cannot be imagined as a religious project.

If the word 'saint' has a designation today it will be through the revolutionary of compassion, Stan Swamy. These days, the miracle is to be courageous, thoughtful and kind-hearted in an oppressive regime. Stan Swamy performed this miracle every day for thousands of days. Saint he is, and he will re-join the struggle for respect, dignity and equality in that capacity.

But what about us? As long as we remember to ask the question—When will we become an egalitarian polity through the annihilation of caste?—these events will not appear confusing. If we are honest in our remembrance and open ourselves to the thought of equality, we will soon have the redemption of democracy.[18]

27

DISHA RAVI, GRETA THUNBERG AND THE EXISTENTIAL REBELLION

THE WORLD NEEDS TO SAVE ITSELF

As a theoretical biologist who studies ecology, I have traced the ways in which India is a land of extraordinary biodiversity. Having spent some time in the Himalayas I found that the villagers themselves have a certain way of life which understands the wild as a part of themselves. This culture of seeing the natural world as not too sharply separated from the human world is a powerful way to combat the climate crisis. But things are not so simple. The climate crisis and ecological destruction are discussed in relatively hushed tones in India. Modi himself used to deny climate change. Climate and ecological activists are tormented by state legal machinery. As a student, Dwivedi herself participated in the militant ecological movement NBA (Narmada Bachao Andolan, or Save Narmada Agitation) to protect the Narmada river valley and its farmers and Adivasi inhabitants. The movement failed tragically. However, the discussions of climate in the political works of Dwivedi and Mohan are careful. Philosophically they had been active partners with me in the projects created by Bernard Stiegler to protect the world from climate crisis. This text changes all that.

When the farmer's strike and their occupation of Delhi was receiving international support, Disha Ravi, a young climate activist, was arrested by the police on 14 February 2021 for sharing a 'tool kit' online which educates people who are engaged in protest movements. The police in Delhi would also file charges against several others, alleging 'international conspiracy', including Greta Thunberg. As a member of the organisation AAGT (Association des Amis de la Génération Thunberg) I was following these developments keenly. An atmosphere of fear had already been created among those who speak out against ecological destruction. Dwivedi and Mohan had planned to publish this text initially in international media, including AAGT. However, when they learned of the charges the police were making against a young woman—'The call was to wage economic, social, cultural and regional war against India'—they decided that it was urgent to publish it in India.

The text openly mocks at the culture of a state which is indistinguishable from the mafia. It is also a philosophical text which demands a deeper political awareness and activism, almost revolutionary, to be integrated into the extinction rebellion led by young climate activists everywhere, as a necessity—existential rebellion and extinction rebellion.

> *I would like my books to be a kind of tool box which others can rummage through to find a tool which they can use however they wish in their own area.*
>
> –Michel Foucault

On 14 February, Disha Ravi, a 22-year-old woman from Bangalore, was arrested by the Delhi police and charged with sedition and criminal conspiracy. We are told that she is participating in a global social media campaign to support the farmers protesting across India against the new farm laws and that this equals attempting 'to wage economic, social, cultural and regional war against India'. Particularly, she is accused of modifying a document which is classified as a 'toolkit' created for coordinating social media campaigns and protests to help the protesting farmers of India. We should note that 'toolkit' may now appear to be an incendiary term for many

Indians, however it is an ordinary document used by any organisation of people to coordinate and make their actions effective.[1]

The worldwide dimension of the campaign for India's farmers which received support from Greta Thunberg, Rihanna, and Meena Harris among others should be understood properly. The crises of our world—climatic, democratic, technological, financial, epidemic—can no longer be understood or be contained within the logic of nation states. Rather, everything befalls everyone everywhere such that *pandemic*—that which befalls the demos (the people) of the *pan* (the whole)—is the name for the state of the world. Even to begin a resolution towards addressing these crises would require the beginnings of a *democracy of the world*,[2] of which the movements led by Thunberg are a part. This is not the utopia of 'world government' but a cause that is shared by everyone.

The global dimension of capitalistic exigencies is somewhat known to the rulers and their supporters who seem to work according to the 'toolkit' of the day in television studios, newspaper columns and social media. After all, when it comes to the very farm laws, which will deprive the farmers of whatever autonomy and minimal existential assurances they have today, the supporters of the laws cite the globalised food market and American farming practices as examples. In India, the 'urgency' which made the government dubiously bypass parliamentary procedures in order to bring in the new laws seems to point to the insatiable urges of just two corporations, and soon, criticising them might constitute sedition as is already being suggested.[3]

However, our attention in India should be on a more important question—what is the name for the political arrangement that we now are? To say that this is not democracy is not abominable to the high officials and the lowly trolls of the present dispensation, though it might be difficult to hear for those who continue to hope for a tolerable regime to appear in the near future.

There is a story which expresses the substance problem in philosophy, which is about that which makes a particular thing what it is. In the story, a man in Washington DC sells George Washington's axe everyday. One day, someone asks the salesman, 'Sir, I'd like to buy this axe, but the blade seems too new to me. Is it really the axe of

George Washington?' The salesman replies, 'Of course it is the very same axe of Washington, I just changed out the blade twice when it was rusty and the handle thrice because of termites'. The question then is what is it that we are selling to our young students and activists, increasingly women, who are languishing in our prisons?

There is never anything like a 'democracy' in the sense of a political arrangement where the wishes of all individuals are fulfilled or even those of a majority of individuals; the former is ruled out by the finitude of existence and the latter is potentially the very abolishment of such an arrangement, for that is how democratic arguments are used in order to end democratic systems. Instead, democracy is a very young promise of a very young experiment in human history. It relies on mutually agreed protocols and rules for collective deliberations and actions with the additional protocols to criticise and verify these very rules of collective action.

A functioning democracy, which is always going to be an inadequate democracy, is made up of components which are more or less autonomous with respect to one another such as the legislature, judiciary, executive, the media, the universities, and electoral procedures. The components have their own laws. For example, in the house of legislature a member can speak that which cannot be spoken outside it, as shown by the Member of Parliament Mahua Moitra recently.[4] An academic can critically comment on the component laws and functions of the judiciary unlike a member of the judiciary itself.

The law which comprehends all these components is not the constitution, but something that exceeds it towards the open and unknown concerns of the future, still guided by the very promise of maintaining this very system of collective deliberations and actions. In other words, the comprehending law[5] of a political arrangement, as long as it is worthy of being called a *democratic experiment*, cannot be stated exhaustively.

Democracies exist so long as they guard the *democratic promise* which exceeds the democratic arrangements. However, the many laws, state actions and court judgments which we have witnessed in India over the past few decades have systematically betrayed this democratic promise by misusing the very democratic institutions and procedures. No political party in India can be exonerated from this crime against democratic promise.[6]

When one of the components of the political arrangement seizes all the other components of a political arrangement, it initiates the end of the very system. The Greeks called it *stasis*, which is one of the designations of evil. That is, we continue to misname that in which we are. This condition of *stasis*—which can be specified as totalitarianism, authoritarianism, fascism, Nazism, dictatorship—certainly enables some men of business. Legislations which are delayed and made uncertain by deliberative democratic processes are bad for their business. Now, many governments across the world are merely the market places for the laws.

We have found in recent years that the charges raised and the evidence presented against activists who are convinced of their critique, and who continue to adhere to the *democratic promise*, are almost always ludicrous. Recently we learnt of the planting of evidence in the computers of activists to arrest them under extraordinary provisions of the law. Last year, a young girl was made to suffer in prison for raising slogans,[7] and several young women are languishing in our prisons without bail for attempting to break Brahminical patriarchal chains.[8] When we look at the sickening anti-miscegenation laws brought by the states and the anti-miscegenation vigilante action against inter-caste and inter-religious relations across the country, something appears clearly. There is an attempt at ethnic/religious purification for which all societies have crushed the freedoms of women.

In India the non-governmental paramilitary '*organisational famiglia*',[9] also known as the 'Sangh parivar', is fantasising about the ideal Indian woman who will be the domestic goddess to those outside her homes and merely the devoted supplicant to her father, brother, husband and son inside.

The latest arrest of Disha Ravi too should be seen in the same light. It is no different from the incarceration of young women fighting for their freedom of movement and other rights. All these prisons reveal the true wall of democracy today—it bears the names Disha Ravi, Nikita Jacob, Loujain Al-Hathloul, Devangana Kalita, Safoora Zargar, Natasha Narwal, Hadiya, Nodeep Kaur, Ishrat Jahan,

Rhea Chakravarty among countless others, and they are spilling over. The prison guards should know that women broke free of the oldest of prisons and these new ones are a day's work in comparison.[10]

Democracy is a collective deliberation and action based on rules and protocols which are themselves open to perpetual examination. In a functioning democracy, the courts would have laughed at the officials and governments which parade these innocents under ludicrous charges and fantastical evidence. But in India, day after day charges which try to outdo one another in ridiculousness are brought before our judges and they continue to bring the hammer down on poor souls, abdicating their judicial duties. If sharing 'toolkits' is a crime then Michel Foucault, Gilles Deleuze and other philosophers might soon emerge as global conspirators who will then be charged by the police under sedition laws.

Notwithstanding the tolerable outcomes which emerge from the courts from time time—bail here, a stay order there—the fact is that each and every component of what was the Indian experiment in democracy today is competing to enable an extra-constitutional Sangh parivar[11] to destroy the final remaining functions and institutions of the experiment. Which component will become the most rewarded arm of the fascist state is the question.

In spite of all the examples of global authoritarianism, we know that human beings—with their drive for freedoms, their ever-growing shared concerns in the face of global crises—cannot survive within totalitarian arrangements. Totalitarianisms are paranoid about the very thing which allows humanity to accrue the mutations through which it will meet the exigencies of the future – that is, the creation of knowledge and freedoms. They fear anything which may weaken their ever-rusting iron fists, especially this new generation of thinkers and activists who are able to acutely perceive the imminent crises of this world. If the present turn away from democracy continues any longer it will indeed be catastrophic for all, whether in India or elsewhere—including for those who today defend this turn in the name of market efficiency and the so called 'success' of the 'Chinese model'. The fact is that totalitarianisms everywhere are the most serious threat to the very existence of human beings today.

The 'extinction rebellion' of Greta Thunberg and her friends[12] correctly perceives in the ecological crises an impending disaster which threatens to extinguish humanity itself. However, it is evident that the ethos of Thunberg's civil disobedience model presupposes democratic conditions. Therefore, the concerns of the activists of extinction rebellion must necessarily expand, especially in this context of the hunting down of the young women and men who believe in the democratic promise. The world needs an existential rebellion of all peoples everywhere against totalitarianisms of all kinds. The *existential rebellion* will then be the revolt everywhere against those who are attempting to shatter the democratic promise.

28

ON TEESTA SETALVAD

This is another unpublished text which reminds me of the modern adage, if you kill a man you are a murderer, when you kill many you are a conqueror, and when you kill them all you become god.

Teesta Setalvad is a human rights campaigner and activist who had been struggling to secure legal aid and justice for the victims of the anti-Muslim pogrom of 2002 in Gujarat where Modi was the chief minister. Modi remains accused in courts outside India, including in the United States of America. He is able to travel freely around the world today because he is the prime minister of India, while 'low intensity' pogroms, oppression of the lower caste people, and destruction of democracy continue. The article is a defence of Setalvaad and it also presents a grim picture of the law.

On 25 June 2022, Teesta Setalvad, a respected senior human rights activist, was arrested by the Anti-terrorism Squad (ATS).[1] She was also a contributor to the special issue of the journal *Revue des Femme Philosophes*. The special issue was titled 'Intellectuels, Philosophes, Femmes en Inde: des espèces en danger',[2] and released in 2018 at the Unesco headquarters in Paris. Along with Anand Teltumbde,

Setalvad is the second contributor to this special issue who is now prison.[3]The title of this special issue is sadly prophetic in these hours.

Setalvad's arrest was in preparation for a long time, so will be the arrests and persecutions of many more who clamour of human rights in India very soon. In 2002, when Narendra Modi was the chief minister of the state of Gujarat in India, an anti-Muslim pogrom took place in which more than 2,000 people were killed.[4] The pogrom was condemned by the countries of the world, and America denied Modi a visa for the same reasons until he was elected as the prime minister of India[5] in 2014. That is, the culpability of the head of a state who controlled the police during a pogrom which ran for weeks on end can never be doubted anywhere in the world.[6] Modi is able to move around the world without fear of juridical consequences for extraordinary crimes only because he is the head of a state, and that fact is important to consider when observing the democratic collapse in India, because Modi cannot afford to be out of power.

When the pogroms began in Gujarat, a senior politician and former member of parliament, Ahsan Jafri, offered protection to a large number of Muslim people in his house. Jafri had been a staunch opponent of Modi and the paramilitary organisation to which he belongs, named RSS (National Self-server's Corp). As a senior politician of the Congress party he felt assured of protection. While three mobile police vehicles were stationed outside his house, 69 Muslims under his protection were killed. Jafri had called Modi asking for help but to no avail.[7] Jafri himself was dismembered and burnt alive.[8] His wife Zakia Jafri filed a petition in the Supreme Court of India accusing Modi of culpability, and Setalvad was one of the petitioners in this case. Her petition was denied by the Supreme Court on 24 June 2022. But the court's judgement contained something of an additional favour to Modi by accusing the petitioners of committing a crime in having even approached the court, and the very next day Setalvad was arrested.

Two consequences follow from this for India given that Supreme Court judgments create precedents: there is no rule of law anymore when one is not free to petition the courts; and any discussion in the future about the carnage in Gujarat in 2002 can be treated as a crime.

However, the intimidation by the state and assassinations by paramilitary organisations are not new in India. In January 2021, we were threatened with decapitation[9] for exposing the causes of the political and civilisational collapse in India. The majority of the people of India continue to suffer due to a severe misunderstanding about its politics by the rest of the world, which believes that there is a majority religion called 'Hindu' and that these 'Hindus' are oppressing the religious minorities. The reality is that Hindu religion was constructed in early twentieth century by the minority upper castes (10 per cent of the population) to mask their continuing racialised oppression of the majority lower caste people (90 per cent).[10] Pogroms against Muslims are often preceded by the demands for rights from lower caste people; that is, the oppression of Muslims and Christians is performed as a distraction from a real power struggle between upper and lower caste people. This has also prevented the world from seeing India as the country which entertains the oldest racist apartheid system.[11]

Since 2018 several lower caste intellectuals, anti-caste activists, and academics were arrested and imprisoned using faked evidence[12] under terrorism charges. One of them was a Jesuit priest named Stan Swami, aged 84 years, who died in prison.[13] Indian media and academia are dominated by the minority upper castes who are reluctant to report everyday caste oppression and to give space in the public forums for lower caste intellectuals to express their political ambitions, of which the most important are dignity and equality before the law. Further, by the force of law and of media power, to include the lower caste majority into the offensive false term 'Hindu majority' the lower caste people are framed into the histories of crimes in which they do not have the power to participate. Therefore, so long as caste oppression of millennia remains the reality of India other religious groups will continue to suffer as the sacrificial lambs.

29

ROMILA THAPAR

THE MODERN AMONG HISTORIANS

For a long time, the upper caste supremacists had been attacking the specialists of ancient India, including the physical attack on Wendy Doniger in London. But their animosity towards the historian of ancient India, Romila Thapar, is far more serious as she is a rationalist with a secular politics (without the Indian twist, for she means by this term the separation of religion from politics), and a public intellectual of courage. These attacks still continue towards Thapar. In 2019, her academic credentials were challenged and an attempt was made to revoke her emeritus status at JNU. She was attacked in social media.

This text is a defence of Romila Thapar, the ancient historian and dear friend of Dwivedi and Mohan. At the same time it is an exposition and defence of the very meaning of history and historiography. While doing so it integrates three domains: it provides a conceptual sketch of what continues from ancient to modern India, beginning with the spoked wheel and the 'Aryan' population which invaded India; it is a summary of the central concerns of Thapar's historiography which the authors show as the force of the caste order preventing the appearance of a modern state; and it is a revolutionary point of view of politics as the fight for freedom.

> *'It is impossible to come to terms with National Socialism on an intellectual basis, because it is simply not intellectual.'*
>
> *–Die Weiße Rose, Leaflet 2*

Romila Thapar is among the Indian cultural figures who are recognised and highly esteemed globally, yet there are those in India who wish to subject her *curriculum vitae* to scrutiny.[1] They do so not because they are unaware of her intellectual contributions but because they conflict with every myth they want to perpetuate in their crusade against history.[2]

What is a body of work, or *a corpus*?[3] A collection of writings—in Thapar's case it comprises thousands of pages—is not yet a corpus if it does not express something alive that is reaching out towards the possible developments of thought and also towards the impossible which it seeks to realise. The summary of all the possibilities and impossibilities of a thing is called its essence, and essence defines a corpus.

The essential and history

The essential—the exchange between the possible and the impossible[4]—is seen in the histories which occupy Romila. When a circle is carved into a block of wood, it is a heavy wheel, and its impossibilities are speed and manoeuvrability. About 4,000 years ago in the Ural region, the round block of wood became the spoked wheel (*Which of Us are Aryans?*, ed. Thapar 2018, p. 6). The wheel then carried on it the hordes, the words, the rituals and the poem of its own construction—*ratha cara*—to Asia Minor and what would be Pakistan.[5] In another domain, when Musa al-Khwarizmi[6] used letters and numerals to define the general forms of equations, there was born something which was impossible for Greek geometers—algebra.

The historian is someone who gathers the past from the point of view of the essential, such that we may continue to realise the impossible. That is, *history is the event when the possible crosses over to the impossible*. Thapar expresses it in her book *Early India* as 'a more integrated understanding of a complex society, its various mutations, its creativity and its efforts at enhancing its contributions to civilisation'. Recently, in the context of the destruction of educational institutions in India, she presented the same thesis: 'The essence of university education is to teach students to ask questions, to enable them to question existing knowledge, and through this process of questioning, to advance knowledge'.

We can see that this essential concern, which is to *enhance* and to *advance*, is continuous between Thapar's historical works and political works. Now we can think of the historian in the following way—*Romila Thapar, the ancient historian, works without relent in order to keep history itself alive*. Rather, Thapar is not concerned merely with chronicling the past but with expressing historic sense as a power which articulates politics. The unfolding travesty of morons seeking to assess the contributions of Thapar in order to raise another calumny is the continuation of an ancient conflict between *historic sense* and the recursive ceremonial social order.[7]

Ceremonial social order

We find the concern with the opposition between the essential and the ceremonial order in her early works where she posed a problem: can a society which is made up of *inherited communities*—caste order and clan-based rule—realise something like *the state* which is indifferent to the birth of men?

In the work *From Lineage to State,* she found that the opposition between the state and lineage-based systems, or inherited communities,[8] is an opposition at the level of functions. For example, if everyone inherits the functions played by their ancestors, this prevents the appearance of new functions which would enhance the contributions to civilisation. She found that in the subcontinent, something in-between began to take form which she would mark as a 'transition' that stubbornly persists as an incomplete one—like a train in an endless tunnel.

We continue to find in her political writings that such a transition from the lineage-based societal order to the freedom of something like a state is yet to happen—rather, political history has been in stasis in an essential sense in the subcontinent for centuries while its rulers came and went.

Ceremonial societies do not change in any essential sense, instead they repeat themselves year after year, faithfully. Their repetition is made possible through a peculiar logic—they identify means with ends, and vice versa. For example, the caste order which conserves itself through miscegenation rules and untouchability practices is both the means and end. The caste order observes itself as the means in order to repeat itself as the end.

Thapar writes about the necessary conditions of the ceremonial order of the subcontinent founded on caste, saying that it is one in which social and economic 'inequalities should be legitimised through a theoretically irreversible hierarchy and the imposition of the hierarchy claim to be based on a supernatural authority'. In other words, Thapar has been at work for decades to reverse the irreversible.

The moron who stubbornly persists in the ceremonial order is also immured, or confined, to a world of his own making. The word 'moron' is related to the Sanskrit '*mura*'. These two terms have a relation through the speculative etymological roots (*Proto Indo-European*) to 'immurement', that is, to be enclosed within a wall.

The moron, lacking in historic sense, finds that everything interesting had already happened in the mythic past which he faithfully repeats. Hence he keeps on finding the 'symbolic presence' of the new in the mythic past such that tensor algebra, the internet, plastic surgery and quantum computation are found archived in the tired idols of his divinities. The moron gazes into the eye of cow, where he finds the inverted image of history[9] and the archives of the present setting in, and thus he misses the essential.

We must then recapitulate in order to catch up with Romila Thapar. We find that when the possible crosses over to the impossible, history is written, such as when Einstein presented his General Theory of Relativity in 1915. When the possibilities unfold, we chronicle—such as the accounts of the day-to-day functioning of a government. And when ceremonial social order repeats, little is written, which perhaps explains the delayed onset of writing in the subcontinent.

To be modern

The attention to the essential in the past, or to historic sense, too has a history, which we usually refer to as the appearance of modernity. The writing and reading of history became necessary in order to be modern. The appearance of the modern attitude in the nineteenth century gave us two great philosopher-historians—Hegel and Marx. But what does it mean to be modern? Can one be modern today?

To begin with, to be modern is to not be a moron, someone who is blind to the essential or to that passage from the possible to the impossible which is gathered as history. The moron enters politics with the assumption that only the past can be the origin; rather, everything has been exhausted in the past. *Modernity is the confidence in humanity that the present can be the origin of new and impossible orders and, that the essential is available every moment*. In this sense, the attitude of modernity is characterised by the breaking down of walls and by breakthroughs.

Romila, then, is not only an ancient historian, nor just the historian of the ancient world, but she is the modern among historians. She has remarked on the practice of politics as a fight for freedom in the very sense of the term *modern*, which is an impatience with all forms of ceremonial orders, saying in an interview to *The Wire*, 'You cannot have a democracy where you have pre-determined majorities of whatever kind. In a democracy, an issue comes up, and the majority comes from every part of society and takes a decision and the next issue that comes up has a totally different constituent of majority.'[10]

30

INTELLECTUAL INSURGENCY

FOR MAHESH RAUT

When the activists and academics were arrested for commemorating the Bhima Koregaon battle, there was less attention paid in the media to the youngest detainee, an intellectual and activist named Mahesh Raut. Raut had been suffering from various ailments for the past five years in prison and I have not been able to find any prominent voices writing or campaigning for his release in Indian mainstream media, whereas I could find a greater level of mainstream support for other activists arrested on other cases.

This text was composed in July 2023 and as of this moment in October it has not yet found a publisher. There is a philosophical examination of the meaning of education under way in this text continuing from their tribute to Aron Schwartz. It points to the 'interest' invested in all forms of formal education. The goals or ends of education projects are set in place by those who control the syllabus and the conditions of academic instruction to suit their own interests. Instead, Dwivedi and Mohan ask for a pedagogical insurrection which is able to put in place ends or goals as they emerge from out of the very process of learning and researching. Such a process of 'intellectual insurgency' may be the need of the hour in most parts of the world right now.

'I shall speak of ghost, of flame, and of ashes'
—Jacques Derrida, *Of Spirit: Heidegger and the Question*

It is not easy to write about the scholar and activist Mahesh Raut without sorrow and rage. Raut was a fellow of the Prime Minister's Rural Development programme; it has been five years since he was arrested on 6 June 2018. He is the youngest prisoner in the Bhima Koregaon case, currently awaiting the mercy of the judiciary for bail in Taloja central jail. His health has been deteriorating in prison. The evidence presented in the Bhima Koregaon case was found to be spurious and was planted onto the computer of another accused activist Rona Wilson.

It will be imprudent and immoral to write about Mahesh Raut without recalling the circumstances which have been keeping him in prison, and above all it would usher in the evil of cowardice. These very circumstances are now articulating the macabre events unfolding in the tribal areas of Manipur which augur what may spread soon to different corners of India; the atrocities against the lower caste people and Adivasi (tribal) people which are recurring across the country; the simmering hate campaign against Muslims in Haryana which are reaching the neighbouring states (given, as Khalid Anis Ansari showed, that the Muslims who are killed in pogroms are mostly lower caste); and the *moronisation* of the education system in India.

The Bhima Koregaon case, in which Raut has been incarcerated, is related to the very origins of the upper caste supremacist RSS (National Self Service Corps) which is rooted in the anxieties of the Brahmins in the face of the political mobilisations of the lower caste majority in the nineteenth century in Maharashtra. Brahmins were the oppressors of the lower caste people in Maharashtra, as Joti Rao Phule wrote: 'The poor subjects, according to the Bhat rulers were specially created (by God) to serve the Bhat Peshwas and their castemen as helots'.

In January 1818, an army comprising of Dalit soldiers defeated the army of the Brahmin Peshwa, and the East India Company created a pillar to memorialise the soldiers who died in that battle. Especially since Ambedkar and his followers gathered around the pillar in 1927, it became a locus of the lower caste political mobilisation. In 2018, the memorial event was called 'anti-national', which stands for *against Brahmin interests*, by the Akhil Bharatiya Brahmin Mahasangh (All India Brahmin Congress). The event was disrupted by a mob led by upper caste supremacist groups and was marred by the riot which followed. The very first FIR filed in this case named Sambhaji Bhide, a former RSS worker. This man is highly regarded by the major political parties.

In the nineteenth century, the power of Brahmins began to wane in proportion to the modern colonial reforms which included unprecedented recruitment of the lower caste people in the army, their right to employment, and the Caste Disabilities Removal Act of 1850. But above all, these reforms created the opportunity for receiving modern education through the military schools. Phule would reiterate that before colonial rule the deprivation of education or enforced ignorance kept the lower caste people in ritualised slavery: 'The Aryan Brahmins forbade the Shudras to take education, which was the root-cause of their wretched condition.'

This degradation and depravation are part of the *denigrate-dominate function*, which is the principle of the 'Aryan doctrine'.

The significance of Bhima Koregaon is not just the memorialisation of the event in which the lower caste people defeated the upper caste army. It symbolises the promise that through modernity—the assertion that the present can be the origin for a better world without any sanction of the past—the lower caste people across religions can rise together and raise a new and egalitarian world from the ruins of the 'Aryan doctrine'.

Raut was neither an organiser of this memorialising event in 2018 nor a participant in it. His real crime was that he educated those who were forbidden to receive education and thus were held 'to the (meanest) level of the beasts (of the field)'. Raut was working among the Adivasi (the original inhabitants or tribal people) and educating them about their constitutional rights and human rights—'Raut has worked extensively to strengthen gram sabhas [village councils], guiding them on how they can safeguard their own rights over forest produce and their land'. His arrest compels us to ask of the meaning of the relation between the India and the Adivasi people.

The relationship of upper caste supremacists of today towards the Adivasi people is not that different from that of the 'Aryans' who arrived in the subcontinent millennia ago. It is mediated by 'the denigrate-dominate function'. In the already racialising casteist texts of the 'Aryans', the Adivasi people are often described as forest-dwelling blood-thirsty demons. The subjugation and at the same time the distancing of the Adivasi people abound in the *Mahabharata*—the killing of Hidimba (who may have been the god of a pre-'Aryan' civilisation as evidenced by his continuing presence in the Himalayas), the mutilation of the tribal boy Ekalavya, the burning of forests, and the sacrifice of the tribal warrior Ghatotkacha. The evidence for these ancient interactions exist within the Vedic language which borrowed terms for geographical features from Adivasi languages.

When the RSS stubbornly refers to the Adivasi people as 'Vana vasi' (forest dwellers) the ancient denigrating meaning is invoked. The killings and humiliations of the Adivasi people receive little media attention, since that would challenge the upper caste supremacist idea of India as the land of the 'Aryans' of northern India who have the right to enforce their social codes, language, and oppressor narratives upon the rest of India.

The BJP and most other political parties including the Congress have continued their relation to the Adivasi people through the ancient denigrate-dominate function. They have never encouraged critical, theoretical and jurisprudential discussions on the relation between the modern constitution of India and the rights of the Adivasi people. If one cares to look, there is extraordinary suffering, state sponsored or directed oppression, and exploitation taking place in the Adivasi lands distributed across India. Through all institutions which they control, the upper castes maintain *the denigrate-dominate function*.

In July 2023, a man named Pravesh Shukla urinated on the face of an Adivasi man in the state of Madhya Pradesh, a BJP-ruled state in which such crimes are not the exception. In 2018, an Adivasi man was beaten to death by a mob in Kerala for stealing food. Last year, an Adivasi was killed in Rajasthan for the crime of drawing water. In the state of Jharkhand, 122 Adivasi people were arrested and kept in prison for five years under false charges of terrorism, and they were released in July 2022 by a court which observed that:

> No evidence or statements recorded by the prosecution was able to establish that the accused were members of the Naxal wing and was involved in the crime. No arms or ammunition seized by the police were proved to be found from the accused.

Upper-caste supremacy transcends political party boundaries and the majority lower caste people and those who work from the lower caste majority position can often be beaten, humiliated, killed or imprisoned with ease. Mahesh Raut certainly violated the ancient norms of the 'Aryan doctrine' when he brought education to the lower caste people and the Adivasi people.

In India, we have never engaged in a sustained discussion on the meaning of education although some of the most important leaders of politics before 1947 were concerned with it. These days, we mostly discuss education in the most deplorable terms, that is, of having to defend the reservation given to the lower caste majority in educational institutions. These discussions are often puerile and occasionally vulgar in the mainstream media, as seen on the issue of the reservation provisions for the lower caste Muslims and Christians who constitute the majority of these groups. It reveals a 'miraculous' situation where the lower caste majority are being oppressed by the upper caste minority, and yet the minority people find it their right to grant reservations to the majority as if it were an undeserved pittance.

There are two opposing tendencies with respect to education in India—*the lower caste majority position* and *the upper caste supremacist position* across religions including Islam, Sikhism and Christianity. The latter seeks to deprive the lower caste majority of education and academic positions in the educational institutions of India, as evident in the upper caste (mostly Brahmin) membership of the recently created NCERT committee which has been entrusted with 'investigating in' what the lower caste majority (of all religions) should learn in schools.

M. K. Gandhi stands for the latter position on education. Gandhi wrote about giving education to the peasants (who are not Brahmins):

> What do you propose to do by giving him a knowledge of letters? Will you add an inch to his happiness? Do you wish to make him

> *discontented* with his cottage or his lot? And even if you want to do that, he will not need such an education.

Further Gandhi argued in favour of the 'traditional' Brahminical education, 'Our ancient school system is enough'.

The terms 'discontent' and 'unrest' in Gandhi are complex and we have dealt with them elsewhere. Gandhi found that 'just as *the state between sleep and awakening* must be considered to be necessary, so may the present unrest in India be considered a necessary and therefore, a proper state' and 'Unrest is, in reality, discontent'. Then, discontent is the state which precedes the *fight for freedom*, which is the meaning of politics. For Gandhi, political unrest is a necessity but only for a few since his views on education reveal that he wanted the lower caste majority to remain asleep while the upper caste minority decided the lower caste majority's destinies. Hence, he wished to reserve the power of discontent, and the education in necessary discontent, for the upper caste minority.

On the other hand, the intellectual leaders of the lower caste majority had always argued for the egalitarianism of the restlessness or the unrest of thought which precedes all creations of freedom and the fights for freedom. Today, when the unity between the postcolonial and decolonial academic project and upper caste supremacism (which masks itself as Hindu majoritarianism) is asserting itself through the imposition of Hindi, and the upper caste codes of diet, we should meditate on Joti Rao Phule's text on unrest, discontent, modern education and the effects of colonial rule. Phule wrote that God himself:

> has sent the English to our country to end the Brahmin's proscription of education for the Shudras and Atishudras and to empower them [...] the newly *educated Shudras and Atishudras will establish their own state* and, like the Americans, will govern it themselves.[1]

Narayana Guru in Kerala had demanded that the lower caste majority become the masters of English language and modern knowledge systems.

Later, B. R. Ambedkar, the most educated politician in Indian history said something similar: 'if you give education to the lowest strata of Indian Society which is interested in blowing up the Caste System, *the Caste System will be blown up*'. Indian politics since the nineteenth century had been nothing other than the battle of these two positions—the lower caste majority position and the upper caste minority position—across religions. The educational imperators of the upper caste minority are trying desperately to prevent another beginning from out of a 'blown up' caste system. Rather, we are witnessing a pretend politics which lives on the time borrowed from a deferred revolution.

The conflict between these two tendencies of education articulated the political awakenings in many university campuses. It began in 2015 with the ban imposed by the central government on the lower caste majority education project Ambedkar-Periyar Study Circle, which since then has sprung up in other campuses. Eventually these movements were diverted into upper caste discourses on nationalism. While the television networks debated the difference between 'Hindu' and 'Hinduness' (Hindutva), the crushing of these intellectual currents continued away from attention. Today, intellectual acts are themselves forced into a certain *intellectual insurgency* through the terms such as 'urban naxal', 'urban Maoist', 'Khan Market gang' and so on.

But then, we must begin to think what it means to pursue and share education today such that we ourselves come to excel at intellectual insurgency. In the Kantian sense, education is the training of the faculty which allows us to encounter the world under un-anticipatable circumstance, it is a preparation for the obscure. For Kant, it is founded on courage—the opposite of which is being cultivated by the bands of cowards—to think without the crutches of religion and superstitions. That is, education never finishes, for it creates humanity anew each time someone's thought breaks boundaries.

Education in that sense also discards the ends (*telos*) or goals which are external to it, and imposed on it. Education generates its own ends and opposes the imposition of ends and goals from outside it. *These endogenous ends of education* threaten fascisms. For example, the imposition of the ends (*telos*) of Hindi language and upper caste supremacism (Hindu nationalism) for the Indian union enforces the goals of the minority upper castes of northern India upon shockingly diverse and divergent cultures which exist in the Indian subcontinent. Instead, education can create new collective faculties to attune to one another as if one were harmonising, deviating, and creating new tonal relations in a concert.

And that brings us to the other important component of education. In order to play a musical instrument one must train one's fingers (for example, a piano or a fiddle) to reach the correct positions so that the intended notes are heard. For playing alongside the many instruments and many kinds of tonal cultures such as raga and scales, one must master the musical instrument and the theory. In politics, the equivalent of praxis and theory is organisation and the knowledge of constitution and political theory. When someone joins any political organisation whatsoever with the goal of being trained in political praxis, but without surrendering to the ends imposed by that organisation, it is equivalent to training the fingers to play the piano.

However, an intellectual insurgency must keep knowledge alive the way *Fahrenheit 451* taught us, through external and internal memories. More importantly, intellectual insurgency is learning to *read poetically* (more than what is said by the letters) *and critically* (by asking why those words were written, and from which position). Today this training and intellectual insurgency can be conducted through the sharing of science and humanities text books, video lessons, social media, blogs, and the creation of websites. There are many academics and intellectuals in India who would join and teach for the gatherings of learners forced into the underground of education. Intellectual insurgency is generosity and egalitarianism at work (*energeia*).

The present regime is run by the political offspring of an organisation led by barely educated Brahmins, and several of these political leaders have either questionable or scant literacy. The present regime has removed evolutionary biology and the periodic table from 9th and 10th classes from schools, whereas these items should have been introduced much earlier. This regime has also removed portions on Mughal history, caste oppression, and the 2002 pogrom against Muslims in Gujarat when Modi was the chief minister.

We can anticipate what is coming through the newly constituted upper caste NCERT committee from the example of Modi's Gujarat.

In 2004, the students in Gujarat were already reading chapters titled 'Hitler, the Supremo' and 'Internal Achievements of Nazis'. The textbook goes on to say that Hitler 'lent dignity and prestige to the German government' and 'instilled the spirit of adventure in the common people.' The concern of an intellectual insurgency should be that the vegetarianism of Hitler and the instilled 'spirit of adventure' which resulted in millions of deaths should not be repeated as farce in India.

However, the composition of the NCERT committee, which was earlier led by the likes of Romila Thapar, now forebodes the same 'spirit of adventure' continuous with Nazi Germany and Gujarat since 2002. It includes a Tamil Brahmin praise poet of Modi. The inclusion of Sudha Murthy, the 'pure' vegetarian Brahmin who happens to be the wife of a billionaire and the mother in law of the current British prime minister should be worrying. For Murthy is also 'a member of the Board of PM CARES Fund Trust', which is a constitutionally dubious 'non-state' organisation that received 'Rs 2,913.6 crore between 2019–20 and 2021–22' from government-run companies. In November 2022, Murthy prostrated before Sambhaji Bhide (the former RSS worker named in the first FIR filed in the Bhima Koregaon case) and took his blessings in public.

The word 'insurgency' is often used to refer to the refusal by people to obey orders and to recognise authority. For example, the call for a 'total revolution' by Jaya Prakash Narayan in the 1970s which was heeded by the RSS was in effect a political insurrection. It remained short of what Marx, in *The Poverty of Philosophy,* called 'total revolution'—'a struggle of class against class, a struggle which carried to its highest expression'.

The philosophical concept of insurgency is related to but distinct from the statist notion. Insurgency comes from the Latin roots 'in', 'sub' and 'rego'. 'Rego' meant 'to correct', 'to make something right', and also 'rules' and regulations in the way in which Descartes used it, 'Regulae ad directionem ingenii' (Rules for the direction of imagination).

Philosophically insurgency means to rise up or to raise from below in order to constitute new Regulae, or to create another beginning.

NOTES

INTRODUCTION

1. See Divya Dwivedi, 'The Evasive Racism of Caste and the "Aryan Doctrine"', *Critical philosophy of Race* vol. 23 no. 1 (2023): 209–245.
2. See Shaj Mohan, 'Teleography and Tendencies: Part 2 History and Anastasis', *Philosophy World Democracy,* vol. 3 no. 4 (April 2022), https://www.philosophy-world-democracy.org/articles-1/teleography-and-tendencies-part-2-history-and-anastasis. In simpler terms, the past reveals itself according to the interests (or ends understood as telos) the historian has in the future. History does not allow a god's eye view, and this fact is marked by Mohan through the concept of 'teleography'.
3. Mohan would argue in another context that 'resistance and protests are no longer very helpful. Instead, we should be thinking in terms of systemic transformation, more precisely revolution'. The difference between resistance and revolution was developed rigorously by Dwivedi and Mohan in their book *Gandhi and Philosophy*. Later I will provide a sketch of this theory in one of the chapter introductions. See 'The silence on the streets should never be mistaken for a quiet submission in politics'—An interview with Shaj Mohan, *Crisis and Communitas*, https://crisisandcommunitas.com/?crisis=the-silence-on-the-streets-should-never-be-mistaken-for-a-quiet-submission-in-politics-an-interview-with-shaj-mohan
4. Abhish K. Bose, 'Class, Caste and Communism: An Interview With J. Reghu', Counter Currents, 5 April 2023, https://countercurrents.org/2023/04/class-caste-and-communism-an-interview-with-j-reghu/

5. Ibid.
6. Ibid. See also the special issue of the journal *Episteme* on the philosophy of Divya Dwivedi and Shaj Mohan, *Episteme*, Issue number 4, February 2021, https://positionspolitics.org/episteme-4/
7. See Maël Montévil, 'Penser au-delà de l'identité : philosophie et sciences', *Philosophy World Democracy*, vol. 3 no. 6 (June 2022), https://www.philosophy-world-democracy.org/other-beginning/penser-au-dela-de-lidentite-philosophie-et-sciences
8. The TV network was recently acquired by the Adani group which is proximate to Modi, to the point that the opposition leader Rahul Gandhi said 'Modi is Adani'. See 'Adani Stock Scam An Opportunity To Curtail Hindurashtra Conspiracy', *Counter Currents*, 30 March 2023, https://countercurrents.org/2023/03/adani-stock-scam-an-opportunity-to-curtail-hindurashtra-conspiracy/
9. N. K. Raveendran, 'Two Philosophers and a Political Theorist: An Allegory of Indian Public Sphere', *Mathrubhumi*, 15 November 2022, https://english.mathrubhumi.com/features/specials/two-philosophers-and-a-political-theorist-an-allegory-of-indian-public-sphere-1.8048901
10. Ibid.
11. See 'In support of Divya Dwivedi and Shaj Mohan', *Mediapart*, 7 November 2022, https://blogs.mediapart.fr/les-invites-de-mediapart/blog/071122/support-divya-dwivedi-and-shaj-mohan
12. See the article 'Philosopher Divya Dwivedi Among Latest Targets of India's Right Wing' by Anthony Ballas, *Protean* (5 October 2023), https://proteanmag.com/2023/10/05/philosopher-divya-dwivedi-among-latest-targets-of-indias-right-wing/
13. Ibid.

1. THE PATHOLOGY OF A CEREMONIAL SOCIETY

1. See M. K. Gandhi, *Hind Swaraj Or Indian Home Rule*, Ahmedabad: Navajivan Publishing House, 2008.
2. Refers to the Nazi occupation of Czechoslovakia from 1938. The Nazis killed more than 300,000 people, mostly Jews.
3. Referring to the 'Wehrkraftzersetzung' laws of the Nazi regime which found all criticisms of the regime and its ideological positions seditious. From 2016 several Indian activists, journalists and politicians have been imprisoned under similar conditions.
4. These are the rationalist philosophers of India assassinated by the Hindu right since 2013.

5. The article is an enactment of the refusal to say the fascistic slogan 'Long live mother goddess India'. See 'Kandhamal: Nun rape trial begins', *Indian Express*, 27 July 2010, http://archive.indianexpress.com/news/kandhamal-nun--rape-trial-begins/652248/
6. Kumar was the president of Jawaharlal Nehru University (JNU) students union, as a member of the students wing of the Communist Party of India. Later he joined the Indian National Congress or the Congress party.
7. The Yoga teacher and businessman Ram Dev demanded that there should be a law which makes it mandatory to chant the fascist slogan. See 'Everyone must chant "Bharat Mata Ki Jai", amend law: Baba Ramdev', *Indian Express*, 24 March 2016, https://indianexpress.com/article/india/india-news-india/everyone-must-chant-bharat-mata-ki-jai-amend-law-baba-ramdev/
8. The chief of the RSS (Rashtriya Swayam Sevak Sangh, or National self-server's corp) publicly stated that it was the wish of the organisation to see to it that the whole world chanted their slogan, that is the whole world belonging to the RSS in future as a part of the would be Hindu empire. See 'We Want the whole world to chant 'Bharat Mata ki Jai': RSS chief Bhagwat', *Hindustan Times*, 28 March 2016, https://www.hindustantimes.com/india/want-the-whole-world-to-chant-bharat-mata-ki-jai-rss-chief-bhagwat/story-tuj1Vwv8BmX1omz4MKtnJL.html
9. The uniform of the Hindu or upper caste supremacist organisation similar to the Nazi organisations was khaki shorts until recently. The organisation practices drills and weapons training, often in public grounds.
10. Perumal Murugan is a Tamil language novelist who writes about caste oppression. In 2015, he declared that he will no longer be a writer when the levels of threats against him from the upper caste supremacist organisations increased. See https://www.theguardian.com/books/2015/jan/15/indian-author-perumal-murugan-hindu-protests
11. This text was and still may be one of the most aggressive writings against the RSS. Its open challenge to the RSS and the Hindu right government makes it dangerous for its authors.

2. HIDDEN BY HINDU

1. Author's note: The term 'religion' in the various senses in which we use it today has come through Kant's conception of a universal

religion and the need felt by Christian missionaries to classify the customs and beliefs of the people they encountered during the era of 'colonialism'.

2. 'Syndicated Hinduism', Romila Thapar, *Hinduism Reconsidered*, editors Sontheimer and Kulke, Delhi: Manohar Press, 1989.
3. See https://www.ndtv.com/tamil-nadu-news/tamil-nadu-couple-hacked-to-death-allegedly-over-inter-caste-marriage-2064779 and https://www.thehindu.com/news/national/other-states/up-honour-killing-dalit-man-burnt-alive/article29431184.ece
4. *Gandhi and Philosophy: On Theological Anti-politics*, London: Bloomsbury Academic, 2019.
5. On 15 March 2018 the Government of India issued a directive prohibiting the use of the term 'Dalit' in the media. The self-description of the oppressed castes as 'Dalit' is threatening since it has enabled greater political mobilization of the lower castes.
6. We must note that manual scavenging is an everyday practice in India. At least one Dalit dies every five days in sceptic tanks, which is a conservative estimate. See https://indianexpress.com/article/india/official-data-shows-one-manual-scavenging-death-every-five-days-5361531?
7. Dalits are still killed for entering the upper caste temples. See https://www.hindustantimes.com/india/dalit-man-attacked-set-on-fire-for-entering-temple-in-up/story-oZTmIGHAhck4jLi7lB4mMO.html
8. See https://www.bbc.com/news/world-asia-india-48265387
9. 'The Sacred in Modern Hindu Politics', Robert Eric Frykenberg, *Hinduism In India*, edited by Will Sweetman and Aditya Malik, London: Sage Publishers, 2016.
10. 'Patriotism without People', Sukumar Muralidharan, *Social Scientist*, Vol. 22, Nos. 5–6, May–June 1994.
11. Romila Thapar, 1989.
12. 'Socio-economic Caste Census', Rajesh Ramachandran, *The Economic Times*, 12 July 2015, https://economictimes.indiatimes.com/news/politics-and-nation/socio-economic-caste-census-numbers-not-being-revealed-to-hide-upper-caste-dominance-in-governance/articleshow/48034215.cms?from=mdr

3. THE 'ARYAN DOCTRINE' AND THE DE-POST-COLONIAL

1. Hypo- being the Greek prefix for all these prepositional meanings.
2. See 'Ce que l'hindouisme recouvre,' by Divya Dwivedi and Shaj Mohan, *Esprit*, June 2020.

3. See Divya Dwivedi, Shaj Mohan, and J. Reghu, 'The Hindu Hoax: How upper castes invented a Hindu majority', *The Caravan,* January 2021.
4. See Khalid Anis Ansari, 'Revisiting the Minority Imagination: An Inquiry into the Anticaste Pasmanda-Muslim Discourse in India,' *Critical Philosophy of Race*, vol. 11 no. 1 (2023), p. 124-25, (Special Issue: 'Caste and Racism in India', guest edited by Divya Dwivedi).
5. Author's note: The commission was created in 1953 to examine the backward caste groups, other than Dalits and Adivasis, who required reservations. The report was rejected by the government.
6. Author's note: Named after the ancient 'Aryan' tribal chief of the upper caste epics, fables, and myths through which it is asserted that the land of India is owned by the upper caste supremacists where the lower caste majority and other religious groups have an uncertain status.
7. See the entry *Idyllic a priori* in the Glossary.

4. NEVER WAS A MAN TREATED AS A MIND

1. The title is borrowed from a phrase in the suicide note of the Dalit doctoral scholar Rohith Vemula. The part referenced in the title of the says 'The value of a man was reduced to his immediate identity and nearest possibility. To a vote. To a number. To a thing. Never was a man treated as a mind. [...] My birth is my fatal accident.' For the full text, see https://thewire.in/caste/rohith-vemula-letter-a-powerful-indictment-of-social-prejudices
2. In Tamil, freedom.
3. This expression 'orienting star' returns in the corpus of Dwivedi and Mohan, which is in reference to Hegel's remark that Mercury is the orienting star for the departed souls, in his *Philosophy of Mind*. With Dwivedi and Mohan, the goal of philosophy is to constitute disorientation and at the same time to give the power to exist and proceed in freedom in such a state of disorientation. For a technical articulation of this concept established through Kant, see 'On the Relation Between the Obscure, the Cryptic and the Public', in *The Public Sphere From Outside the West*, London: Bloomsbury Academic, 2015.
4. 'Auschwitz trial: survivor urges guard to reveal his role at death camp', *The Guardian*, 11 February 2016, https://www.theguardian.com/world/2016/feb/11/auschwitz-guard-trial-concentration-camp-germany-reinhold-hanning

5. Translates to 'An order is an order' which was an excuse of many Nazis who were tried after the 2nd world war.
6. See Alain Badiou, *Being and Event*, Translated by Oliver Feltham, London: Continuum, 2005.
7. See Martin Heidegger, *Philosophical and Political Writings*, New York: Continuum International Publishing Group, 2003, and Martin Heidegger, *Introduction to Metaphysics*. The philosophical and political oeuvre of Dwivedi and Mohan has a complicated opposition to Heidegger. They refer to Heidegger, often to refute his interpretations of the history of philosophy and politics. At the same time they take the phenomenological and deconstructive aspects of Heidegger's works as points of departure. Mohan has disclosed the invalidity of some of the philosophical axioms of Heidegger, including 'ontico-ontological difference' and 'the end of philosophy'. With Jean-Luc Nancy, Dwivedi and Mohan initiated a project to begin philosophy again with an openness to the other through the project 'The Other Beginning of Philosophy'. See the journal *Philosophy World Democracy* for more https://www.philosophy-world-democracy.org/other-beginning
8. Narendra Modi, the prime minister of India, was the chief minister of the state of Gujarat in 2002 when the events known as the Gujarat pogrom took place. Thousands of Muslims were killed, hundreds lost their homes and livelihood. Modi is widely held to be politically responsible for his provocative speeches, and administratively responsible for the pogrom and its cover ups. When asked about his guilt Modi replied that he felt as sad as anyone would when they see a puppy run over by a car. See 'Modi's "puppy" remark triggers new controversy over 2002 riots', 12 July 2013, *Reuters*, https://www.reuters.com/article/narendra-modi-puppy-reuters-interview-idINDEE96B08S20130712. See note 6 above.
9. The excuse of Lal Krishna Advani, who is a member of the RSS and a founder of the BJP (Bharatiya Janata Party) for serious crimes committed by him. Advani took out a procession across India to mobilise masses to demolish the sixteenth century Babri Mosque in the state of Uttar Pradesh, to build a temple for the mythical king Rama. Modi was an organiser of this movement. The mobilisations were widely supported by upper caste Indians, including some intellectuals, because it diverted attention from the rising demands from the lower caste majority of India for rights and opportunities. The mosque was demolished on 6 December 1992 and the pogroms and the riots that followed killed hundreds of people across India. The effects of religious polarisation allowed the BJP to obscure the

demands of the lower caste majority and come to power in many states of India, and eventually form national governments from 2002. Advani himself became a deputy prime minister of India. The judiciary allowed the culprits including Advani to go scot free. See 'Babri masjid demolition saddest day in life: L. K. Advani, *One India*, 29 March 2011, https://www.oneindia.com/2011/03/29/lk-advani-apology-gujrat-riot-babri-demolition-aid0102.html

10. The re-construction and re-deployment of 'Aryan' identity in European philosophy and politics from the eighteenth century, and its effects on India and vice versa, are themes in the philosophical works of Dwivedi and Mohan. Dwivedi has investigated the philosophical crimes of 'Aryanised' racism and presented a critique in several of works. Especially important in this regard are the special issue of the journal *Critical Philosophy of Race* edited by Dwivedi, and her lectures at École Normale Supérieur and forthcoming book, both of which the editor was privy to.
11. This is an interpretation of the ancient text 'Gita' or 'Bhagavad Gita'. Dwivedi and Mohan present an interpretation of the text as one that enforces caste rules.
12. These are terms found in the upper caste religions of India, and in Buddhism, designating a domain where those released from the burdens of existence will arrive provided they fulfil their existential duties, which are often given by caste rules.

5. THE MACABRE MEASURE OF DALIT-BAHUJAN MOBILIZATIONS

1. See 'Why Hathras happened: Answer lies in NCRB data, crime against women up 7.3%', *India Today*, 1 October 2020, https://www.indiatoday.in/news-analysis/story/hathras-gangrape-murder-ncrb-data-crime-against-women-1727250-2020-10-01
2. See the suicide note of Rohith Vemula, 'My Birth is My Fatal Accident: Rohith Vemula's Searing Letter is an Indictment of Social Prejudices', *The Wire*, 17 January 2019, https://thewire.in/caste/rohith-vemula-letter-a-powerful-indictment-of-social-prejudices
3. See the report 'UP Police Now Claims Hathras Victim Wasn't Raped, Matter 'Twisted' to 'Stir Caste Tension'', *The Wire*, 1 October 2020, https://thewire.in/women/hathras-victim-forensic-report-uttar-pradesh-police-caste-tension-rape
4. On the attempted destruction of evidence, see 'Exclusive: Aligarh Hospital MLC Report on Hathras Victim Shatters UP Police's 'No

Rape' Claim', *The Wire*, 3 October 2020, https://thewire.in/women/aligarh-jnmch-hathras-victim-mlc-report-up-police-rape

5. For Dwivedi and Mohan upper caste supremacy is made 'palatable' for the international audience through the terms 'Hindu nationalism' and 'Hindu supremacy'. All these terms, as Dwivedi shows here, are 'Aryan supremacy'. For a detailed account of 'Aryan supremacy' and 'Aryan doctrine' still operating in India and the world see Divya Dwivedi, 'The Evasive Racism of Caste—and the Homological Power of the 'Aryan' Doctrine', Critical Philosophy of Race Penn State University Press Volume 11, Issue 1, 2023 pp. 209-245.
6. See the news report, 'NCRB data: 7% rise in crimes against women', *Indian Express*, 30 September 2020, https://indianexpress.com/article/india/ncrb-data-7-rise-in-crimes-against-women-6636529/
7. Author's note: Editors Aloysius Irudayam S. J., Jayshree P. Mangubhai, and Joel G. Lee, *Dalit Women Speak Out: Caste, Class and Gender Violence in India*, Delhi: Zubaan Books, 2014.
8. Author's note: Ibid.
9. Author's note: Ibid.
10. Author's note: The text continues, which reads like present day India, 'These people drove us, the poor mangs, and mahars, away from our own lands, which they occupied to build large buildings. And that was not all. They would make the mangs and mahars drink oil mixed with red lead and buried our people in the foundations of their buildings, thus wiping out generation after generation of our poor people. The brahmans have degraded us so low; they consider people like us even lower than cows and buffaloes'. Mukta Salve, 'Mang Maharachya Dukhvisayi (About the grief of the Mangs and the Mahars)', *Dalit Web*, https://www.dalitweb.org/?p=2947
11. Author's note: Rosalind O'Hanlon, *Caste, Conflict and Ideology Mahatma Jotirao Phule and Low Caste Protest in Nineteenth-Century Western India*, Cambridge: Cambridge University Press, 1985.
12. Since 2022 caste oppression, lower caste political movements, lower caste intellectuals and leaders have been removed from Indian school and university syllabi by the Modi led government, although most of the public discussions were focused on the removal of portions discussing the Mughal rule in India. See 'Exclusive: Citing COVID Burden, NCERT Drops Mentions of Caste Discrimination From Sociology Textbook', *The Wire*, 18 June 2022, https://thewire.in/education/ncert-deletes-mentions-of-caste-discrimination-anti-caste-movement-from-class-12-sociology-book

13. Author's note: Ramdas says 'what is Brahminism? It is composed of humans that are supremacists at birth and for all times to come'. See Anu Ramdas, 'Feminism is Brahminism', *Round Table India*, 30 May 2020, https://www.roundtableindia.co.in/feminism-is-brahminism/
14. See 'India's #MeToo Is Here, Has Prodded Action Against Accused', *News Click*, 11 October 2018, https://www.newsclick.in/indias-metoo-here-has-prodded-action-against-accused And the chapter 'Sex and Postcolonial Values' in this anthology.
15. See Priyanka Sami, 'Hathras Case: The Intersecting Factors Behind Structural Violence Against Dalit Women', *The Wire*, 1 October 2020, https://thewire.in/caste/hathras-case-structural-violence-dalit-women-intersecting-factors
16. Rupali Bansode, 'Dalit Girls Negotiate Women's Studies', *Round Table India*, 8 December 2013, https://www.roundtableindia.co.in/dalit-girls-negotiate-women-s-studies/
17. Author's note: Editors Sukhdeo Thorat and Umakant, *Caste Race and Discrimination: Discourses in International Context*, Jaipur: Rawat Publications, 2004.
18. A term of colonial origin, meaning the region is controlled by mafia organisations.
19. Michel Foucault, *Power (The Essential Works of Foucault, 1954-1984, Vol. 3)*, The New Press, 2001.
20. See 'FIR against Bhim Army chief Chandrashekhar Azad, 400 others over Hathras visit', *Indian Express*, 5 October 2020, https://indianexpress.com/article/india/hathras-rape-case-bhim-army-chief-chandrashekhar-azad-fir-6703460/
21. International plot is the mark of tinpot dictatorships and autocracy in general, be it the Soviet Union, India, or North Korea. See 'In fresh FIR, Hathras police claims 'international plot' to defame Yogi govt', *Indian Express*, 5 October 2020, https://indianexpress.com/article/india/hathras-gangrape-case-fir-yogi-adityanath-6703740/
22. Thakur is an upper caste similar to Kshatriya, who control land and other resources. 'Ex-BJP MLA holds meeting in Hathras to back accused', *Indian Express*, 5 October 2020, https://indianexpress.com/article/india/ex-bjp-mla-holds-meeting-in-hathras-to-back-accused-6703130/
23. See 'Elgar Parishad: NIA Arrests Hany Babu, "Pressured Him to Implicate Colleagues, Others," Says Wife', *The Wire*, 28 July 2020, https://thewire.in/government/nia-bhima-koregaon-hany-babu-arrest-gn-saibaba

24. United Nations responded to these troubling reports from India. See 'CAA protesters' arrest "designed to send chilling message": UN asks India to free activists', *The Print*, 26 June 2020, https://theprint.in/india/caa-protesters-arrest-designed-to-send-chilling-message-un-asks-india-to-free-activists/449401/

6. THE MEANING OF CRIMES AGAINST MUSLIMS IN INDIA

1. See the report in *The Guardian*, 'Prophet Muhammad remarks embroil India in row with Gulf states', https://www.theguardian.com/world/2022/jun/06/prophet-muhammad-remarks-embroil-india-in-row-with-gulf-states
2. A report in *The Telegraph* says '"She will bounce back once the heat settles down," a BJP leader said, underlining Sharma's "deep connections" within the party and the Sangh parivar at large.' See 'After suspension from BJP, Nupur Sharma withdraws statement', *The Telegraph*, 6 June 2022, https://www.telegraphindia.com/india/after-being-suspended-nupur-sharma-withdraws-controversial-statement/cid/1868517
3. See '"Muslims Should Be Set Ablaze Just as Hindus Burn Ravana Effigies on Dussehra": BJP MLA', *The Wire*, 8 May 2022, https://thewire.in/communalism/muslims-should-be-set-ablaze-just-as-hindus-burn-ravana-effigies-on-dussehra-bjp-mla
4. Bulldozer is an idol among the followers of the RSS. For example 'With Khargone, Shivraj Singh Chouhan Drives Home Dream of 'Bulldozer Justice"', *The Wire*, 12 April 2022, https://thewire.in/government/khargone-ram-navami-violence-bulldozer
5. It is such a symbol as Americans in New Jersey discovered, Tracey Tully, 'An Anti-Muslim Symbol From India Is Paraded on Main Street, New Jersey', *New York Times*, 25 September 2022, https://www.nytimes.com/2022/09/25/nyregion/bulldozer-indian-parade-new-jersey.html
6. See the translation of Dwivedi's interview to *Le Monde*, https://www.lemonde.fr/international/article/2022/02/11/divya-dwivedi-en-inde-les-minorites-religieuses-sont-persecutees-pour-cacher-que-la-veritable-majorite-ce-sont-les-castes-inferieures_6113301_3210.html
7. Kshatriya are the warrior caste group.
8. See 'Anti-fascism is a crime in India' in this anthology. Also 'Sauver l'Inde du nationalisme', *Libération*, 7 January 2020, https://www.liberation.fr/debats/2020/01/07/sauver-l-inde-du-nationalisme_1771899/

9. See Divya Dwivedi: 'En Inde, les minorités religieuses sont persécutées pour cacher que la véritable majorité, ce sont les castes inférieures' in this anthology. Also, Hannah Ellis-Petersen, '"Shoot them": Indian state police accused of murdering Muslims and Dalits', *The Guardian*, 22 February 2022, https://www.theguardian.com/global-development/2022/feb/22/uttar-pradesh-elections-hindu-nationalist-yogi-adityanath-police-accused-unlawful-deaths-muslims-dalits

7. WHO GETS TO KILL WHOM IN THE UNION OF INDIA?

1. In 1984, following the assassination of the Indian prime minister Indira Gandhi, a pogrom ensued killing thousands of Sikh religious followers. It was not a spontaneous event as investigators found later. It was led by the members of the Congress party at that time, which fell into the leadership of Rajiv Gandhi. An enquiry found that 'at some places the RSS people did play a role'. See https://thewire.in/diplomacy/rajnath-called-1984-killings-genocide-now-mea-objects-canada and also https://scroll.in/article/766550/rss-was-silent-during-the-1984-riots-at-places-it-was-implicated-in-the-violence The Sikh politician from the state of Punjab asserted that RSS men were guilty of the crimes against Sikhs in the 1984 pogrom. See 'Amarinder names BJP, RSS leaders involved in 1984 riots', https://www.dailypioneer.com/2014/state-editions/amarinder-names-bjp-rss-leaders-involved-in-1984-riots.html
2. In 1989, an anti Muslim pogrom took place in the North Indian state of Bihar. 'Official sources put the death toll at around 1,000. Others sources say nearly 2,000 were killed. According to the PUDR report, 93% of the dead were Muslim.' See https://scroll.in/article/747650/the-forgotten-riot-how-bhagalpur-1989-left-a-memory-trace-in-bihar-politics
3. Refers to the anti-Muslim pogrom in December 1992 in Bombay which was led by the 'Hindu' organisations, especially the Shiv Sena. The leader of the organisation was Bal Thackeray, a former cartoonist. 'Bal Thackeray died in November 2012—nearly 20 years after the violence. He was accorded a state funeral. The Indian national flag draped his corpse.' See https://scroll.in/article/745603/to-understand-why-thousands-attended-yakubs-funeral-you-have-to-recall-the-bombay-riots
4. Refers to the anti-Muslim pogrom in the state of Gujarat which was then under the leadership of Modi. It is through this event that Modi

ascended to national and international importance. See 'Narendra Modi "allowed" Gujarat 2002 anti-Muslim riots', *BBC*, 22 April 2011, https://www.bbc.com/news/world-south-asia-13170914 Also consult the 2023 BBC documentary, banned in India by Modi, *India: The Modi Question*, https://www.bbc.co.uk/iplayer/episode/p0dkb2kx/india-the-modi-question-series-1-episode-2

5. These pogroms against Christians were led by the subsidiary organisations of the upper caste supremacist organisation RSS. See 'Three pogroms held together by a common thread' https://www.thehindu.com/opinion/op-ed/Three-pogroms-held-together-by-a-common-thread/article15901626.ece
6. Refers to the provocative actions of the most widely recognised Bollywood film star Amitabh Bachchan during the anti-Sikh pogrom of 1984. In recent years, Bachchan had been proximate to Modi. See '1984 riots: "Why nobody noticed Amitabh Bachchan spewing venom in India"', *Times of India*, 21 October 2011, https://timesofindia.indiatimes.com/india/1984-riots-Why-nobody-noticed-Amitabh-Bachchan-spewing-venom-in-India/articleshow/10429011.cms
7. The anti-Muslim pogrom in Gujarat took place in 2002. Since Modi came to power at the centre as the prime minister all discussions and protests about the events known as 2002 became 'restricted'. The most recent episode is the judicial summons issued to the BBC by an Indian court for airing a documentary on the 2002 pogrom accusing Modi of culpability on the basis of a UK government report. See 'BBC gets India court summons in defamation case over Modi film', *Al Jazeera*, 22 May 2023, https://www.aljazeera.com/news/2023/5/22/bbc-gets-india-court-summons-in-defamation-case-over-modi-film
8. A mocking remark on the idea of 'mother India' projected by the RSS, because many upper caste leaders of the BJP believe that the place of a woman is home. See 'Do We Need to Rethink the Idea of the Bharat "Mata"?', *The Wire*, 8 March 2023, https://thewire.in/women/bharat-mata-india-women-respect-safety-discrimination
9. The Modi government has criminalised the consumption of beef in most states of India. It is a strategy aimed at hurting the physical and economic well being of Muslims and Dalits. For many lower caste people it is an easily available source of nutrition and the leather trade provides regular source of income. See 'Indian beef ban hits "untouchable" Dalits hardest', *World Watch Monitor*, https://www.worldwatchmonitor.org/2015/03/indian-beef-ban-hits-untouchable-dalits-hardest/

10. Dwivedi and Mohan are mocking the RSS and the BJP for their unfamiliarity with the 'epics' of India such as 'Mahabharata' and 'Ramayana'. They suggest that the RSS knows only the televised tales derivative of these old texts. The 'Rama temple movement' and the eventual destruction of the Babri mosque were prepared through the television series 'Ramayana'. See 'Ramanand Sagar's "Ramayan" Has Once Again Helped Televise BJP's Ram Revolution', *The Wire*, 24 May 2020, https://thewire.in/politics/ramayan-bjp-hindutva
11. In 2017, during an election campaign in the state of Uttar Pradesh, Modi made the the opposition between burial grounds for Muslims and cremation ground for 'Hindus' the central question. See 'If a kabristan can be constructed, a shamshaan too should be built: PM Modi', *Hindustan Times*, 20 February 2017, https://www.hindustantimes.com/assembly-elections/if-a-kabristan-can-be-constructed-so-should-a-shamshaan-pm-modi/story-obPfbdpUwPZm98wBKdZmTN.html
12. The common practice amongst many 'liberal' centrist political commentators is to dismiss the importance of vitriolic statements and hate speeches of the upper caste supremacist organisations such as the RSS and the BJP.
13. In 2016, a Muslim trader Akhlaq was lynched to death by 'cow vigilantes' controlled often by the RSS. Soon the police seized the meat from his refrigerator instead of investigating his murder. See 'Dadri lynching: Meat sample changed before test, says Akhlaq's son', *Indian Express*, 27 July 2016, https://indianexpress.com/article/india/india-news-india/dadri-lynching-meat-sample-changed-before-test-says-akhlaqs-son-2937851/
14. When the Dalit scholar Rohith Vemula committed suicide due to caste oppression at his university, the government investigated the caste records of Vemula's family, instead of investigating the circumstances of his suicide and apprehending the culprits. See 'The Law is Clear: Radhika Vemula and Her Children Are Dalits', *The Wire*, 18 February 2017, https://thewire.in/law/legal-precedent-establishes-radhika-vemula-and-her-children-are-dalits
15. Even before Modi became the prime minister of the Indian Union in May 2014, many news networks already began to campaign aggressively for him. Today the control of the media by the RSS and the BJP is nearly absolute. For a recent account read 'Modi's Final Assault on India's Press Freedom Has Begun', *New York Times*, 8 March 2023, https://www.nytimes.com/2023/03/08/opinion/india-kashmir-modi-media-censorship.html

16. Pierre Clastres is an important influence on the works of Dwivedi and Mohan, while they maintain a subtle critical distance from him. See the appended dictionary entry 'Regularity' and *Gandhi and Philosophy* for more.
17. Dwivedi and Mohan are often described as 'leftists', however they are critical of nearly all the political parties in India, who they interpret as the perpetrators of upper caste dominance over the society. See 'Over four decades on, the Marichjhapi massacre needs more attention', *Indian Express*, 18 February 2023, https://indianexpress.com/article/opinion/over-four-decades-on-the-marichjhapi-massacre-needs-more-attention-8453100/#
18. The Supreme Court of India has since allowed the construction of a Rama temple at the site where the Babri mosque stood. The perpetrators of the crime of the demolition of the mosque were never punished.
19. In imitation of the Nazi campaigns against the Jewish people, the upper caste supremacist organisations of India (also known as Hindu nationalists) have created the hoax that Muslim men seduce 'Hindu'girls and convert them to Islam. The judiciary in India has denied the existence of such a 'love jihad'. Dwivedi and Mohan have said time and again that these campaigns have two goals, to prevent the liberation of the lower caste majorities through religious conversion, and to control the sexuality of women. See '"Love jihad": War on romance in India', *Al Jazeera*, 14 October 2014, https://www.aljazeera.com/features/2014/10/14/love-jihad-war-on-romance-in-india/
20. The meaning of 'life' as a life in politics, and politics as the fight for freedom animates many of the texts of Dwivedi and Mohan, including their popular interventions, often against Giorgio Agamben, in the pandemic debates. See *Coronavirus, Psychoanalysis, and Philosophy*, edited by F. Castrillón, T. Marchevsky, London: Routledge, 2021.

8. COURAGE TO BEGIN

1. 'Philosopher en Inde', available as podcast, https://www.radiofrance.fr/franceculture/podcasts/les-chemins-de-la-philosophie/philosopher-en-inde-3220645
2. Hindu nationalism and why 'being a philosopher in India can get you killed', Mediapart, 27 May 2018, https://www.mediapart.fr/en/journal/international/270518/hindu-nationalism-and-why-being-philosopher-india-can-get-you-killed

3. Mohan's philosophical works have been reclaiming reason while also introducing radical changes to reason, and the principle of reason. The basis of this reconception is the rejection of classical laws of thought to enable reason to be the power or faculty to think, examine and experience that which comes without any plan or familiarity, 'Reason is the power to be free; politics is the training through the categories of the public and the private to be the obscure animal. The sense we might get in Kant's clarification of man into the obscure animal is of a being subject to no plan, but, in fact, it is characterized by a preparedness for any plan', Shaj Mohan, 'On the Relation Between the Obscure, the Cryptic and the Public', *Public Sphere from Outside the West*, London: Bloomsbury Philosophy, 2015. Consult also the interview available online '"But, there is nothing outside of philosophy": Conversation between Shaj Mohan and Rachel Adams', *Episteme*, https://positionspolitics.org/conversation-between-shaj-mohan-and-rachel-adams/
4. The concept of 'stasis' is derived by Dwivedi and Mohan as one of the names of 'evil', from Ancient Greek political thought. In the Greek state, as they show 'stasis referred to a specific situation in the polis where two or more groups of men either claim or seek control over the creation of laws which would order the life of the city' (*Gandhi and Philosophy*, p. 216). However, it is also an abstract concept describing any system of components, as in a component of a system seeking to be the law which guides the system of several components. For example, the RSS which represents the upper caste interests seeking to determine legislation is stasis. For this reason Dwivedi would say that caste order is the stasis of the subcontinent. See also the appendix entry on 'stasis'.
5. Chimera for Dwivedi and Mohan are any arrangement of components which do not form a system or where the components cannot have regular relations with each other, or where they do not have a comprehending law, as with anomia. Chimera is a situation of evil.
6. Dwivedi and Mohan argue in other texts that India is not yet independent and the so called Indian independence movement was really a transfer of power movement which resulted in the British elites transferring the power to rule under modern conditions to the upper caste elites of India. The real independence, they argue, will be when the oppressive caste system is destroyed.
7. See appendix entry on 'calypsology'.
8. See the article 'Hidden by Hindu' in this anthology for a more detailed discussion.

9. Through criticisms the article suddenly arrives at a moment of admiration for M. K. Gandhi. This passage shows the complex and critical relation Dwivedi and Mohan maintain to all 'traditions' of philosophy and to the important thinkers, which is explainable in terms of their system. This relationship extends in Mohan's works to Aristotle, Duns Scotus, Leibniz and Gilbert Simondon among others; for Dwivedi it is Plato, St Augustine, Hölderlin, Fichte, and Roman Jakobson; and for both it is with Kant, Heidegger, Derrida, and Wittgenstein.

9. ASSEMBLIES OF FREEDOM

1. 'Two Years Later, Delhi Police Plans Reward to Identify Cops Who 'Assaulted, Forced Muslims to Sing', *The Wire*, 20 June 2022, https://www.thequint.com/news/india/bhima-koregaon-violence-sambhaji-bhide-milind-ekbote-hindutva-leaders, https://thewire.in/government/delhi-riots-2020-crime-branch-reward-to-identify-police-faizan-anthem.
2. 'Nuh Villages Live in Fear after Nocturnal Raids and Mass Arrests of Muslim Youth', *The Caravan*, 13 August 2023, https://caravanmagazine.in/crime/nuh-haryana-bajrang-dal-communal-violence-arrest-muslim-youth; https://thewire.in/communalism/nuh-mosques-arson-internet-remains-suspended; 'Christians Attacked and Bible Torn in Church Attack in Delhi During Sunday Service', *The Wire*, 21 August 2023, https://thewire.in/communalism/christians-attacked-in-delhi-church-during-sunday-service.
3. 'Profile: The Vishwa Hindu Parishad', *BBC*, 7 March 2002, http://news.bbc.co.uk/2/hi/south_asia/1860202.stm
4. 'Reality Belies Modi Govt Claims of Implementing Swaminathan Commission's Report', *The Wire*, 27 December 2020, https://thewire.in/government/reality-belies-modi-government-implementing-swaminathan-commission-recommendations.
5. 'PM Modi should express grief in Parliament over death of 750 farmers during protests: Rakesh Tikait', *New Indian Express*, 9 October 2021, https://www.newindianexpress.com/nation/2021/oct/09/pm-modi-should-express-grief-in-parliament-over-death-of-750-farmers-during-protests-rakesh-tikait-2369732.html.
6. 'Wrestlers' Protest: Jat BJP Leader Says Party Will Suffer Politically if Issue Is Dragged', *The Wire*, 4 June 2023, https://thewire.in/politics/wrestlers-protest-jat-bjp-chaudhary-birender-singh; 'Why

is a BJP minister blaming the VHP for the Nuh violence?', *Scroll*, 3 August 2023, https://scroll.in/article/1053711/how-the-nuh-communal-violence-may-impact-electoral-politics-in-haryana.

7. 'BJP leaders face boycott in Haryana over Samrat Mihir Bhoj statue controversy', *The Hindu*, 23 July 2023, https://www.thehindu.com/news/national/other-states/bjp-leaders-face-boycott-in-haryana-over-samrat-mihir-bhoj-statue-controversy/article67113089.ece.
8. See the Scroll article in note. 6 above.
9. https://documents-dds-ny.un.org/doc/UNDOC/GEN/G20/232/15/PDF/G2023215.pdf?OpenElement.
10. https://www.un.org/sites/un2.un.org/files/2021/03/udhr.pdf.
11. https://districts.ecourts.gov.in/sites/default/files/fctwrkshop.pdf.
12. 'Under new Bill, marrying woman by concealing identity will invite 10 years jail', *Hindustan Times*, 12 August 2023, https://www.hindustantimes.com/india-news/under-new-bill-marrying-woman-by-concealing-identity-will-invite-10-years-jail-101691808075638-amp.html.
13. 'Why are the twenty-two vows necessary for neo-Buddhists?', *Counter Currents*, 12 October 2022, https://countercurrents.org/2022/10/why-are-the-twenty-two-vows-necessary-for-neo-buddhists/.
14. See Dwivedi, Mohan and Reghu, 'The Hindu Hoax'.
15. Sagar, 'Scriptural Economy', *The Caravan*, 23 July 2020, https://caravanmagazine.in/politics/narendra-modi-atmanirbhar-bharat-rss-hindu-economics-rashtra.
16. 'BJP slams AAP over conversion "oath", minister hits back at "propaganda"', *Hindustan Times*, 8 October 2022, https://www.hindustantimes.com/cities/delhi-news/bjp-slams-aap-over-conversion-oath-minister-hits-back-at-propaganda-101665167118302.html.
17. 'Amid row over mass conversion, AAP Minister Gautam apologises', *The Hindu*, 8 October 2022, https://www.thehindu.com/news/cities/Delhi/amid-row-over-mass-conversion-aap-minister-gautam-apologises/article65982444.ece; see also note 16 above.
18. https://archive.org/details/encyclopediaofmo0000atki/page/264/mode/2up?q=RSS+1947+banned&view=theater
19. '"Inching Closer to a Police State": We20 Summit Organisers After Police Refuses Permission on Day 3', *The Wire*, 20 August 2023, https://thewire.in/rights/inching-closer-to-a-police-state-we20-summit-organisers-after-police-refuses-permission-on-day-3.
20. 'People and Nature over Profits for a Just, Inclusive, Transparent and Equitable Future', *Working Group on IFIs*, 20 August 2023, https://

wgonifis.net/2023/08/20/people-and-nature-over-profits-for-a-just-inclusive-transparent-and-equitable-future/.

21. 'PM's Rural Development Fellows Come Out in Support of Mahesh Raut', *The Wire*, 9 June 2018, https://thewire.in/rights/pms-rural-development-fellows-come-out-in-support-of-mahesh-raut.
22. See various reportages on this: https://caravanmagazine.in/law/did-pune-police-tamper-evidence-against-bhima-koregaon-accused; https://www.wired.com/story/modified-elephant-planted-evidence-hacking-police/; https://thewire.in/tech/security-researchers-claim-link-between-pune-police-and-hacking-campaign-against-bhima-koreagon-accused; https://caravanmagazine.in/politics/many-plots-to-assassinate-narendra-modi.
23. See the chapter 26 in this anthology.
24. 'Violence in Maharashtra as Dalits protest death of 28-year-old in Bhima Koregaon clashes, bandh called in state', *Hindustan Times*, 2 January 2018, https://www.hindustantimes.com/india-news/violence-in-maharashtra-as-dalits-protest-death-of-28-year-old-in-bhima-koregaon-clashes/story-zerVWqrSjLjF2x53oHMVXL.html.
25. See 'The Hindu Hoax'.
26. 'Former Delhi Police Officer Who Let Kapil Mishra Make Fiery Speech before Delhi Riots Seeks Medal', *The Wire*, 3 July 2021, https://thewire.in/government/former-delhi-police-officer-who-let-kapil-mishra-make-fiery-speech-before-delhi-riots-seeks-medal.
27. 'Freedom of speech the 'bulwark' of democracy: Why the Andhra HC struck down order seeking to regulate public assemblies, processions', *Indian Express*, 20 May 2023, https://indianexpress.com/article/explained/explained-law/andhra-hc-government-order-struck-down-processions-8616123/.
28. See chapter 29 in this anthology.
29. 'Activists' Arrests: Supreme Court Rejects Review Petition Filed by Romila Thapar and Others', *The Wire*, 27 October 2018, https://thewire.in/rights/activists-arrests-supreme-court-rejects-review-petition-filed-by-romila-thapar-and-others.

10. LOOMING OBJECTS AND THE ANCESTRAL MODEL OF HISTORIOGRAPHY

1. Heinrich Wölfflin, *Principles of Art History*, translation by Jonathan Blower, Los Angeles, Getty Research Institute, p. 97.
2. Concepts refer to components and componential relations. The objective field of historiography of a region, depending on the

interests and the investments in a particular historiography, may include or exclude some components or componential relations.

3. That which prehends, seizes, and through the seizure sets ranges and limits.
4. See the extensive discussion in Shaj Mohan, 'Teleography and Tendencies: Part 2 History and Anastasis,' *Philosophy World Democracy*, vol 3. no. 4 (April 2022), https://www.philosophy-world-democracy.org/articles-1/teleography-and-tendencies-part-2-history-and-anastasis.
5. Richard Woodman, *The History of the Ship*, London: Conway Maritime Press, 1997, p. 6.
6. See Divya Dwivedi, 'The Evasive Racism of Caste—and the Homological Power of the "Aryan" Doctrine'.
7. Bush said, 'God would tell me, 'George go and fight these terrorists in Afghanistan'. And I did. And then God would tell me 'George, go and end the tyranny in Iraq', 'George Bush: "God told me to end the tyranny in Iraq"', *The Guardian*, 7 October 2005, https://www.theguardian.com/world/2005/oct/07/iraq.usa And I did.' See, Shaj Mohan, 'Teleography and Tendencies: Part 1 Ukraine', *Philosophy World Democracy,* vol. 3, no. 2 (March 2022), https://www.philosophy-world-democracy.org/articles-1/teleography-and-tendencies-part-1-ukraine and 'Teleography and Tendencies: Part 2 History and Anastasis'.
8. See Maël Montévil, 'Remarques sur les corps', in *Jean-Luc Nancy: Anastasis de la pensée*, edited by Divya Dwivedi, Jérôme Lèbre and François Warin, Paris: Ed. Hermann, 2023.
9. Author's note: The term 'myth' requires a longer explanation in this situation, which cannot be attempted in this short text. But it should be noted that the knowledge of the 'ancient Greeks' and 'Ancient Greek knowledge' arrived in Europe through Arabic texts and scholars, and that in many parts of what is Europe today Arabic or its versions were spoken.
10. Wilhelm Worringer, *Abstraction and Empathy*, Ivan R. Dee, Chicago: Inc Publisher, 1997, p. 135.
11. Aristotle, *Politics*, Book VII, 35.
12. A minor incident of this moment is of an American citizen of Indian origin attempting to attack the presidential residence in America, carrying a Nazi flag. See https://www.aljazeera.com/news/2023/5/23/man-arrested-after-crashing-truck-into-barrier-near-white-house
13. See Philippe Lacour-Labarthe and Jean-Luc Nancy, 'The Nazi Myth.' *Critical Inquiry*, vol. 16, no. 2 (1990): 291–312.

14. See Dwivedi, 'The Evasive Racism of Caste—and the Homological Power of the "Aryan" Doctrine.'
15. See Shaj Mohan, 'And the Beginning of Philosophy', *Philosophy World Democracy*, vol. 2 no. 7 (July 2021), https://www.philosophy-world-democracy.org/other-beginning/and-the-beginning-of-philosophy ; and Divya Dwivedi, 'Nancy's Wager', *Philosophy World Democracy*, vol. 2 no. 7 (July 2021), https://www.philosophy-world-democracy.org/other-beginning/nancys-wager
16. Each carrying their homologies of other protests and other dreams of freedom; see Divya Dwivedi, 'May 1968 and Other Dates in the Memories of Imagination' *Interventions*, vol. 23, no. 3 (2021): 379-398.

11. DEMOCRACY AND REVOLUTION

1. Literally 'cremation grounds or burial grounds', but it was given as a choice by Modi to the electorate who were expected to decide whether 'Hindu' interests (cremation) should come first or that of the Muslims (burial). It is without doubt a disturbing indication of thanato-philia in the politics of upper caste supremacism.
2. Elsewhere Mohan has extended this use of the concept of *telos*, 'Telos is not merely an end, as in the goal of an action; it is the limit of the abilities to tolerate or bear changes and responsibilities, and to give reasons [...] When telos is exchanged for eschaton, we surrender our anticipations and ourselves to the orders of survival which are unforgiving to politics which is desirous of freedom; that is, all discourses of anti-politics posit a certain destruction, an eschatology, while politics is the games of the anticipations of freedoms'. See Shaj Mohan, 'What Comes Next: Auguries', *Global Cooperation Research, Käte Hamburger Kolleg—A Quarterly Magazine*, 2/2023, https://www.gcr21.org/publications/gcr/gcr-quarterly-magazine/global-cooperation-research-2-/-2023/qm-2/2023-articles/qm-2-2023-mohan-what-comes-next-auguries
3. See the glossary on 'hypophysics'.
4. Jean-Luc Nancy, *The Truth of Democracy*, translation by Pascale-Anne Brault and Michael Naas, Fordham University Press, 2010, p. 32.
5. See the glossary on 'Anastasis'.

12. THE FUTILITY OF "RESISTANCE", THE NECESSITY OF REVOLUTION

1. A reference to George Orwell's *Animal Farm*.

2. Ludwig Wittgenstein, *Culture and Value*, translated by Peter Winch, Chicago: University of Chicago Press, 1984.

13. FROM PROTESTING THE CAA TO EMBRACING THE DALIT-BAHUJAN POSITION ON CITIZENSHIP

1. Authors' note: Upper caste supremacism, which projects itself as 'Hindu nationalism' or 'Hindu majoritarianism', claims that the upper castes sprung from the soil, and for that reason it also rejects evolutionary theory, and the fact that humanity emerged from Africa and populated the world. The listed populations are among the people who entered the Indian subcontinent from elsewhere. In India, the oldest inhabitants are called 'adivasi', which literally means original inhabitants. The RSS has been demoting and denigrating them by renaming the 'adivasi' as 'vanavasi' or the forest dwellers. There are other population groups who were living in the subcontinent before the arrival of 'Arya' populations with their rituals which are the basis of upper caste religious practices even today. Those older populations include the Dravidian and the Munda.
2. This sentence refers to several far right and liberal upper caste intellectuals and academics who mocked the students who were protesting.
3. See the report 'Workers Building Mass Camp for Undocumented Immigrants Fear They May Be Detained There', *The Wire*, 9 September 2019, https://thewire.in/rights/workers-building-mass-camp-for-undocumented-immigrants-fear-they-may-be-detained-there
4. The criticism of both subaltern and postcolonial theories of historiography is present in other texts in this anthology. Dwivedi and Mohan have each articulated the different facets of these schools. The common thread in their critical remarks is a fact, it is an upper caste supremacist theoretical formation which seeks to restore the pride those groups lost during colonial interruptions. I quote Mohan at length here, 'The de-postcolonial theory is constructed out of the resources and the political intention of the auto-critique which appeared in philosophy in the twentieth century and which examined the fundamental concepts of metaphysics, politics, and history critically. Heidegger, Adorno, Derrida, Foucault and many others participated in this critical praxis. The lesson taken from it by postcolonial theory, especially the Indian kind, suppressed the auto-critique and used the concepts and insights as instruments to construct what is properly a geo-political discourse of which the Nazi

style organisation RSS and its prime minister Modi are beneficiaries. That is, postcolonial theory of the Indian kind masks the fact of auto-critique to create an accusatory discourse which prohibits the critique of upper caste theories. Therefore, it is not a "theory", whatever it means, and certainly not an adequate theory of the epoch of colonialism.' Interview with Shaj Mohan by Rachel Adams, '"I take, and I am taken, by what belongs to philosophy": Philosophy and the redemption of democracy', *South African Journal of Science*, vol.118, spe 2 Pretoria (2022) http://dx.doi.org/10.17159/sajs.2022/15000

5. Chandrashekhar Azad Ravan is a Dalit politician, lawyer, and activist. He is the founder of the organisation Bhim Army. Azad was arrested several times, detained, or kept under house arrest.
6. Hartosh Singh Bal is a mathematician, novelist and editor of *The Caravan*. Bal's name and texts return frequently in the discourse of Dwivedi and Mohan. Bal is an anti-caste intellectual who was one of the earliest from his generation to publicly oppose the false distinction between 'Hinduism vs Hindutva', and 'Hindu vs Muslim' as the problematic of Indian politics. Instead, Bal writes in opposition to all political parties which are slyly upper caste supremacist.
7. *Dalit Camera* and *Round Table India* are among the prominent lower caste publications in contemporary India. They also reflect a reality that it is nearly impossible for the lower caste majority to publish in the national media of India which are owned by upper castes.
8. In 1818, a mostly lower caste army defeated the Brahmin kingdom in the Maratha region. It is experienced as a great shame by Brahmin leaders and the RSS even today, which also holds the possibility that in the future Brahmin dominance over society may come to an end. In 2018, more than hundred thousand lower caste activists gathered to commemorate the events and they were attacked by an upper caste mob with the help of the police. The celebratory march was preceded by an event called 'Elgar parishad'. Many who took part in both events were arrested using the draconian anti-terrorism laws including Varavara Rao, Arun Ferreira, Sudha Bharadwaj, Father Stan Swami and Gautam Navlakha. Father Stan Swami died in prison. Many are still languishing in the prisons. This event shows clearly that upper caste supremacism fears only the organisation and democratic agitations of the lower caste majority. See 'The Compassionate Revolution of Saint Stan Swami' in this anthology.

14. THE CURRENT PROTESTS IN INDIA ARE A TRAINING GROUND FOR A BREAK WITH THE PAST

1. Partha Chatterjee is an Indian historian of the postcolonial subaltern school and has refrained from acknowledging the lower caste majority position in politics and historiography. The article mentioned here is 'True Federalism Is the Counter-Narrative India Needs Right Now', *The Wire*, 18 January 2020, https://thewire.in/politics/india-federalism-protests
2. For the meaning of the 'historian's eye' See Mohan, 'Telecgraphy and Tendencies: History and Anastasis'.
3. Dwivedi has addressed the events of 1967 in India known as Naxal Bari movement and May '68. See Dwivedi, 'May 1968 and Other Dates in the Memories of Imagination'.
4. Jean-Luc Nancy, *The Truth of Democracy*, translated by Pascale-Anne Brault and Michael Naas, New York: Fordham University Press, 2010.
5. This is in reference to the hoax of an anti-corruption movement produced by the RSS and led by Arvind Kejriwal who became the chief minister of Delhi after defeating the Congress party. In several texts Dwivedi and Mohan have argued that these events have had a character of something like a 'regime change'.
6. It is also in reference to the previous chapter 'From Protesting the CAA to Embracing the Dalit-Bahujan Position on Citizenship'.
7. Ambedkar-Periyar Study Circle in IIT-Madras was a courageous development. It created a group which could freely study the logic, the reality and the evil of caste oppression. They were banned in 2015. The circle inspired a movement across Indian campuses where the lower caste majority students created their versions of the movement, and it continues. It was brought to a temporary arrest through the upper caste controlled events known as JNU protests where upper caste students and faculty created a new false opposition between good nationalism and bad nationalism. Dwivedi and Mohan have remarked on it in several texts, especially in the chapter 'Sex and Postcolonial Family Values' in this anthology. Dr B. R. Ambedkar is a Dalit intellectual giant, an economist, political philosopher, and the architect of India's secular constitution. Erode Venkatappa Ramasamy or Periyar was an anti-caste intellectual and activist from the state of Tamil Nadu. In the 1920s, Periyar created the Dravidian movement which was opposed to the North Indian 'Aryan' upper caste movements which had by then acquired the religious respectability of 'Hindu'.

8. It was a movement by girls in colleges and universities seeking more freedom. However, as with many such movements, the lower caste majority students were marginalised by the upper caste leadership. See 'Statement: Why we decided to leave Pinjra Tod', *Round Table India*, 19 February 2019, https://www.roundtableindia.co.in/statement-why-we-decided-to-leave-pinjra-tod/
9. Apter's text makes references to Dwivedi and Mohan's 'Hoax of the Cave', in this anthology. See 'Alphabetic Memes: Caricature, Satire, and Political literacy in the Age of Trump', *OCTOBER* 170, Fall 2019, pp. 5–24, https://doi.org/10.1162/octo_a_00366
10. Several political organisations tried to appropriate or to subvert the anti-CAA protests for their own ends. For example, one of the former leaders of the Congress party demanded that the movement almost surrender to the Congress. See 'States Can't Say "Won't Follow Law Passed By Parliament": Kapil Sibal', *NDTV*, 19 January 2020, https://www.ndtv.com/india-news/citizenship-amendment-act-nrc-congress-kapil-sibal-says-states-cant-say-wont-follow-law-passed-by-pa-2166230
11. A highly influential lower caste intellectual, writer, activist, and organiser from the state of Kerala who took an oppositional stance to the transfer of power movement and to the invention of Hindu religion.
12. The alliance took an anti-caste position that 'the controversial enumeration of citizens may impact Dalits, Adivasis, and OBCs as much as Muslims', *The Wire*, 16 January 2020, https://thewire.in/rights/caa-nrc-dalits-adivasis-obcs
13. This argument was made by Hartosh Singh Bal, and the authors provided a link to the article by Bal. See Hartosh Singh Bal, 'Herding The Hindutva Flock', *The Caravan*, 15 August 2019, https://caravanmagazine.in/politics/for-modi-rss-kashmir-is-tool-consolidate-hold-over-twice-born-castes
14. The reference is not to the novel 'Ignorance' by Kundera, but to an earlier work of non-fiction, 'Testaments Betrayed'.
15. The reference to the hoax of anti-corruption movement suggesting that the then Congress led government could not counter an organised hoax to destabilise it. See Parveen Dhonthi, 'How Ties With The Think Tanks Vivekananda International Foundation and India Foundation Enhance Ajit Doval's Influence', *The Caravan*, 5 November 2017, https://caravanmagazine.in/vantage/vivekananda-international-india-foundation-ajit-doval-influence
16. The RSS and the Modi-led government could destroy the movement through infiltration, sabotage, fake news, and eventually what became

the Delhi pogrom against Muslims which took several lives. The pogrom began on 23 February 2020, with the support of the police force, and since then many of the victims have been charged with serious crimes by the police. Importantly, this pogrom took place when the then American president Trump was on his state visit to India. Trump did not speak a word against it and instead praised Modi for his 'democratic leadership'. See 'Why the 2020 violence in Delhi was a pogrom', *Al Jazeera*, 24 February 2021, https://www.aljazeera.com/opinions/2021/2/24/why-the-2020-violence-in-delhi-was-a-pogrom

17. Author's note: See Pritam Singh, 'Hindu Bias in India's 'Secular' Constitution: probing flaws in the instruments of governance', *Third World Quarterly*, vol. 26, no. 6 (2005): 909-926
18. Author's note: See Alok Rai, *Hindi Nationalism*, Hyderabad: Orient Blackswan, 2001.

15. THE OBSCENITY OF TRUTH: ARREST THE ANTI-FASCIST!

1. See, 'Elgaar Parishad probe: Those held part of anti-fascist plot to overthrow govt, Pune police tells court', *Indian Express*, 30 August 2018, https://indianexpress.com/article/india/elgaar-parishad-probe-those-held-part-of-anti-fascist-plot-to-overthrow-govt-pune-police-tells-court-5331832/
2. 'SC allows rights activists to remain under house arrest', 30 August 2018, *The Hindu*, https://www.thehindu.com/news/national/sc-allows-rights-activists-to-remain-under-house-arrest/article24813876.ece
3. For a note on The Caste Disabilities Removal Act, 1850, see *India Kanoon*, https://indiankanoon.org/doc/466892/
4. See 'Hidden by Hindu' in the same anthology for a detailed account.
5. Unbelievable as it may seem, this is only the surface of present day Indian regime's relation to the Nazis. For an account see 'In Modi's Gujarat Hitler is a Text Book Hero', *The Times of India*, 30 September 2004, https://timesofindia.indiatimes.com/india/In-Modis-Gujarat-Hitler-is-a-textbook-hero/articleshow/868469.cms For a more detailed account please consult Divya Dwivedi edited special issue of the Unesco journal, Review of Women Philosophers.
6. For a deeper understanding of the relation between the 'Aryan doctrine', upper caste supremacism in India, and neo-Nazi movements around the world see Divya Dwivedi, 'The Evasive Racism of Caste—and the Homological Power of the 'Aryan' Doctrine'.

7. Megan Clark, 'Ten Years Later, Indians Remember Worst Violence Against Christians', *Religion Unplugged*, 31 August 2018, https://religionunplugged.com/news/2018/8/31/ten-years-later-indians-remember-worst-violence-against-christians
8. 'Uttar Pradesh Police admit youth was lynched', *The Hindu*, 30 August 2018, https://www.thehindu.com/news/national/other-states/uttar-pradesh-police-admit-youth-was-lynched/article24823061.ece
9. See 'India's caste system: 'They are trying to erase dalit history. This is a martyrdom, a sacrifice'', *The Guardian*, 24 January 2016, https://www.theguardian.com/world/2016/jan/24/student-suicide-untouchables-stuggle-for-justice-india
10. Mr Ravan was eventually released. For a report on the arrest, see 'Bhim Army chief Chandrashekhar, accused in Saharanpur violence, arrested by UP STF in Dalhousie', *Indian Express*, 8 June 2017, https://indianexpress.com/article/india/bhim-army-founder-chandrashekhar-arrested-up-stf-in-dalhousie-4694312/

17. THE TERROR THAT IS MAN

1. This was Narendra Modi's remark when asked about having any regrets about the mass killings which took place in the state of Gujarat in 2002 within his administrative responsibility and the provocative actions led by him. See 'India's Narendra Modi lets politics go to the dogs', *Washington Post*, 12 July 2013, https://www.washingtonpost.com/news/worldviews/wp/2013/07/12/indias-narendra-modi-lets-politics-go-to-the-dogs/
2. Hegel's statement does not refer to India directly however it could apply to India where political concept of freedom arrived rather late, and as the article shows it is a concept which remains at odds with the social order of caste. 'The Orientals have not attained the knowledge that Spirit-Man as such is free; and because they do not know this, they are not free. They know that one is free. But on this very account, the freedom of that one is only caprice; ferocity-brutal recklessness of passion, or a mildness and tameness of the desires, which is itself only an accident of Nature-mere caprice like the former. That one is therefore only a Despot; not a free man'. See G. W. F. Hegel, *Lectures on the Philosophy of World History*, Oxford: Oxford University Press, 2019.
3. The phenomenon of 'honour killings' refers to a wide range of social practices which are illegal, including the well known example of 'sati'

or 'widow burning'. When caste laws which enforce strict endogamy are broken people are killed even today in India, usually its victims are women. Further, 'the majority of the honour violence victims are members of Scheduled Caste communities' who are people belonging to the lowest castes of India. See https://thewire.in/caste/caste-honour-killings-cases-laws. The statistics about the killings are harder to come by due to the resistance to legislate against such practices in India, however the numbers are assumed to be staggeringly high. The Indian government did not recognise and record honour killings as a crime until 2014. 'India's Supreme Court recorded 288 honor killings in India between 2014 and 2016. However, Evidence, a non-government organization, found that between 2012 and 2017 there were 187 cases in the state of Tamil Nadu alone.' See also https://legalserviceindia.com/legal/article-8389-honor-killing-in-india-an-analysis-on-indian-statutes.html

4. Malankara Mar Thoma Syrian Church takes its name from the Aramaic 'Mar Thoma' meaning St. Thomas, the Apostle and it is older than the Catholic Church. The Syrian church practices strict caste discrimination against the lower caste Christians in India.
5. This remark implies an interpretation of computation as a technical implementation of Kurt Gödel's theorems on incompleteness. Gödel himself employed an abstract system of proof checking analogous to the computer in his theorems.

18. THE HOAX OF THE CAVE

1. See Shaj Mohan and Anish Mohammed, 'The New Secret', *Economic and Political Weekly*, vol. XLVI, no. 13 (16 March 2011): 13-15, https://archive.org/details/TheNewSecretVault7AndDNCLeaks
2. Emily Apter discussed the theoretical dimensions of this text in her article on memes. See note 9 of chapter 14 above.
3. The idol drinking milk turned out to be capillary action, that is, a fluid in a narrow tube forced to the top by the effects of surface tension. For a contemporary report see 'Hindu world divided by a 24-hour wonder', *The Independent*, UK, 22 September 1995, https://www.independent.co.uk/news/uk/hindu-world-divided-by-a-24hour-wonder-1602382.html
4. Hypophysics is a term used in passing by Kant which Dwivedi and Mohan developed into an analytical tool, in certain ways similar to Heidegger's use of 'metaphysics' to analyse history of philosophy. Hypophysics refers to the identification of a value with its nature. This

very concept has a relation to the concept of 'functional isolation'. See the glossary on 'hypophysics' and 'functional isolation'.

5. An online version of the text is available. Michel Foucault, 'Foucault' in *Dictionnaire des philosophes*, 1984, https://foucault.info/documents/foucault.biography/#:~:text=To%twentiethe%20extent%twentiethat%20Foucault,a%20Critical%20History%20of%twentiethought.
6. See Jawaharlal Nehru, 'We Want No Caesars: Nehru's Warning to Himself', *The Caravan*, 14 November 2016, https://caravanmagazine.in/vantage/want-no-caesars-nehrus-warning
7. See Max Weber, *Politics as a Vocation*, edited and translated by H. H. Gertha nd C. Wright Mills, New York: Oxford University Press, 1946.
8. This passage clearly refers to Modi. Modi said to a group of children that there was no climate change and that our sensitivity to the weather has increased due to our 'weakness'. See 'Teachers Day speech: PM Modi says no climate change', *India Today*, 5 September 2014, https://www.indiatoday.in/india/north/story/teachers-day-speech-pm-modi-says-no-climate-change-207413-2014-09-05
9. Modi actually said 'Now, this man had an idea. He took a small utensil, inverted it, made a hole in it and put a pipe through that. Gas used to emanate from the gutter and using that pipeline, he used the gas for his tea stall. An easy technique.' See '"Liquid Nala Gas": Twitter cracks up on Narendra Modi's comment about making tea from gutter fumes', *Scroll*, 14 August 2018, https://scroll.in/article/890416/liquid-nala-gas-twitter-cracks-up-on-narendra-modis-comment-about-making-tea-from-gutter-fumes
10. See 'Serial gaffes put Modi on back foot', *Hindustan Times*, 11 November 2013, https://www.hindustantimes.com/india/serial-gaffes-put-modi-on-back-foot/story-whYTpwSMzt2tnVaTVBWOFI.html
11. According to a later report, 'There is no subject known as "entire" political science or "entire" anything, as anyone with the minimal exposure to education would know. But the university has so far refrained from issuing either a corrigendum to or a revision of this case of seeming duplicity. And whenever there has been a move to get some clarity on the matter, Gujarat's courts have stonewalled it.', *The Wire*, 12 April 2023, https://thewire.in/government/narendra-modi-degree-entire-political-science
12. A report says 'The cloudy sky, Modi said, could be advantageous as the IAF planes would then escape detection by Pakistani radars. Modi also said he relied on his "raw wisdom" to dispel the doubts of the

experts.' See 'It was raining, was scared his plane would disappear: Rahul Gandhi takes jibe at PM Modi's cloud-radar theory', *India Today*, 17 May 2019, https://www.indiatoday.in/elections/lok-sabha-2019/story/it-was-raining-was-scared-his-plane-would-disappear-rahul-gandhi-takes-jibe-at-pm-modi-s-cloud-radar-theory-1527620-2019-05-17

13. Some of the hoaxes and pseudoscience peddled by the parent organisation of Modi, the RSS, includes the presence of stem cell technology, airplanes, mobile telephones, internet, and nuclear weapons in ancient India. For an account of some of these claims Meera Nanda, 'Saffronized Science: Rampant Pseudoscience in "Vedic Garb" in the Indian Subcontinent', *Social Epistemology Review and Reply Collective*, 2015, Vol. 5, Number 1, 39 - 47. See also, Sanjay Kumar, 'Hindu nationalists claim that ancient Indians had airplanes, stem cell technology, and the internet', *Science*, 13 February 2019, https://www.science.org/content/article/hindu-nationalists-claim-ancient-indians-had-airplanes-stem-cell-technology-and
14. Dwivedi and Mohan are alluding to the fact that the politicians and ministers, including Modi himself, are culpable for the crimes of the anti-Muslim pogrom of 2002 are walking free today. See for example, 'Naroda Patiya case: Gujarat ex-Minister Maya Kodnani walks free', *The Hindu*, 20 April 2018, https://www.thehindu.com/news/national/naroda-patiya-riots-case-maya-kodnani-acquitted/article23612196.ece
15. The assassinations and murders of Dalit activists are discussed in other texts in this collection. The reference is made to the decision of Modi to ban overnight a range of currency notes without any warnings to the people, which led to the collapse of rural economies and damaged the savings of the poor. Many died standing in the summer sun waiting to exchange these worthless notes of rupees. For an introduction, see 'Demonetisation drive that cost India 1.5m jobs fails to uncover "black money"', *The Guardian*, 30 August 2018, https://www.theguardian.com/world/2018/aug/30/india-demonetisation-drive-fails-uncover-black-money
16. While the article speaks of Modi as a 'large man', Modi himself projected that he was a body builder with a chest circumference of 56 inches, which is of course an embarrassing and obscene claim for any political leader to make. Many military experts have said that these boasts and hoaxes hide his inability to confront the threat of China along India's borders. See 'Military veterans slam Modi's "56-inch chest" boast, S Jaishankar's comment on China', *The Telegraph*,

24 February 2023, https://www.telegraphindia.com/india/military-veterans-slam-modis-56-inch-chest-boast-s-jaishankars-comment-on-china/cid/1918541

17. In the Indian legal system, as a continuation of the British colonial law, the idols of the temples are legal persons.
18. In 2011, the congress-led government of the Indian union was nearly destabilised and weakened through a series of unproven charges of corruptions. Eventually, many parts of the national capital Delhi were paralysed by an anti-corruption agitation led by Anna Hazare and Arvind Kejriwal. Eventually, it was revealed that this agitation was stage managed by the RSS through its proxy Vivekananda Foundation. The man who planned most of the operations, Ajit Doval, is today the national security advisor of the government. Arvind Kejriwal himself launched a political party whose name imitates the slogan of the Congress party, and today he is the chief minister of Delhi. This sense of 'unbelievability' of the events of Indian politics returns as theme, entirely rooted in evidence, in this anthology. See Praveen Dhonthi, "How Ties With The Think Tanks Vivekananda International Foundation and India Foundation Enhance Ajit Doval's Influence', *The Caravan*, 5 November 2017, https://caravanmagazine.in/vantage/vivekananda-international-india-foundation-ajit-doval-influence

19. SEX AND POST-COLONIAL FAMILY VALUES

1. Anish Mohammed, Shaj Mohan, 'The New Secret'.
2. '61 Indian academics on crowd-sourced list of "harassers"', *Indian Express*, 7 October 2017, http://indianexpress.com/article/india/61-indian-academics-on-crowd-sourced-list-of-harassers-4908459/
3. https://en.wikipedia.org/wiki/Rani_Karnavati
4. https://en.wikipedia.org/wiki/Ek_Duuje_Ke_Liye
5. Shruti Chaturvedi and Utpala Shukla, 'Khurshid Anwar's Suicide: Some Unanswered Questions', *Counter Currents*, 13 July 2014, http://www.countercurrents.org/shukla130814.htm
6. 'Delhi: Man commits suicide after being accused of sexual harassment', *LA Times*, 25 July 2017, http://www.asianage.com/metros/delhi/250717/delhi-man-commits-suicide-after-being-accused-of-sexual-harrasment.html
7. 'Family of UC Davis official who killed himself after sexual harassment accusation sues university', *LA Times*, 26 October 2017, http://www.latimes.com/local/lanow/la-me-uc-davis-suicide-20171026-story.html

8. 'Important to name perpetrators, says V Geetha on Raya Sarkar's crowd-sourced list of sexual harassers', *New Indian Express*, 27 October 2017, https://www.newindianexpress.com/nation/2017/oct/27/important-to-name-perpetrators-says-v-geetha-on-raya-sarkars-crowd-sourced-list-of-sexual-harasser-1684340.html
9. http://wildcatdispatches.org/2017/10/25/priyamvada-gopal-on-love-and-sex-in-academia-and-beyond/
10. 'How to Make Sense of the Radical Challenge to Sexual Harassment in Academia', *The Wire*, 25 October 2017, https://thewire.in/gender/facebook-sexual-harassment-south-asian-academics
11. 'Long-distance Kissing and Licking? Prototypes Reveal the Future of Virtual Make-out Sessions', *Future of Sex*, 23 December 2016, https://futureofsex.net/remote-sex/long-distance-kissing-licking-prototypes-reveal-future-virtual-make-sessions/
12. 'Future of Sex Report: Detailed Predictions on the Impact of Technology on Human Sexuality', *Future of Sex*, https://futureofsex.net/future-of-sex-report/
13. http://we-consent.org
14. 'Sex robots with "resistance setting" let men simulate rape and should be outlawed, say campaigners', *The Independent*, 2 September 2017, https://www.independent.co.uk/tech/sex-robots-that-let-men-simulate-rape-should-be-outlawed-says-campaigner-a7959071.html
15. *What the Nation Really Needs to Know: The JNU Nationalism Lectures*, Edited by JNUTA, Delhi: Harper Collins, 2017.
16. Menon, 'As Jodhpur University Goes on "Anti-National" Witch-Hunt, Here's the Incredible Backstory', *The Wire*, 17 February 2017, https://thewire.in/109643/nivedita-menon-rss-ignorance-jodhpur-university-ranawat-jnu/
17. Marzia Casolari, 'Hindutva's Foreign Tie-up in the 1930s Archival Evidence' *Economic and Political Weekly* vol. 35, no. 4, (2000): 218–28.

20. OUR WANDERING SENSES

1. Some of their texts of the Pandemic were published in the anthology *Coronavirus, Psychoanalysis, and Philosophy*.
2. See also Shaj Mohan and Divya Dwivedi, 'Ahoratos, Palestine', *Philosophy World Democracy* vol. 4 no. 11 (November 2023), https://www.philosophy-world-democracy.org/articles-1/ahoratos-palestine and 'Let The World Speak: An Interview with Shaj Mohan', *Protean*, 2 December 2023, https://proteanmag.com/2023/12/02/let-the-world-speak-an-interview-with-shaj-mohan/

21. 'HE HAS LIT A FUNERAL PYRE IN EVERYONE'S HOME'

1. Author's note: The video has English subtitles and it should be viewed to grasp the indifference of the Indian government towards the lives of the 4.7 million who died. 'Delhi's cremation ground', *The Caravan*, https://www.youtube.com/watch?v=XspQv5Y-OEg

22. A GREAT INTOLERANCE

1. Simone Weil is an unusual presence in the works of Mohan even as he engages with Weil critically. The concept of 'metaxu' in Weil marks the region between life as an intolerable burden and grace as a release from life which is at the same time never liveable for anyone. The concept of 'Metaxu' can be seen in the discussions of tolerance and range in both Dwivedi and Mohan, which is their negotiation of the liveability and unbearability involved in political actions. That is, they have re-animated Weil the political philosopher through Weil the nihilist. See Shaj Mohan, 'The Between: The Dangerous Occupation of the Philosopher', *Revue des femmes philosophes*, no. 4-5, https://unesdoc.unesco.org/ark:/48223/pf0000265538
2. This is a reference to the concept of the 'chimera' and also 'comprehending law'.

23. 'IN INDIA, RELIGIOUS MINORITIES ARE PERSECUTED TO HIDE THE FACT THAT THE REAL MAJORITY ARE THE LOWER CASTES'

1. Author's note: See Stefan Arvidsson, 2006. *The Aryan Idols: Indo-European Mythology as Ideology and Science*, translated by Sonia Wichmann, Chicago: University of Chicago.
2. See the discussion of analogies and homologies between caste and race in Divya Dwivedi, 'The Evasive Racism of Caste—and the Homological Power of the 'Aryan' Doctrine.' *Critical Philosophy of Race*.
3. See Heinrich von Stietencron, *Hindu Myth, Hindu History*, Delhi: Permanent Black, 2005.
4. *Collected Works of Mahatma Gandhi*, vol. 68, p. 382–3.
5. *Collected Works of Mahatma Gandhi*, vol. 68, p. 318–39.
6. See Ornit Shani, *Communalism, Caste, and Hindu Nationalism: The Violence in Gujarat*, Cambridge: Cambridge University Press, 2007.
7. Gael Omvedt, *Dalits And The Democratic Revolution: Dr. Ambedkar And The Dalit Movement In Colonial India*, Delhi: Sage India, 1994.

24. THE WINTER OF ABSOLUTE ZERO

1. Mohan in fact calls for a 'democracy of the world' which is different from a 'world government'.
2. It is an elite college in Delhi university founded during colonial rule in 1854 modelled after and in relation with Cambridge university. The criticism of the college is that it is an elite institution which caters to the children of the elites who are able to rise to positions of power and prestige through the networks of alumni without any political commitments.
3. It is an allusion to Joseph Goebbels.
4. In India the movement for the demolition of the Babri mosque and its demolition took place when the Congress party was in power at the central government.
5. The position of Khaldun with a difference, in that historiography is autonomous, is present in Mohan's texts on history. This is a passage which echoes Khaldun, 'Anastasis escapes history. Anastasis belongs to philosophy. It is this relation between philosophy and history that is needed today. Historiography escapes philosophy due to the latter's concern with essences which deprives the philosopher of the drawing power of teleography'. See Mohan, 'Teleography and Tendencies: Part 2 History and Anastasis'.

25. CARGO CULT DEMOCRACY

1. Edited by Divya Dwivedi, *Revue des femmes philosophes*, Special issue: 'Intellectuals, Philosophers, Women in India: Endangered Species'.
2. News report in *Le Monde*, 'En Inde, le mensuel "The Caravan" est harcelé par la police', 2 February 2022, https://www.lemonde.fr/international/article/2021/02/02/en-inde-le-mensuel-the-caravan-est-harcele-par-la-police_6068474_3210.html
3. See Giorgio Agamben, *Remnants of Auschwitz: The Witness and the Archive*, Translated by Daniel Heller-Roazen, New York: Zone Books, 2002.
4. See Divya Dwivedi and Henrik Skov Nielsen, 'The Paradox of Testimony and First-Person Plural Narration in Jensen's We, the Drowned', *CLCWeb: Comparative Literature and Culture* vol. 15, no. 7 (2013): <https://doi.org/10.7771/1481-4374.2388>
5. Babasaheb Dr. B.R. Ambedkar, *Annihilation of Caste*, Archive.org, https://archive.org/stream/HindSwaraj-Ambedkar-01/Ambedkar_Volume_01_djvu.txt
6. See 'On Teesta Setalvad' in this anthology.

7. For a report on caste rules in prisons, see Sukanya Shantha, 'From Segregation to Labour, Manu's Caste Law Governs the Indian Prison System', *The Wire*, 10 December 2020, https://thewire.in/caste/india-prisons-caste-labour-segregation
8. See 'The Compassionate Revolution of Saint Stan Swami' in this anthology.
9. The English translation of the same interview in this anthology.
10. The interviewer is referring to the text 'Courage to Begin', included in this anthology.
11. See Hartosh Singh Bal, 'Spare me the good Hindu: The Hindu vs Hindutva battle is meaningless in shaping our politics', *The Caravan*, 6 July 2018, https://caravanmagazine.in/politics/hindu-vs-hindutva-battle-meaningless-in-shaping-our-politics
12. One of the most prominent intellectuals and academics from the lower caste majority position in the last hundred years.
13. See Ornit Shani, *Communalism, Caste and Hindu Nationalism: The Violence in Gujarat*, Cambridge University Press, 2009, https://doi.org/10.1017/CBO9780511607936
14. See 'Hindu Hoax'.
15. Jotirao Phule, *Selected Writings of Jotirao Phule*, edited by G.P. Deshpande, New Delhi: Leftword Books, 2002.
16. Richard P. Feynman, 'Cargo Cult Science', Caltech, http://calteches.library.caltech.edu/51/2/CargoCult.pdf
17. A phrase used by Dwivedi and Mohan to refer to the RSS as a mafia organisation with its family organisations. As they are rooted in the western state of Maharashtra, 'the west coast'.
18. Author's note: See Aarushi Punia, 'Calypsology of Caste through Metaphorization: A Review of Isabel Wilkerson's Caste', *Philosophy World Democracy*, vol. 1, no. 1 (November 2020), https://www.philosophy-world-democracy.org/book-reviews/calypsology-of-caste.

26. THE COMPASSIONATE REVOLUTION OF SAINT STAN SWAMY 1937–2021

1. See, *On Bernard Stiegler Philosopher of Friendship*, edited by Jean-Luc Nancy, Introduction by Shaj Mohan, London: Bloomsbury Academic, 2024.
2. See 'After 20 Days, NIA Says It Doesn't Have Stan Swamy's Sipper and Straw', *The Wire*, 26 November 2020, https://thewire.in/rights/stan-swamy-straw-sipper-nia-elgar-parishad

3. Often the oppositional position of Indian columnists and intellectuals align them with the Congress. The criticism of the Congress party which ruled India for several decades is constant in the writings of Dwivedi and Mohan. They argue that the Congress is primarily responsible for the present fascistic control of the state exercised by RSS. See 'Who Gets to Kill Whom in the Union of India?' in this anthology for more.
4. Several of the draconian provisions of law used by the BJP today were enacted by the Congress when they were in power. The former Congress prime minister Manmohan Singh also preceded and legitimised the BJP's claim that the organisations of the lower caste people and the tribals for their rights are the greatest threat to India. See 'Manmohan: naxalism the greatest internal threat', *The Hindu*, 11 October 2009, https://www.thehindu.com/news/national/Manmohan-naxalism-the-greatest-internal-threat/article16886121.ece See also 'Minutes after opposing it, Congress backs UAPA Bill in Rajya Sabha', *Indian Express*, 3 August 2019, https://indianexpress.com/article/india/minutes-after-opposing-it-congress-backs-uapa-bill-in-rajya-sabha-5873977/
5. Teltumbde was released from prison after languishing in it for almost a thousand days. See 'Anand Teltumbde gets bail after 949 days in jail under UAPA', 7 December 2022, https://indianexpress.com/article/cities/mumbai/sad-we-spent-time-in-jail-in-fake-case-anand-teltumbde-8291797/
6. See 'The Obscenity of Truth: Arrest the Anti-Fascist!', in this anthology.
7. See Divya Dwivedi and Shaj Mohan, 'En Inde, les troubles s'expliquent en partie par la Constitution du pays', *Le Monde*, 24 January 2020, https://www.lemonde.fr/idees/article/2020/01/24/en-inde-les-troubles-s-expliquent-en-partie-par-la-constitution-du-pays_6027035_3232.html
8. See chapter 27 in this anthology.
9. This is a conceptual move similar to Nietzsche's. That is, the experience of 'novelty' can be created through not educating a generation about the past or through forgetting. See the interview with Mohan 'But, there is nothing outside of philosophy', Shaj Mohan and Rachel Adams, *Positions Politics: Episteme*, no. 4 (February 2021) special issue on the philosophy of Dwivedi and Mohan, 'Philosophy for another time', edited by Kamran Baradaran, https://positionspolitics.org/conversation-between-shaj-mohan-and-rachel-adams/

10. Several of the texts of Dwivedi and Mohan rely on the reports of the journalist Sukanya Shantha who investigates crimes against and the criminalisation of the lower caste people. See Sukanya Shantha, 'Incriminating Letters Were "Planted" on Rona Wilson's Laptop: US Digital Forensics Firm', *The Wire*, 10 February 2021, https://thewire.in/tech/rona-wilson-elgar-parishad-letters-planted-us-firm
11. For evidence planted on Swami's computer, see 'Documents Planted On Computers: New Report After Stan Swamy's Death', *NDTV*, 6 July 2021, https://www.ndtv.com/india-news/arsenal-consulting-report-stan-swamy-others-said-evidence-was-fabricated-new-report-backs-that-2480532?pfrom=home-ndtv_bigstory
12. See 'Hidden by Hindu' in this anthology.
13. Sukanya Shantha, 'Elgar Parishad: NIA Claims Arrested Accused Were Attempting to Create a "Dalit Militia"', *The Wire*, 20 October 2020, https://thewire.in/rights/elgar-parishad-nia-chargesheet-dalit-militia
14. See the report from *Human Rights Watch* for an understanding of caste oppression as the basis for the violence against Christians in India, https://www.hrw.org/reports/1999/indiachr/christians8- 03.htm
15. See 'Christians seek justice seven years after Kandhamal riots', *Reuters*, 8 September 2015, https://www.reuters.com/article/india-christians-justice-idINKCN0R821W20150908?edition-redirect=in
16. An Australian missionary who lived among the tribal people or the adivasis of the state of Odisha. In 1999, while he slept in his car with his two sons, Philip aged 10 and Timothy aged 6, and he were burned alive by the members of the Hindu terrorist organisation Bajrang Dal, which is a wing of the paramilitary organisation RSS. See '"The Graham Staines Story" a grim reminder of horrors of religious persecution', *The Week*, 1 April 2019, https://www.theweek.in/leisure/society/2019/04/01/graham-stained-story-grim-reminder-horrors-religious-persecution.html
17. In 2018, in the state of Kerala, a Dalit Christian boy was killed by upper caste Christians for marrying from their community. See 'Protests After Alleged "Honour" Killing of Kerala Man by Wife's Kin', *The Wire*, 29 May 2018, https://thewire.in/communalism/protests-after-alleged-honour-killing-of-kerala-man-by-wifes-kin
18. It is important to note that the terms 'Saint' and 'redemption' have been given a new semantic field through democracy by Dwivedi and Mohan.

27. DISHA RAVI, GRETA THUNBERG AND THE EXISTENTIAL REBELLION: THE WORLD NEEDS TO SAVE ITSELF

1. Delhi police soon filed a case against Greta Thunberg. See 'Delhi Police FIR on Greta Thunberg "Toolkit" Is Not Just a Futile Exercise but an Embarrassment', *The Wire*, 13 February 2021, https://thewire.in/law/delhi-police-greta-thunberg-protest-toolkit-fir
2. See 'The Winter of Absolute Zero' in this anthology.
3. For the subversion of parliamentary procedures to pass the farm laws, see 'Farm Bills: English Newspapers Condemn RS Deputy Chairman's Decision to Hold Voice Vote', *The Wire*, 23 September 2020, https://thewire.in/media/english-newspaper-editorials-rajya-sabha-voice-vote For the two corporations, of Ambani and Adani, and their gains from the proposed farm laws see the report on the speech of Rahul Gandhi in the parliament. "Hum do, hamare do': Rahul Gandhi attacks govt over farm laws, says "4 people" running the country', *Indian Express*, 11 February 2021, https://indianexpress.com/article/india/rahul-gandhi-farm-laws-lok-sabha-7184519/
4. Mahua Moitra is a defiant opponent of the Modi government and a parliamentarian. For the incident mentioned here, see 'Ruckus in House After Mahua Moitra's Remarks on Ex-CJI's Sexual Harassment Case', *The Wire*, 9 February 2021, https://thewire.in/politics/ruckus-in-house-after-mahua-moitras-remarks-on-ex-cjis-sexual-harassment-case
5. See the glossary on comprehending law.
6. See 'The Hindu Hoax'.
7. See 'The Necessity of Revolution' in this anthology.
8. The reference is to two young women, Devangana Kalita and Natasha Narwal, who were arrested for their work with 'Pinjra Tod' (break the shackles) movement. They have since been released in June 2021 on bail.
9. A phrase used by Dwivedi and Mohan to describe the upper caste ('Aryan') supremacist paramilitary organisation. This phrase 'organisational famiglia' refers to two aspects; firstly, the RSS is at the head of a family of organisations including terrorist outfits; secondly, in Italian it refers to the mafia. In an interview, included in this anthology, Dwivedi would expand it as 'organisational mafia famiglia'.
10. Authors' note: The pathbreaking autobiography of Baby Kamble tells the history of strong women who fought the oppressive caste system before the power and rage of Dr B. R. Ambedkar arrived. See Baby

Kamble, *Prisons We Broke*, translated by Maya Pandit, Hyderabad: Orient BlackSwan, 2009.

11. What was referred to earlier, the family of the organisations controlled by the upper caste supremacist RSS.
12. This is a reference to the Association des Amis de la Génération Thunberg (AAGT) created by the philosopher Bernard Stiegler, a friend of Dwivedi and Mohan. For a history, see https://generation-thunberg.org/projet/histoire Later Dwivedi and Mohan dedicated a text to AAGT which is not included in this anthology. Divya Dwivedi and Shaj Mohan, 'Trash: Evil', *Philosophy World Democracy*, vol. 4, no. 3 (March 2023), https://www.philosophy-world-democracy.org/articles-1/trash-evil

28. ON TEESTA SETALVAD

1. 'Gujarat Police Arrest Teesta Setalvad, Activist Who Pursued 2002 Riots Case Against Modi', *The Wire*, 25 June 2022, https://thewire.in/government/gujarat-police-arrest-teesta-setalvad-activist-who-pursued-2002-riots-case-against-modi
2. This special issue was edited by Divya Dwivedi.
3. In 2 September 2022 Setalvad received interim bail from the Supreme Court of India.
4. 'Communal Riots in Gujarat: The State at Risk?' by Christophe Jaffrelot, *Heidelberg Papers in South Asian and Comparative Politics*, South Asia Institute Department of Political Science University of Heidelberg, 2003.
5. 'Narendra Modi's US visa secure despite Gujarat riots guilty verdicts', Simon Tisdall, *The Guardian*, 2 June 2016, https://www.theguardian.com/world/2016/jun/02/narendra-modis-us-visa-secure-despite-gujarat-riots-guilty-verdicts. See also 'Issue of Gujarat Chief Minister Narendra Modi's Visa Status', Statement by David C. Mulford, U.S. Ambassador to India, March 21, 2005, https://2001-2009.state.gov/p/sca/rls/rm/2005/43701.htm
6. See 'Why it is important to remember Ehsan Jafri', by Christophe Jaffrelot, *The Indian Express*, March 1, 2022, https://indianexpress.com/article/opinion/columns/why-it-is-important-to-remember-ehsan-jafri-7795207/
7. See 'Harsh Mander: Whatever happened To Ehsan Jafri on February 28, 2002?', *Scroll*, 20 July 2022, https://scroll.in/article/1028354/harsh-mander-whatever-happened-to-ehsan-jafri-on-february-28-2002

8. 'Gulbarg Society massacre verdict: "Mob dragged out Ahsan Jafri, burnt him alive"', *The Indian Express*, 18 June 2016, https://indianexpress.com/article/india/india-news-india/gulberg-society-massacre-verdict-details-mob-dragged-out-ahsan-jafri-burnt-him-alive-2859757/
9. 'En Inde, le mensuel "The Caravan" est harcelé par la police', *Le Monde*, 2 February 2021, https://www.lemonde.fr/international/article/2021/02/02/en-inde-le-mensuel-the-caravan-est-harcele-par-la-police_6068474_3210.html. See also Jean-Luc Nancy, 'La religieuse manipulation du pouvoir', *Libération*, 7 March 2021. https://www.liberation.fr/idees-et-debats/tribunes/la-religieuse-manipulation-du-pouvoir-20210307_LYR4ECBNONBPLLDV4GZOZNZFYI/
10. See 'The Hindu Hoax'.
11. See chapter 2 in this anthology.
12. 'Police Linked to Hacking Campaign to Frame Indian Activists', *The Wired*, June 2022, https://www.wired.com/story/modified-elephant-planted-evidence-hacking-police/
13. See chapter 26 in this anthology.

29. ROMILA THAPAR

1. See the report in *The Wire*, 'JNU Asks Romila Thapar to Submit Her CV For "Evaluation"', 1 September 2019, https://thewire.in/education/jnu-asks-romila-thapar-to-submit-her-cv-for-evaluation
2. This text implies a theory of history already discussed in other works. In *Gandhi and Philosophy*, Dwivedi and Mohan write in their opposition to M. K. Gandhi, 'Active force generates history and writes it. History is the interruptions in the natural span of mankind; it abandons man into the desert of freedom, where he is free to bind the values of his choice to the things of his desire', p. 108. In later texts, Mohan has developed his concept of history. 'In the same way that one hesitates to call the chronicle of the movement of traffic its history, the transformations of an object in a field are not 'historical', unless the objectivity itself were to undergo transformation. When the field itself and the theory of its objectivity undergoes changes we also speak of theoretical or scientific revolutions; on such occasions, history is the experience of the prodigious.' See Mohan, 'Teleography and Tendencies: Part 2 History and Anastasis'.
3. Corpus, body, chimera, components, organs are concepts in the works of Dwivedi and Mohan. They point out that when there is no

resonance or well determined relation between the components of any system, it results in anomia or the absence of law. It is similar to various forms of sickness in living organisms. In the context of a corpus of writings too the conceptual schema is the same. A body of writing risks being 'an anonymous cadaver' until a group of concepts in relation, a system, gathers each and every word, 'When the thoughts of a thinker are not well understood the corpus is of no one'. See *Gandhi and Philosophy*, p. 21.

4. See 'Teleography and Tendencies: Part 2 History and Anastasis'.
5. The upper caste supremacist claim is that India is the land of the Vedas and the 'Aryans' who composed them are autochthonous to India. Dwivedi and Mohan rely on the accumulated evidence of Indology and archeology to assert that the land where the Vedas were completed is present day Pakistan. That is, Pakistan which is opposed in everyday politics in India by the upper caste supremacists is the very land where their 'common ancestors' lived and died.
6. Muhammad ibn Musa al-Khwarizmi (780 - 850) was a mathematician who lived in the city of Baghdad. The disciplines of algorithms and algebra are named after him.
7. The concept of 'ceremonial society' is invoked here. In this case, it suggests that all attempts at self-conservation in societies risk slipping them into the dangers of ceremonial order. Caste order is shown to be such a self-conserving supremacism perpetrated by the upper castes of India.
8. This theme is continuous in the works of Dwivedi and Mohan. Inherited communities are exemplified by caste in that Brahmins maintain social relations exclusively with Brahmins, for example, while the Dalits are prevented from the entering the social sphere of the Brahmins. But their use of 'inherited communities' also includes class structure, wealth as that which is heritable, aristocratic privileges, and poverty. Politics is opposed to inherited communities.
9. This remark on the 'inverted image' is an obvious reference to Marx, who is regarded by Mohan as the first philosopher to liberate history from theological capture. While Dwivedi and Mohan do refer to Marx frequently, their engagement is always critical. Marx says, 'Consciousness can never be anything else than conscious existence, and the existence of men is their actual life-process. If in all ideology men and their circumstances appear upside-down as in a camera obscura, this phenomenon arises just as much from their historical life-process as the inversion of objects on the retina does from their physical life-process', *The German Ideology*.

10. This interview itself was part of a project led by Divya Dwivedi for the *Revue des Femmes Philosophes,* 'Intellectuals, philosophers, women in India: endangered species', edited by Divya Dwivedi, with contributions from Anand Teltumbde, Hartosh Singh Bal, Flavia Agnes, Subhashini Ali, Ravish Kumar, Shahid Amin, and Perumal Murugan among others.

30. INTELLECTUAL INSURGENCY: FOR MAHESH RAUT

1. *The Third Eye and Other Works: Mahatma Phule's Writings on Education*, New Delhi: Orient Blackswan, 2023, p. 107.

BIBLIOGRAPHY

Shaj Mohan and Divya Dwivedi, *Gandhi and Philosophy: On Theological Anti-politics*, Foreword by Jean-Luc Nancy, London: Bloomsbury Academic: 2019.

Dwivedi, 'The Evasive Racism of Caste—and the Homological Power of the "Aryan" Doctrine', *Critical Philosophy of Race*, Penn State University Press, vol. 11, no. 1, 2023, pp. 209-245.

Dwivedi, 'A Mystery of Mysteries!–' *European Journal of Psychoanalysis*, 2021, https://www.journal-psychoanalysis.eu/articles/a-mystery-of-mysteries-d-dwivedi/

Dwivedi, 'Homologies in Freud and Derrida: Civilization and the Death Drive', *Eco-Ethica*, vol. 9, 2020.

Dwivedi, 'May 1968 in the Memories of Imagination', *Interventions: International Journal of Postcolonial Studies*, vol. 22, 2020.

Dwivedi, 'Modal of Lost Responsibilities', in *Virality of Evil Philosophy in the Time of a Pandemic*, London: Rowman & Littlefield , 2022.

Dwivedi, 'Nancy's Wager', *Philosophy World Democracy*, vol. 2. no. 7 (July 2021), https://www.philosophy-world-democracy.org/other-beginning/nancys-wager

Mohan, 'Deconstruction and Anastasis', *Qui Parle* vol. 31, no. 2 (2022): 339–344.

Mohan, 'The Obscure Experience', *Coronavirus, Psychoanalysis, and Philosophy*, edited by F. Castrillón and T. Marchevsky, London: Routledge, 2021.

Mohan, 'On the Bastard Family of Deconstruction', *Philosophy World Democracy*, 2021. Text of public seminar in École Normale Supérieure on 23 November 2021.

Mohan, 'Teleography and Tendencies: Part 2 History and Anastasis', *Philosophy World Democracy*, vol. 3, no. 4 (April 2022), https://www.

philosophy-world-democracy.org/articles-1/teleography-and-tendencies-part-2-history-and-anastasis

Mohan, 'But, there is nothing outside of philosophy', Shaj Mohan and Rachel Adams, *Positions Politics: Episteme*, no. 4 (February 2021) special issue on the philosophy of Dwivedi and Mohan, 'Philosophy for another time', edited by Kamran Baradaran, https://positionspolitics.org/conversation-between-shaj-mohan-and-rachel-adams/

Mohan, 'Be held in the gaze of the stone' (the text of the lecture delivered on the 10th of June at the children's hospital in St. Denis), *Philosophy World Democracy*, vol. 3, no. 6 (June 2022), https://www.philosophy-world-democracy.org/other-beginning/be-held-in-the-gaze-of-the-stone

Mohan, 'I take, and I am taken, by what belongs to philosophy': Philosophy and the redemption of democracy, *South African Journal of Science*, vol.118, spe 2 Pretoria 2022.

Dwivedi and Mohan, 'The Endogenous Ends of Education: For Aaron Swartz', *European Journal of Psychoanalysis*, 2021.

Dwivedi, Divya, Shaj Mohan, and J. Reghu, 'The Hindu Hoax: How upper castes invented a Hindu majority', *The Caravan*, January 2021.

Dwivedi, Divya, Shaj Mohan, 'Parentheses of Philosophy,' *Economic and Political Weekly* vol. 54, no. 40, (5 October 2019).

Secondary literature

Robert Bernasconi, 'Welcoming Divya Dwivedi and Shaj Mohan's *Gandhi and Philosophy*', *Positions Politics*, from the special issue on the philosophy of Dwivedi and Mohan, 'Philosophy for another time', edited by Kamran Baradaran, February 2021.

Maël Montévil, 'Penser au-delà de l'identité : philosophie et sciences', *Philosophy World Democracy*, vol. 3, no. 6 (June 2022).

Daniel J. Smith, 'Hypophysics and the Comparison between Caste and Race', *Positions Politics*, February 2021.

Reghu Janardhanan, 'The Deconstructive Materialism of Dwivedi and Mohan: A New Philosophy of Freedom', *Positions Politics*, February 2021.

Reghu Janardhanan, 'Deconstructive Materialism: Einsteinian Revolution in Philosophy', *Philosophy World Democracy*, vol. 2 no. 11 (November 2021).

Michel Bitbol, 'Reply to: The Principles of Beginning, by Shaj Mohan', *Philosophy World Democracy*, vol. 4, no. 1 (January 2023).

Ivana Perica, 'Transformative Imagination and the Need for Law', *Positions Politics* issue 4: philosophy for another time, February 2021.

Rex Butler, 'An Other Beginning: A New Thinking of the End', *Philosophy World Democracy*, vol. 3, no. 2 (February 2022).

N. K. Raveendran, 'Two philosophers and a political theorist: An allegory of Indian public sphere', *Mathrubhumi*, 15 November 2022.

Marguerite La Caze, 'Cocktails more lethal than Molotovs: Freedom, Indestinacy, and Responsibility in Gandhi and Philosophy', *Positions Politics*, February 2021.

GLOSSARY OF CONCEPTS

Analogy — The concept of analogy retains the classical meaning of the comparison of proportions, what A is to B is C is to D. But it recovers the deeper meaning implied in the practice of analogy in the history of philosophy. Analogy is derived from the fact that functions are transferable from one arrangement of components to another. Biology clearly shows it, the construction of the function of flight in birds and bats are altogether different, but they are the same flight function. The compound eye of bees and the spherical eye of mammals perform the same sight function, but they are analogous. Dwivedi and Mohan, therefore took the concept of analogy to its roots in a new and complex theory of functions.

Anastasis — The term is introduced as ana-stasis (see *Gandhi and Philosophy*) as leading out of stasis (See entry *stasis* below). One of the earlier uses of this term referred to the resurrection of Jesus Christ, which was deconstructed by Jean-Luc Nancy who denied that anastasis has any relation to the raising of the dead. Stasis is the arrest of any complex system when one of its components draws all the other components towards itself. Military dictatorships are a good example in politics. Stasis closes the system from developing new possibilities and creating new relations with the outside. For Dwivedi and Mohan, stasis can lead to criticalisation and the self-destruction of the system. A biological example is 'bleeding out'. Anastasis itself takes place when a system in stasis which presents itself as a ruin is seized by a new comprehending law. The implication of a new comprehending law is that not all components and componential relations from a previous epoch will continue to exist in the new system. Dwivedi and Mohan assert that one cannot enforce anastasis, because anastasis always come from the other (See *anomia, criticalisation,* and *ruin*)

Anomia — It signifies the absence of a regular relation between the components of a system. It also creates transient and monstrous arrangements of components. A variation of this term and concept, *anomie*, was important in French sociology from the nineteenth century. In the works of Dwivedi and Mohan, anomia is derived from Ancient Greek societies. The example, of Typhaon which is half snake and half man, and the centaurs are composed of components which cannot be comprehended or unified by a comprehending law. Societies enter anomia through crisis, criticalisation or stasis. Mohan reminds us to think of Thucydides who wrote about the anomia of Athens which was seized by the plague. Anomia is therefore not merely lawlessness, but the presence of relations or arrangements among components which are impossible to endure. Anomia does not ever appear by itself, but accompanies stasis and criticalisation. (Also see *Ruin*)

Aryan doctrine — It refers to the set of dogmatic beliefs that there is an 'Aryan' race to which white people, Iranians and Indians belong, and that this is the most superior race which has created the greatest civilization in the world. Although it has been associated in popular consciousness with orientalist research, race theories and then Nazism, in Europe and with Germany in particular, Dwivedi and Mohan deploy this term to invoke the longer history of the idea of 'Arya' in India, where it has been a self-designation of the upper castes for centuries and literally means 'high', 'noble', and 'superior'. Dwivedi has traced the way this term in the upper caste discourse and Brahmancial texts later spread to Europe with the active agency of the upper caste 'native informers': 'Caste was the empirical, conceptual, and textual resource for Europeans as it showed that large groups could be dominated as well as excluded through the self-designated superiority, supplied by the Brahminical texts, of the oppressing group'. Its attraction for European race theorists lay precisely in how it expressed the upper caste sense of their own supremacy. The term declares what she calls the 'denigrate-dominate function' where the majority population was oppressed and dominated by being denigrated as born inferior. Hence, this is first of all a doctrine of the caste system and only then and therefore, also a racist concept that still produces terrifying effects in politics up to today.

Caste as racism — The critical necessity of comparing caste and race can be traced to the great lower caste activist Jotirao Phule in the nineteenth century, and then the 'caste school of race' in the USA in the twentieth century. The comparative framework from studying caste and race has been deployed by Dalit social scientists to produce sharp critiques of the past as well as present maintenance of the caste order. The acme of this critique was the 2001 Durban WACR conference of UN, where Dalit scholars asserted that caste should be considered among the kinds of racist discriminations. However, the then Indian government led by the BJP, and eminent postcolonial sociologists strenuously tried to suppress any reference to race and racism while discussing caste. Dwivedi has shown that a non-critical and positive evaluation of caste already inspired race theorists in the eighteenth century and was being actively pursued throughout the past centuries. Therefore, in addition to the comparative framework she adds the homological framework to show that caste is not just similar to racism but has been at the origins of race theory. The long pre-colonial history of caste gives both material and textual evidence that it had all the components and logic of the denigrate-dominate function that came to be developed in race theories. Dwivedi and Mohan oppose the recent fiction that caste is a colonial construct, since this shifts the blame and responsibility on the foreign coloniser rather than on the old oppressors, the upper castes. They never stop reminding that the caste order is the 'oldest racism'.

Ceremonial society — It is a general concept for a type of society which repeats its actions with regularity in such a manner that even after centuries it would appear more or less the same. For Dwivedi and Mohan, the oppressive caste order creates ceremonial society which forces its members to ceremonially repeat their sexual relations and social functions. The concept is a critical appropriation of both ethnological conceptions of tribal societies and cybernetic theories, especially autopoiesis. To repeat a society ceremonially, the society should see to it that the rules which allow the reproduction of itself as the very goal of that society. In this way it again characterises caste oppression in the works of Dwivedi and Mohan. Conserving the caste rules is the very goal of the upper castes, which ensures that caste oppression is ceremonially repeated. Elsewhere Dwivedi and Mohan have said that all *inheritable communities* are ceremonial societies.

Calypsology — It is a concept related to ceremonial society, but not restricted to it. The concept is derived from the myth of Calypso who imprisoned Ulysses in her island and made him functionally isolated into a companion/prisoner. The concept can be defined as follows: A system which deploys its means as its ends repeats itself faithfully. It was developed in opposition to Gandhi's thesis that means and ends must be one and the same. Dwivedi and Mohan, through a deconstruction of the means and ends concept, gave a new power to the Kantian thesis that man must be treated only as an end. But they show that all things come to be means or ends depending on their componential relations and functional isolations. The ethics is to keep the polynomia of everything open. (See *Polynomia*)

Componential law — The law which refers to the regularity of something which is in a relation to other things. The podium of a lecture room in Mohan's example, is a component in the system of education, which has its own law in that only designated faculties can occupy it regularly. Components themselves can be polynomial, that is capable of many different regularities. The component of hand has a set of componential laws in human activities, as it can be in a componential relation with a piano and also in another componential relation with surgical instruments. In politics Dwivedi and Mohan show that the lower caste people are not allowed to enter into componential relations with academic institutions, media, and the judiciary. (See *Law*)

Comprehending law — A system of components in relation is held together by 'something' which is not a thing, or a component. It refers to the regular relations and also the varying intensities of relations among a system of components. For these reasons, comprehending law can never be exhaustively stated. The concept is derived from many different thinkers and domains, including Marx, Derrida, Freud, cosmology, and ecology. These concepts—functional isolation, homology, analogy, componential law, comprehending law, corpus—together overcome the distinction between boundary conditions and dynamics as used in philosophy of physics. That is, the pinpointing of a boundary conditions begins with at least a functional isolation, for which a telos has to be given, or reason should be rendered. (See *Law and Reason*)

Corpus/Body — The word body has many meanings depending on the disciplines from particular periods and depending on the philosophers. Corpus can be said of a system of components in a regular relation, which appears from outside as a unity and with a telos. Each corpus has limits to the polynomia possible due to their essences. But the power of a corpus can be extended through addition and subtraction of component relations. The body of a man who has trained well for deep sea diving is a different corpus compared to that of a woman trained to be a mathematician. A collection of writings and a collection of protest movements are also corpus, provided a reason can be given through which a unity or purpose can found.

Criticalisation — Systems eventually reach a point where components may not be able to sustain the required demands of regularity, and the relations among components may lack regularity. It is impossible to reanimate a criticalised system as it was with the identity associated with it. Instead, when such systems are recovered by the additions and subtractions of components they will be qualitatively different. Dwivedi and Mohan often give the example of the critical care unit in hospitals. Stasis often leads to criticalisation and criticalisation is accompanied by anomia. (See *Anomia* and *Stasis*)

Deconstruction — Deconstruction as a word appears infrequently although in many situations the work of deconstruction is underway. The use of the concept is not the same in any philosopher of this tradition—Heidegger, Derrida, Nancy, Stiegler, Dwivedi, Mohan—but the root meaning is that of exposing the force through which alone complex systems can be given unity and totality (see Mohan's 'Be Held in the Gaze of the Stone'). Their arguments through the title 'Hindu hoax' in several texts are a deconstruction, for example. Dwivedi and Mohan show anastasis to be more than deconstruction. For Mohan, deconstruction still relies on classical laws of thought to derive contradictions which suspend a system, whereas for Dwivedi and Mohan, the classical laws of thought are themselves unexamined and they reject them. Thus, deconstruction performs a stage in their works, while in the next they are able to give new powers to the deconstructed systems. This is evident in these texts as the 'lower caste majority position'.

Field —There are several meanings to the word in English and many of these meanings are implied in these texts. It is also complicated by the different terms used in French to designate many different kinds of fields. Primarily a field is analogous to something like an algebraic field. In an algebraic field all the terms and relations obey the field laws of algebra. However, field also implies the relation between two fields, where one of the examples given is that of electro-magnetic fields. At the same time philosophy is not a field and there are no field laws in philosophy. In politics, the use of the field is to show the caste system as a field which has caste laws as field laws, determining who is who, and what relations are possible among who.

(An unpublished seminar on the field by Mohan given at École Normale Supérieure in the winter of 2021 clarifies these ranges of meanings with respect to metaphysics).

Function — In mathematics function is a relation. If A is a Function of B, the value of A depends on B. The mathematical meaning is implied. But so is the biological meaning of functions, such as digestive function, or grasping function. Identity itself is a function because it requires restricting other meanings and uses of a particular thing through functional isolation of that thing. The same function can be performed by different componential relations, and this is the meaning of analogy. The same function can also be used to develop other functions. The function of tapping is extended into the function of typing. Therefore functions themselves have homological powers (see *homology*). The fact that the same group of components can perform several functions is designated by *polynomia*.

Functional isolation — A thing has a particular use or meaning only due to its functional isolation, there is neither substance nor substrate underlying things to give them unity. It is neither restricted to texts nor to things. This concept clarifies deconstruction and also transforms it from being a theoretical suspension of the meaning of metaphysical texts. Biologically, the beak of birds perform many functions. In the functional isolation *to probe*, the beak is used differently and in the functional isolation *to grasp* it used in another way. This applies to even everyday objects through which the belief in identity is ingrained. A chair can be for sitting when it is functionally isolated, but it is also used for the function of climbing when no ladder can be found. A ladder can be functionally isolated to climb and it can also be functionally isolated to be a bridge. There is a relation between functional isolation and the use of pharmakon in the works of Bernard Stiegler.

In politics caste functionally isolates human bodies to make them priests, warrior, scavenger, and untouchable. The task in politics is to release the functionally isolated bodies, components and institutions towards *polynomia*, which is freedom. (See *Polynomia*)

Hoax — It is a concept related to the project of deconstruction of truth. Hoaxes are enduring constructions which are sustained by many men in concert. The agreement of many people concerning a matter is often taken as an established fact, which can be used as truth function later. Hoaxes, if unchallenged can have the same function of truths, that is, those propositions which can be taken for axioms. The fact of hoaxes being a collaborative enterprise show that they are evil in politics, in the meaning similar to it in the works of Hannah Arendt. In politics 'Hindu', 'Hindu majority', 'Hindu supremacy',

'Hindu nationalism' are hoaxes which hide the reality that the lower caste people are the majority who had been deprived of their rights for millennia.

(Consult footnotes to 'Hoax' in this volume)

Homology — The concepts of homology, analogy and functions together substitute the stance of materialism. Homology is closer to the concept of matter as it is commonly used, but it differs from matter in that homology can also be abstract. Homological power is that which allows the construction of more than one function from out of the same thing or concept. Biologically, opsins are receptor protein molecules which are able to perform visual transduction and several other functions including registering temperature. Melanopsin is involved in circadian rhythms while in the retina opsins function as photoreceptors. Homological investigation shows the powers in a component for being home to many functions. In politics, Dwivedi and Mohan often refer to the political institutions and organisations such as the constitution of India and the Congress party as homological powers for the lower caste majority.

Hypophysics — This concept comes from a remark in Kant's *Groundwork for Theory of Morals* (Dwivedi and Mohan wrote a humorous defence for its appropriation, see *Parentheses of Philosophy*). Heidegger had used a particular concept of metaphysics—metaphysics is that discourse which determines Being as a particular being—as an instrument to study the history of philosophy and to correct its course. The use of hypophysics is often made to remove the confusions created by the Heideggerian use of metaphysics. Hypophysical systems are characterised by the identification of a thing with a value. For example, the statement 'nature is good' is hypophysical. Dwivedi in particular has been investigating the hypophysics in German philosophical tradition which entwines it with the 'Aryan doctrine'. Hypophysics in politics shows caste order to be founded on a hypophysical theory which identifies the colour of the skin with its value (Brahmin-white-good) and the birth of a person with his or her inferiority. That is, all racisms are hypophysical but the way the hypophysics is articulated in each system of racism differs.

Idyllic a priori — It is a humorous term which was coined by Mohan. *A priori* in its philosophical meaning is that which is prior to experience which conditions the experience. It suggests that the idylls of the past are often used as *a priori* for arguments in politics and philosophy. Such idylls may never have existed or if they did they could be sustained always at the cost of many others. It was first used in a text opposing Agamben. For Giorgio Agamben, it was the era of the scholars who went to university and lived an idyllic life of freedom and held discussions. Dwivedi and Mohan showed that such idyllic eras of scholars were reserved for the elites of Italian society which exploited the labours of the poor. In the Indian context, postcolonial theory, subaltern theory, and the decolonial projects are based on the *idyllic a priori* of the upper castes, especially the Brahmins.

Law — Law does not have the usual meanings, which restrict it often to the legal meaning. The theory of law has a relation to the 'regulae' in Descartes (Mohan's exposition in the Anastasis seminars clarifies it further) but there are no strict rules of thought. Law is also mathematical and physical, while Dwivedi and Mohan refer to Feynman in *Gandhi and Philosophy*, it is not strictly a realist concept. Instead, law is the shortest (or shorter) statement possible that describes a regularity. Laws are observed in everyday life including in the regularities of children going to school, adults going to offices, and in the traffic flow which depends on the office and school hours. Politically, laws that are hidden or unstated should be discovered, such as the regularity with which the lower caste majority are kept out of important institutions such as the media and university, which Dwivedi and Mohan often show through statistics. Such laws should be changed. There are laws (*componential laws*) which are in relations with other laws, the relations between these componential laws also have regularity. The laws of the house, office and school are met in the traffic which has its own laws. In their examination of metaphysics, Dwivedi and Mohan find certain componential laws continuing to dominate across various epochs.

Looming objects — Objects which can change the comprehending law. Looming objects are found more or less unchanging from one epoch to another. For example, Brahminical ceremonies as legitimising power in India have been continuing for millennia. When a looming object vanishes or when it is radically transformed, the comprehending law of the system itself will change. The most accessible and immediate example presently is of large scale computational systems, which can change the relation among other components of contemporary society, as seen with the anxiety around AI technology. (Looming objects and Ersatz projects were discussed in the Anastasis seminars, being prepared for publication, held at at École Normale Supérieure in summer 2022).

Obscure/Obscure experience — It is a term originally found in the works of Mohan. The 'obscure' is taken from the post-Cartesian classification of Ideas (especially Malebranche and Leibniz). It is an Idea which is distinct but not directly given to intuition. For Mohan, the obscure experience (which is a kind of *inexperience*) is the limit which simultaneously reveals the freedom and the responsibility of thought. One such example is that it is possible to anticipate many events in the world including the arrival of certain comets and climate change, for these events we can form an 'anticipatory system' (a concept appropriated from Robert Rosen). But the disappearance of the world as such is outside the order of anticipations. The obscure experience gives humility and responsibility to thinking.

Politics — Politics does not have almost any of the usual meanings in Dwivedi and Mohan, and yet retains the distinction from other meanings and uses. Politics is related to freedom, 'politics is the fight for freedom, and freedom is inseparable from the fight for it'. If there is no struggle for greater freedoms politics begins to slide towards stasis and criticalisation. Freedom is evidenced by the release of the polynomia of societies and institutions. In the Indian context, the goal of politics is the annihilation of caste because it alone can release the polynomia of the subcontinent.

Polynomia — It refers to the fact that all things are capable of multiple regularities. This fact of polynomia is also the basis for the definition of politics as concerned with freedom. The realisation of polynomia is the evidence for the achievement of freedom in politics; that is, only then can we state that politics is taking place. The concept is itself a component in relation with *analogy, homology, functional isolation* and *comprehending law*. In *Gandhi and Philosophy* Dwivedi and Mohan call these concepts and others (corpus/body, plan, force) by the philosophical term *Faculties*, or powers. Polynomia is a concept which refers to multiple regions of knowledge including mathematics, physics, biology and technology.

Reason — The new theory of reason distributed across the texts, especially of Mohan. Reason has a relation to the Ancient Greek logos as the 'gathering power', the conception of reason as both drive and faculty in Leibniz and Kant, and also the mathematical theory of conditions. It is the drive to think that is not determined by the classical laws of thought. Reason is a drive without ground and conditions, and it has an object which Mohan calls 'the obscure experience', which is a limit experience of thinking that shows the fragile relation we have with what is really the world. Reason implies an ethics that we should give reason for everything we do and everything we take from or modify in nature and in politics. This is one of the aspects of the principle of sufficient reason that is emphasised, *reason must be given*. Reason is also the faculty which is closest to the essence of all things. Essence 'is the ratio of the kinds of actualities, regularities, modalities, and the reasons for the specific ratios. Thus, essence is where we give reasons and bear responsibilities for the ratios' (See the texts *History and Anastasis* and *The Looming Objects and the Ancestral Model of Historiography* which is the final text in this anthology).

Revolution — There is a theory of revolution in Dwivedi and Mohan, but it is articulated indirectly (this caution is very understandable). Revolution and anastasis are both described as the way out of stasis, revolution is a political activity, but anastasis is that power which raises all kinds of systems from stasis. Revolution is preceded by the discovery of the hoaxes and other forms of truth functions which form the basis for oppressive societies, that is, deconstruction of the truths and norms which are the foundation of oppressive theories. Revolution also requires a revolutionary image of history up to that point and after with the clarity of a telos (a category of reason) for which one must bear responsibility. In these texts the revolutionary image is the division of historiographical perspective between the lower caste majority and the upper caste minority: India as it was imagined was as a land and people owned by the upper caste minority, which was hisoricised through their supremacism; the revolutionary image sees this reality and holds an egalitarian society formed through the destruction of the oppressive caste order as the telos.

Ruin — This concept appears often through synonyms such as the collapsed, destroyed, abandoned, anomon or a system in anomia. Ruin in the texts of Dwivedi and Mohan refers directly to Kant who thought that all philosophers approach the previous philosophies as a ruin from out of which a new system has to be built. Ruin is, in that meaning, what is experienced after anastasis as the past. But philosophy is the specific power which sees the ruin which would form the matter to be raised through anastasis, before it has been raised. Ruin is also the correct experience of historiography. As Mohan said in a lecture 'the past keeps as much secrets and surprises as the future, and we should be careful in our certainty about the past' (The text titled 'Principles of Beginning') is yet to be published although a response to it by Michel Bitbol has already been published in *Philosophy World Democracy*). This attitude is the correct approach to the concept of ruin, and it is a responsible ethos of research in that sense.

Scalology — It is the logic of the values which are measured in a hypophysical system. The familiar example is 'small is beautiful'. The concept derives from 'scala naturae' in the theological classification of nature, which was displaced by the Darwinian revolution. It also refers to various hypophysical hierarchical systems including the 'divine hierarchy' of pseudo Dionysus and the human hierarchy of the caste order (see *Gandhi and Philosophy*). In the caste system, someone's birth as Brahmin is the highest value, and as human beings fall away from the Brahmin in their birth assigned status they lose value. Caste is also colour coded as Dwivedi and Mohan remind us, the white Brahmin is the highest, and the dark skinned Dalit is at the bottom. Dwivedi has produced a new understanding of race and caste through hypophysical analyses and the discovery of scalology in systems of racism.

Stasis — When the components of a system are not able to form regularities together it results in stasis. The concept is drawn out from Ancient Greek political thought, theory of evil, and mathematical modelling. In Ancient Greece, there were many components constituting the polis which included peasants, military, and politicians. When one of the components, such as the military, decides to be the comprehending law of the whole system, they will eventually exhaust all other components for their self-advancement and this results in stasis. Stasis is a form of evil which happens when something necessary is being blocked. The example given from theology by Mohan is about a canal being blocked by a stone. Stasis is also a problem of philosophical systems or any system. Dwivedi and Mohan treat metaphysics as a stasis which endures by changing some of its properties from time to time.

Upper caste supremacism — this term underlines the 'denigrate-dominate function' whereby a group does not only claim superiority over others, nor is it only in a self-other relationship with other groups, but it also deploys the logic of a scale (also called scalology by Dwivedi and Mohan) of superiority by birth in order to gain power over the other people. As opposed to liberals and postcolonialists who disguise this aspect of caste either by speaking of 'diversity' or of 'Hinduism', Mohan and Dwivedi emphasize the supremacism of the upper castes in all spheres of life and in all fields of knowledge.

INDEX